SMP AS/A2 Mathematics

Mechanics 1
for AQA

 CAMBRIDGE
UNIVERSITY PRESS

D1424403

069913

...the School Mathematics Project

SMP AS/A2 Mathematics writing team David Cassell, Spencer Instone, John Ling, Paul Scruton, Susan Shilton, Heather West

SMP design and administration Melanie Bull, Carol Cole, Pam Keetch, Nicky Lake, Cathy Syred, Ann White

The authors thank Sue Glover for the technical advice she gave when this AS/A2 project began and for her detailed editorial contribution to this book. The authors are also very grateful to those teachers who advised on the book at the planning stage and commented in detail on draft chapters.

CAMBRIDGE UNIVERSITY PRESS
Cambridge, New York, Melbourne, Madrid, Cape Town, Singapore, São Paulo, Delhi, Dubai, Tokyo, Mexico City

Cambridge University Press
The Edinburgh Building, Cambridge CB2 8RU, UK

www.cambridge.org
Information on this title: www.cambridge.org/9780521605281

© The School Mathematics Project 2004

First published 2004
5th printing 2011

Printed in the United Kingdom at the University Press, Cambridge

A catalogue record for this publication is available from the British Library

ISBN 978-0-521-60528-1 Paperback

Typesetting and technical illustrations by The School Mathematics Project
Illustrations on pages 54 and 82–83 by Chris Evans

The authors and publisher thank the Lynton and Lynmouth Cliff Railway, Devon, for supplying the photograph on page 106.

The authors and publisher are grateful to the Assessment and Qualifications Alliance for permission to reproduce questions from past examination papers. Individual questions are marked AQA.

Using this book

Each chapter begins with a **summary** of what the student is expected to learn.

The chapter then has sections lettered A, B, C, … (see the contents overleaf). In most cases a section consists of development material, worked examples and an exercise.

The **development material** interweaves explanation with questions that involve the student in making sense of ideas and techniques. Development questions are labelled according to their section letter (A1, A2, …, B1, B2, …) and answers to them are provided.

D Some development questions are particularly suitable for discussion – either by the whole class or by smaller groups – because they have the potential to bring out a key issue or clarify a technique. Such **discussion questions** are marked with a bar, as here.

K **Key points** established in the development material are marked with a bar as here, so the student may readily refer to them during later work or revision. Each chapter's key points are also gathered together in a panel after the last lettered section.

The **worked examples** have been chosen to clarify ideas and techniques, and as models for students to follow in setting out their own work. Guidance for the student is in italic.

The **exercise** at the end of each lettered section is designed to consolidate the skills and understanding acquired earlier in the section. Unlike those in the development material, questions in the exercise are denoted by a number only.

Starred questions are more demanding.

After the lettered sections and the key points panel there may be a set of **mixed questions**, combining ideas from several sections in the chapter; these may also involve topics from earlier chapters.

Every chapter ends with a selection of **questions for self-assessment** ('Test yourself').

Included in the mixed questions and 'Test yourself' are **past AQA exam questions**, to give the student an idea of the style and standard that may be expected, and to build confidence. Occasionally, exam questions are included in the exercises in the lettered sections.

Contents

1 Kinematics in one dimension

In this chapter you will learn how to
- calculate average speed and average velocity
- draw and interpret kinematics graphs
- use the constant acceleration equations to solve problems in one dimension

A Velocity and displacement (answers p 139)

Mechanics is about **forces** and **motion**.

We will start by looking at motion itself, leaving aside questions about how the motion is produced. This part of mechanics is called **kinematics**. Key ideas in kinematics include distance, displacement, time, speed, velocity, acceleration and deceleration.

This chapter will deal with motion in a straight line only.

A1 Jack walks along a straight road at a constant speed of 2 metres per second.

(a) How far has Jack walked after 30 s?

(b) What other information do you need to know in order to fully define his final position?

Many of the situations studied in mechanics are in reality quite complicated. The first step is usually to simplify the situation so as to focus on the most important aspects. For example, Jack's size is ignored and he is assumed to be a moving point. His motion is considered to be in a precise straight line, with any small deviations ignored. The scale of the problem allows these assumptions to be made: Jack is small compared with the distance he has walked, as are any deviations from the straight line.

Notation: 'metres per second' may be written as m/s or as $m\,s^{-1}$. The latter notation will be used in this book.

A2 Jack and Kim start walking from the same point on a straight road at a constant speed of $2\,m\,s^{-1}$.

(a) How far have they walked after 1 minute?

(b) Jack and Kim are not at the same place after 1 minute. Can you explain this?

In question A2, although Jack and Kim started from the same place and walked at the same speed for the same length of time, they ended up in different places. This is because their speeds were the same but their directions were opposite.

K The quantity which includes both speed and direction is called **velocity**.

If Jack's direction is taken as the positive direction then his velocity is $2\,m\,s^{-1}$ and Kim's velocity is $-2\,m\,s^{-1}$.

K The quantity which includes both distance and direction is called **displacement**.

After 1 minute, Jack's displacement is 120 m from the start and Kim's displacement is –120 m.

```
−120 m          0          120 m
  ├─────────────┼─────────────┤
 Kim          start          Jack
```

A3 (a) Write down Jack's displacement from the starting point after 2 minutes.

(b) Write down Kim's displacement from the starting point after 2 minutes.

(c) How far apart are they after this time?

A4 Fran walks 3 km due east and then 1 km due west.

(a) How far did she walk?

(b) Taking east as positive, what is Fran's final displacement?

A5 Jack now runs along the straight road in the positive direction at a constant speed of $3.5 \, \text{m s}^{-1}$ for 2 minutes. He turns around and walks in the opposite direction at a constant speed of $2 \, \text{m s}^{-1}$ for another 2 minutes.

(a) For what distance did Jack run?

(b) For what distance did he walk?

(c) What was his displacement from his starting position after 4 minutes?

A6 This **displacement–time** graph shows the motion of a vehicle travelling at a constant velocity along a straight road.

(a) What is the velocity of the vehicle?

(b) What feature of the graph tells you the velocity?

(c) What feature shows that the velocity is constant?

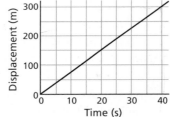

A7 An athlete was in training for the 100 metre sprint.
In March her best time was 14.1 seconds.
By June she had reduced her best time to 13.5 seconds.
She draws this displacement–time graph.

(a) Calculate the gradient of each line.
What are the units for the gradients?

(b) What quantity does each gradient represent?

(c) How does the graph for June show that the athlete had improved her performance?

(d) The graphs are both straight lines. What does this say about her motion?

(e) Are straight line graphs realistic here?
Sketch a more realistic graph for the motion of an athlete in a 100 m sprint.

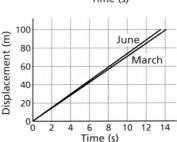

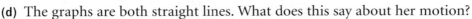

K The gradient of a displacement–time graph gives the velocity.

If the displacement–time graph is a straight line then the motion is at constant velocity.

In the previous question, the athlete **modelled** her motion as a straight line graph. This model, which implies a constant velocity, does not fit the motion exactly.

For example, in the first few fractions of a second, the athlete's velocity increases from zero. So a close-up of the start of the graph would look something like this.

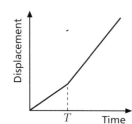

Also it is unlikely that the athlete's velocity would be constant for the whole sprint. She may increase her velocity near the finishing line.

However, the straight line model is still a good approximation for a sprinter. For a much longer race it would be less realistic.

Displacement–time graphs often simplify a real situation. For example, this graph shows a vehicle whose velocity increases instantaneously at time T. In reality, it would take some time for the velocity to change. But if this time is short in comparison with the journey as a whole, then it can be ignored and the change treated as instantaneous.

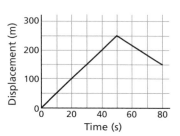

A8 Dan went for a short run.
This displacement–time graph shows his run.

(a) What was his velocity for the first part of the run?

(b) What was his velocity for the last part of the run?

(c) What was his displacement at the end of the run?

K The **average velocity** is the constant velocity at which a journey of the same overall **displacement** could have been completed in the same total time.

$$\text{Average velocity} = \frac{\text{displacement from starting point}}{\text{time taken}}$$

Notation: The letter s is used for displacement and t for time.

A9 What was Dan's average velocity?

A10 What distance did Dan run altogether?

K The **average speed** is the constant speed at which a journey of the same overall **distance** could have been completed in the same total time.

$$\text{Average speed} = \frac{\text{total distance travelled}}{\text{time taken}}$$

A11 What was Dan's average speed?

Example 1

A car travels along a straight road at a constant velocity of $70\,km\,h^{-1}$.
How far does it travel in 45 seconds?

Solution

First convert the velocity into $m\,s^{-1}$.

$$70\,km\,h^{-1} = 70 \times \frac{1000}{3600}\,m\,s^{-1} = \frac{175}{9}\,m\,s^{-1}$$

Leave the velocity as an exact value.

$$\text{Displacement} = \frac{175}{9} \times 45 = 875\,m$$

The car travels $875\,m$ in $45\,s$.

Example 2

A jogger runs for $100\,m$ at a speed of $4\,m\,s^{-1}$ and then walks the same distance
at a speed of $2\,m\,s^{-1}$. What is his average speed?

Solution

Calculate the time spent running.

$$\text{Time running} = \frac{100}{4} = 25\,s$$

Calculate the time spent walking.

$$\text{Time walking} = \frac{100}{2} = 50\,s$$

Average speed = $\dfrac{\text{total distance travelled}}{\text{time taken}}$

$$\text{Average speed} = \frac{200}{75} = 2.7\,m\,s^{-1} \text{ to 1 d.p.}$$

Example 3

This displacement–time graph represents a short cycle ride.
Find the velocity for each part of the journey.

Solution

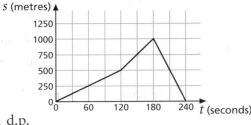

Find the gradient of each line segment.

For $0 < t < 120$, velocity $= \dfrac{500}{120} = 4.2\,m\,s^{-1}$ to 1 d.p.

For $120 < t < 180$, velocity $= \dfrac{500}{60} = 8.3\,m\,s^{-1}$ to 1 d.p.

For $180 < t < 240$, velocity $= -\dfrac{1000}{60} = -16.7\,m\,s^{-1}$ to 1 d.p.

Exercise A (answers p 139)

1 Convert the following speeds into metres per second.

    (a) $36 \, km \, h^{-1}$ **(b)** $45 \, km \, h^{-1}$ **(c)** $54 \, km \, h^{-1}$ **(d)** $75 \, km \, h^{-1}$

2 A jogger runs for 30 seconds at $5 \, m \, s^{-1}$ and then walks an equal distance at $2 \, m \, s^{-1}$. What is her average speed?

3 Find the average speed of a jogger who runs for 30 seconds at $5 \, m \, s^{-1}$ and then walks at $2 \, m \, s^{-1}$ for an equal period of time.

4 Tom walks on a treadmill at $2.5 \, m \, s^{-1}$ for 60 seconds followed by 120 seconds at $1.7 \, m \, s^{-1}$. What distance has he walked altogether?

5 A cyclist travels due west for 45 seconds at $10 \, m \, s^{-1}$ and then turns and cycles due east for 30 seconds at $12 \, m \, s^{-1}$. Take east as the positive direction.

    (a) What distance has the cyclist travelled?

    (b) What is the cyclist's final displacement?

    (c) What is his average speed?

    (d) What is his average velocity?

6 Michelle runs along a long straight road at $4 \, m \, s^{-1}$ for 2 minutes. She turns around and runs in the opposite direction at $5 \, m \, s^{-1}$ for 1 minute.

    (a) What is her average speed?

    (b) What is her average velocity?

7 A car completed a journey of 360 km at an average speed of $80 \, km \, h^{-1}$. The average speed for the first half of the journey's distance was $75 \, km \, h^{-1}$. What was the average speed for the second half of the journey?

8 Marlon went for a walk. This displacement–time graph represents the first part of his walk.

    (a) What happened at time 30 s?

    (b) Find Marlon's velocity for the first 30 s.

    (c) What was Marlon's velocity at time 80 s?

    (d) Find Marlon's average velocity.

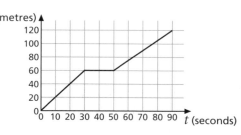

9 Paige jogged along a 100 metre straight track in 20 seconds. She then rested for 10 seconds before walking back to the start in 45 seconds.

    (a) Sketch a displacement–time graph to represent Paige's motion.

    (b) Find Paige's average speed.

    (c) What was her average velocity?

10 Tracy cycles from Aycliffe to Beford, a distance of 3 miles, in 16 minutes.
She rests for 10 minutes before continuing to Ceville, a further distance
of 4 miles, which takes 20 minutes.
Simon walks the same journey, does not stop to rest and takes 2 hours.

If Tracy starts out 50 minutes after Simon, when and where will she overtake him?

11 It is 10 km from Blakesfield to Norton Pond.
Maisie cycles from Blakesfield to Norton Pond, starting at 12 noon,
at a steady speed of 15 km h^{-1} and then immediately turns and
comes back to Blakesfield at a speed of $7\frac{1}{2}$ km h^{-1}.
John sets off on foot from Norton Pond at noon and walks at a steady
speed of 3 km h^{-1} to Blakesfield.

  (a) Draw displacement–time graphs of their motion on the same diagram.

  (b) At what times t_1 and t_2 do Maisie and John pass each other and
how far are they from Blakesfield at these times?

  (c) At what time between t_1 and t_2 are they the greatest distance apart?

B Graphs of motion (answers p 140)

A car travels along a straight road with increasing velocity.
The table shows its velocity at different times.

Time (seconds)	0	10	20	30	40	50	60
Velocity (m s^{-1})	0	2.5	5	7.5	10	12.5	15

This **velocity–time** graph shows the motion of the car.

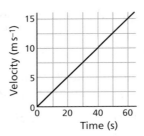

B1 (a) What is the gradient of the graph?

    (b) What are the units of the gradient?

    (c) What do you think this gradient represents?

B2 If the velocity of the car were decreasing
from 15 m s^{-1}, the velocity–time graph
would be as shown.

What do you think the gradient represents
in this case?

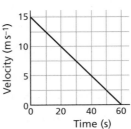

K The rate of change of velocity with respect to time is the **acceleration**.
The units of acceleration are metres per second per second, m/s^2 or m s^{-2}.

The gradient of a velocity–time graph gives the acceleration.
If the velocity–time graph is a straight line, then the acceleration is constant.

$$\text{Acceleration} = \frac{\text{change in velocity}}{\text{time}}$$

Negative acceleration is sometimes described as **deceleration** or **retardation**.
For example, an acceleration of $-3\,\text{m s}^{-2}$ can also be described as
a deceleration of $3\,\text{m s}^{-2}$.

Notation: the letter v is used for velocity and a for acceleration.

B3 A car starts moving from rest with a constant acceleration of $2\,\text{m s}^{-2}$.
Find its velocity after

(a) 1 second (b) 2 seconds (c) 10 seconds (d) 20 seconds

B4 A car moving at $25\,\text{m s}^{-1}$ starts to decelerate at $1\,\text{m s}^{-2}$.
What is its velocity after 10 seconds?

B5 This velocity–time graph shows the motion of a cyclist along
a straight track.
Find the acceleration of the cyclist.

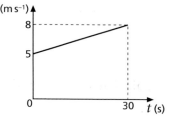

This displacement–time graph shows the motion of a cyclist
who cycles at constant velocity until time t_1, then cycles at
a greater constant velocity until t_2 and then comes to rest.

The graph simplifies the motion, assuming that the velocity
changes instantaneously and the cyclist comes to rest
instantaneously.

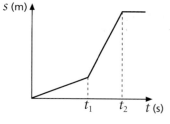

The motion of the cyclist can also be shown in this
velocity–time graph.

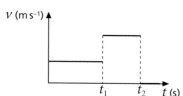

D **B6** How are the following represented on

(i) the displacement–time graph

(ii) the velocity–time graph

(a) the initial constant velocity

(b) the greater velocity

(c) the cyclist at rest

B7 An acceleration–time graph could be drawn for the motion of the cyclist.
Would it give any useful information about the motion of the cyclist?

B8 (a) This velocity–time graph shows the motion of a car along a straight road. Describe the motion of the car.

(b) Sketch the corresponding acceleration–time graph.

(c) How is the displacement of the car changing? Sketch a displacement–time graph for the car.

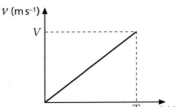

B9 This velocity–time graph shows the motion of a cyclist along a straight track.
Describe the motion of the cyclist at each of the labelled points.

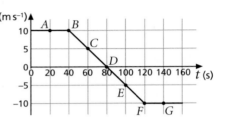

Example 4

A train travelling along a straight track accelerates uniformly from rest for 30 seconds until it reaches a velocity of $20 \, \mathrm{m \, s^{-1}}$.
It then travels at this constant velocity for 120 seconds.
Finally it travels with constant deceleration for 45 seconds until coming to rest.

Sketch a velocity–time graph to show this motion.
Calculate the acceleration in the first 30 seconds and the deceleration in coming to rest.

Solution

Uniform acceleration means that the first part of the graph is a straight line with positive gradient.
Constant deceleration means that the last part of the graph is a straight line with negative gradient.
Sketch the graph, indicating the key points.

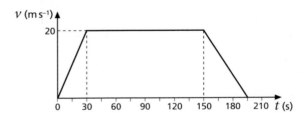

$$Acceleration = \frac{change \ in \ velocity}{time}$$

In the first 30 s, $a = \dfrac{20}{30} = 0.7 \, \mathrm{m \, s^{-2}}$ to 1 d.p.

In the last 45 s, $a = \dfrac{-20}{45} = -0.4 \, \mathrm{m \, s^{-2}}$ to 1 d.p.

The acceleration in the first 30 s is $0.7 \, \mathrm{m \, s^{-2}}$ and the deceleration in coming to rest is $0.4 \, \mathrm{m \, s^{-2}}$.

Exercise B (answers p 140)

1 A cyclist sets off from rest with a constant acceleration of $0.2\,\text{m s}^{-2}$.
  Find his velocity after

  (a) 1 second   (b) 2 seconds   (c) 10 seconds   (d) 1 minute

2 A car decelerates uniformly from a velocity of $30\,\text{m s}^{-1}$ to a velocity of $20\,\text{m s}^{-1}$
  in 20 seconds. Calculate the deceleration of the car.

3 This velocity–time graph represents the motion
  of a cyclist. Find

  (a) the acceleration between A and B

  (b) the acceleration between B and C

  (c) the acceleration between C and D

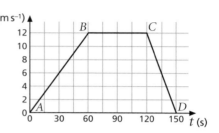

4 For each of the following graphs describe the motion shown and
  sketch the corresponding velocity–time graph.

  (a) 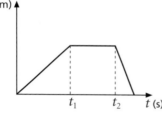   (b)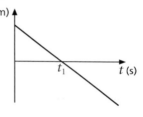

5 For each of the following graphs describe the motion shown and
  sketch the corresponding acceleration–time graph.

  (a) 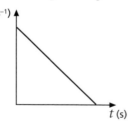   (b)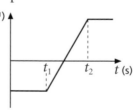

6 A car joins a straight road travelling at a velocity of $12\,\text{m s}^{-1}$ and
  accelerates uniformly for 20 seconds until it reaches a velocity of $18\,\text{m s}^{-1}$.
  It travels at this constant velocity for 2 minutes until it slows down with
  constant deceleration, coming to rest after a further 40 seconds.

  (a) Sketch a velocity–time graph for this motion.

  (b) Calculate the acceleration in the first 20 seconds.

  (c) Calculate the acceleration in the last 40 seconds.

  (d) Sketch an acceleration–time graph for this motion.

C Area under a velocity–time graph (answers p 141)

C1 Aisha runs along a straight road at $4\,\mathrm{m\,s^{-1}}$ for 45 s and then jogs at $3\,\mathrm{m\,s^{-1}}$ for 60 s. This is the velocity–time graph for her run.

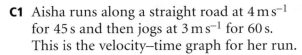

(a) Calculate the area under the graph for $0 < t < 45$.

(b) Calculate the area under the graph for $45 < t < 105$.

(c) What are the units of these areas?

(d) What do you think these areas represent?

Consider a cyclist who accelerates uniformly along a straight road from rest to a velocity of $8\,\mathrm{m\,s^{-1}}$ in 20 seconds. His velocity is continuously increasing as shown in this velocity–time graph.

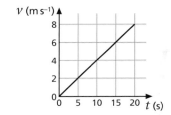

To find his displacement we can simplify the situation by assuming that he has cycled at constant velocity for short periods of time, as shown in this graph. The displacement can then be found by summing the areas under each part of the graph.

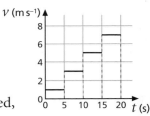

As the times that he cycles at constant velocity are reduced, the simplified graph becomes closer to the actual graph, and the displacement can be found by calculating the area under the true velocity–time graph.

K The area under a velocity–time graph gives the displacement.

C2 Mike runs along a straight track. This is the velocity–time graph for his run.

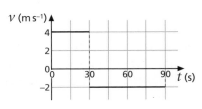

(a) What is the area under the graph for $0 < t < 30$?

(b) What is the area under the graph for $30 < t < 90$?

(c) What is Mike's displacement at time 90 s?

C3 This velocity–time graph shows the motion of a cyclist along a straight track.

Calculate the displacement of the cyclist at time 30 s.

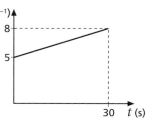

C4 The graph shows the velocity of a car for a short time after it starts from rest at a set of traffic lights.

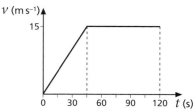

(a) Describe what is happening to the velocity of the car during the journey.

(b) Find the distance travelled by the car in the first 45 seconds of the journey.

(c) What is the total distance travelled by the car in the 120 s?

Example 5

The graph shows part of a cyclist's journey.

(a) What is the cyclist's acceleration between $t = 60$ and $t = 75$?

(b) Find the total distance travelled by the cyclist.

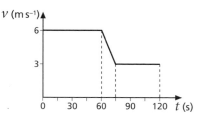

Solution

(a) *The required acceleration is the gradient of the graph between $t = 60$ and $t = 75$.*

Acceleration $= \dfrac{3-6}{75-60} = \dfrac{-3}{15} = -0.2\,\text{m s}^{-2}$

Negative acceleration means the velocity of the cyclist is decreasing.

(b) *To find the total distance, find the sum of the areas under the sections of the graph.*

For $0 < t < 60$,   distance $= 6 \times 60 = 360\,\text{m}$

For $60 < t < 75$,   distance $= \frac{1}{2} \times (6 + 3) \times 15 = 67.5\,\text{m}$

For $75 < t < 120$, distance $= 3 \times 45 = 135\,\text{m}$

So total distance travelled $= 360 + 67.5 + 135 = 562.5\,\text{m}$

Exercise C (answers p 141)

1 This velocity–time graph represents an athlete's pre-race warm up.
Calculate the distance she covered in her warm up.

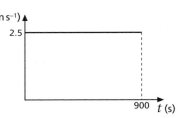

2 This velocity–time graph represents the motion of a cyclist.

(a) Find the displacement of the cyclist at $t = 20$.

(b) Find the displacement of the cyclist at $t = 60$.

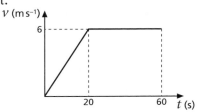

3 As part of his training schedule, Chris runs for 60 seconds at $4.4\,\text{m s}^{-1}$ followed by 90 seconds jogging at $3\,\text{m s}^{-1}$ in the same direction. He repeats this 3 times.

(a) Draw a velocity–time graph for Chris's motion.

(b) Find his total displacement.

4 A car decelerates uniformly from a velocity of $20\,\text{m s}^{-1}$ to a velocity of $13\,\text{m s}^{-1}$ 20 seconds later. It then continues at this velocity for a further 30 seconds.

(a) Sketch a velocity–time graph for this motion.

(b) Find the total distance travelled by the car.

5 A train accelerates uniformly for 20 seconds from rest to a velocity of $9\,\text{m s}^{-1}$. It then travels at this constant velocity for 2 minutes.
Find its total displacement.

*6 These velocity–time graphs show the motion of a car and a van moving from rest along a straight road.

The van accelerates for 30 seconds and then continues on at a steady speed.
The car accelerates at a constant rate.

Find the time when the car overtakes the van.

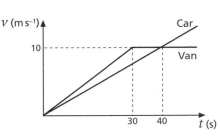

*7 The motion of an object is represented by the graphs shown below.

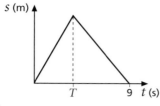 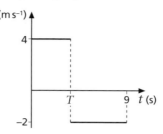

Find

(a) the value of T

(b) the distance covered during the 9 seconds

D Motion with constant acceleration (answers p 142)

A standard set of letters (u, v, a, t, s) is used for the motion of an object moving in a straight line with constant acceleration:

u m s^{-1} is the initial velocity of the object.

v m s^{-1} is the final velocity.

a m s^{-2} is the constant acceleration.

t s is the time for which the object is accelerating.

s m, is the displacement during the time the object is accelerating.

The motion is shown in this velocity–time graph.

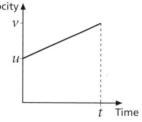

The constant acceleration, a m s^{-2}, is equal to the gradient of the graph.

So $a = \dfrac{v - u}{t}$

D1 Show that the above equation can be rewritten as $v = u + at$.

This equation can be applied to any situation with **constant** acceleration.
If the initial velocity u m s^{-1} is known, the velocity v m s^{-1} at time t s can be calculated.

D2 A tram initially travelling at 10 m s^{-1} accelerates at 0.5 m s^{-2} for 10 seconds. Calculate its final velocity.

D3 A car's initial velocity is 20 m s^{-1}.
It decelerates at 0.4 m s^{-2} for 15 seconds.
Calculate its final velocity.

When an object is decelerating, it has negative acceleration.
The same constant acceleration equations can be applied, but remember
to substitute a negative value for the acceleration.

The area under the velocity–time graph at the start of this section gives the
displacement, s m.

The area is a trapezium, so
$$s = \tfrac{1}{2}(u + v)t$$

Again, this equation can be applied to any situation with **constant** acceleration.
If the initial and final velocities are known, the displacement s m at time t s
can be calculated.

D4 A car travelling with constant acceleration increases its velocity from $15\,\mathrm{m\,s^{-1}}$
to $22\,\mathrm{m\,s^{-1}}$ in 15 seconds.
Calculate the car's displacement.

D5 A train decelerating at a constant rate travels between two marker posts
a distance of 250 metres apart.
When it passes the first post, the velocity of the train is $15\,\mathrm{m\,s^{-1}}$.
When it passes the second post, its velocity is $10\,\mathrm{m\,s^{-1}}$.
Calculate the time taken for the train to travel between the two posts.

> **K** For an object moving with constant acceleration,
>
> $v = u + at$
>
> $s = \tfrac{1}{2}(u + v)t$

Example 6

A car travelling along a straight road at $20\,\mathrm{m\,s^{-1}}$ accelerates at $0.4\,\mathrm{m\,s^{-2}}$ for 25 seconds.
Find the final velocity of the car.

Solution

First list the known values and the unknown. $u = 20,\ a = 0.4,\ t = 25,\ v = ?$

Select the equation that links the letters you have listed.

Use $v = u + at$ to find the final velocity. $v = 20 + 0.4 \times 25$

$v = 30$

The final velocity of the car is $30\,\mathrm{m\,s^{-1}}$.

Example 7

A cyclist applies his brakes for 20 seconds, reducing his speed from $10\,\mathrm{m\,s^{-1}}$ to $6\,\mathrm{m\,s^{-1}}$.
Calculate his deceleration and the distance travelled while braking.

Solution

First list the known values and the unknowns. $t = 20, \; u = 10, \; v = 6, \; a = ?, \; s = ?$

Note that $u > v$ as the cyclist is decelerating.

Substitute known values into $v = u + at$. $6 = 10 + a \times 20$

Rearrange to find a. $a = \dfrac{6 - 10}{20} = -0.2$

The acceleration is negative indicating that the cyclist is slowing down.

Use $s = \frac{1}{2}(u + v)t$ to find the distance. $s = \frac{1}{2}(10 + 6) \times 20 = 160$

He was decelerating at $0.2\,\mathrm{m\,s^{-2}}$ for $160\,\mathrm{m}$.

Exercise D (answers p 142)

1 A motorbike accelerates at a constant rate of $0.5\,\mathrm{m\,s^{-2}}$ from rest.
Calculate its velocity after 20 seconds.

2 A train accelerates at $0.2\,\mathrm{m\,s^{-2}}$ for 45 seconds to a velocity of $21\,\mathrm{m\,s^{-1}}$.
Calculate its initial velocity.

3 A cyclist accelerates uniformly from $5\,\mathrm{m\,s^{-1}}$ to $9\,\mathrm{m\,s^{-1}}$ in 30 seconds.
Calculate the distance the cyclist travels during this time.

4 A car accelerates uniformly from $20\,\mathrm{m\,s^{-1}}$ to $28\,\mathrm{m\,s^{-1}}$ in 40 seconds.
Calculate its acceleration.

5 A car initially travelling at $15\,\mathrm{m\,s^{-1}}$ accelerates uniformly for 16 seconds
covering a distance of $280\,\mathrm{m}$. Calculate its final velocity.

6 A cyclist accelerates uniformly along a straight track.
She takes 20 seconds to cover a distance of $100\,\mathrm{m}$.
Given that her final velocity is $6\,\mathrm{m\,s^{-1}}$, calculate her initial velocity.

7 A train decelerates at a rate of $0.1\,\mathrm{m\,s^{-2}}$ for 30 seconds.
Its initial velocity is $14\,\mathrm{m\,s^{-1}}$.

(a) Calculate its final velocity.

(b) How far has it travelled in this time?

8 A cable car accelerates from rest to its maximum speed of $4\,\mathrm{m\,s^{-1}}$ in one minute.

(a) How far has it travelled in this time?

(b) What is its acceleration?

9 A car decelerates uniformly at $0.4\,\mathrm{m\,s^{-2}}$ from $16\,\mathrm{m\,s^{-1}}$ to rest.

(a) Calculate the time it takes to come to rest.

(b) How far has the car travelled while decelerating?

E Constant acceleration equations (answers p 142)

The equation $s = \frac{1}{2}(u + v)t$ derived in the previous section can be used
to calculate the displacement only if the final velocity is known.
In some cases, only the initial velocity and the acceleration are known and
it would be useful to have an equation for displacement using these two quantities.

E1 Show that $s = ut + \frac{1}{2}at^2$ by substituting $v = u + at$ into $s = \frac{1}{2}(u + v)t$.

E2 A cyclist travelling at an initial velocity of $5\,\mathrm{m\,s^{-1}}$ accelerates at $0.1\,\mathrm{m\,s^{-2}}$.
Calculate the distance she travels in 20 seconds.

E3 (a) Make u the subject of $v = u + at$.

(b) By substituting the expression for u found in (a) into $s = \frac{1}{2}(u + v)t$,
show that $s = vt - \frac{1}{2}at^2$.

The equation $v = u + at$ can be used to calculate the final velocity only if
the time is known. It would be useful to have an equation that can be applied
in cases where the displacement rather than the time is known.

E4 (a) Make t the subject of $v = u + at$.

(b) By substituting the expression for t found in (a) into $s = \frac{1}{2}(u + v)t$,
show that $v^2 = u^2 + 2as$.

E5 A car accelerates at a constant rate of $0.25\,\mathrm{m\,s^{-2}}$ over a distance of $400\,\mathrm{m}$.
If it was initially travelling at $15\,\mathrm{m\,s^{-1}}$, calculate its final velocity.

E6 A train decelerates at a constant rate of $0.15\,\mathrm{m\,s^{-2}}$ for $500\,\mathrm{m}$.
Initially the train was travelling at $20\,\mathrm{m\,s^{-1}}$.
Calculate its final velocity.

K The constant acceleration equations for motion in one dimension are

$$v = u + at$$
$$s = \frac{1}{2}(u + v)t$$
$$s = ut + \frac{1}{2}at^2$$
$$s = vt - \frac{1}{2}at^2$$
$$v^2 = u^2 + 2as$$

These five equations can be applied to any situation involving motion in a
straight line with constant acceleration. In order to decide which equation
should be applied, start by listing the known and unknown values.

Example 8

A car travelling along a straight road at $20\,\mathrm{m\,s^{-1}}$ accelerates at $0.4\,\mathrm{m\,s^{-2}}$ for $625\,\mathrm{m}$. Find the final velocity of the car.

Solution

First list the known values and the unknown. $u = 20,\ a = 0.4,\ s = 625,\ v = ?$

Select the equation that links the letters you have listed.

Use $v^2 = u^2 + 2as$ to find the final velocity. $v^2 = 20^2 + 2\times0.4\times625 = 900$

The velocity will be positive. $v = \sqrt{900} = 30$

The final velocity is $30\,\mathrm{m\,s^{-1}}$

Example 9

A car drives with a constant acceleration of $0.5\,\mathrm{m\,s^{-2}}$ between two marker posts $500\,\mathrm{m}$ apart. It is travelling at $15\,\mathrm{m\,s^{-1}}$ when it passes the first post.

Find the time taken to travel between the posts.

Solution

First list the known values and the unknown. $u = 15,\ a = 0.5,\ s = 500,\ t = ?$

Substitute known values into $s = ut + \frac{1}{2}at^2$. $500 = 15t + \frac{1}{2}\times0.5\times t^2$

$$\Rightarrow\ 0.25t^2 + 15t - 500 = 0$$

This quadratic does not factorise, so use the formula to solve the equation

$$t = \frac{-15 \pm \sqrt{15^2 - 4\times0.25\times-500}}{2\times0.25}$$

$$= \frac{-15 \pm \sqrt{725}}{0.5}$$

$$= 23.85\ldots \text{ or } -83.85\ldots$$

We know the time is positive, so ignore the negative root.

The time taken for the car to travel between the two posts is $23.9\,\mathrm{s}$ (to 1 d.p.).

An alternative method is as follows.

Use $v^2 = u^2 + 2as$ to find v. $v^2 = 15^2 + 2\times0.5\times500 = 725$

Substitute into $v = u + at$ to find t. $\sqrt{725} = 15 + 0.5\times t$

$$t = \frac{\sqrt{725} - 15}{0.5} = 23.85\ldots$$

Exercise E (answers p 142)

1 A cyclist starts from rest and accelerates at $0.25\,\mathrm{m\,s^{-2}}$.
 What is his speed after 30 seconds?

2 A train travelling at $15\,\mathrm{m\,s^{-1}}$ accelerates at $0.3\,\mathrm{m\,s^{-2}}$ over a distance of $750\,\mathrm{m}$. What is its final velocity?

3 A car moves with constant acceleration from rest to $30\,\mathrm{m\,s^{-1}}$ in 12.6 seconds. Find the acceleration and the distance travelled.

4 A car joins a motorway travelling at $14\,\mathrm{m\,s^{-1}}$ and then accelerates at $0.8\,\mathrm{m\,s^{-2}}$ for 20 seconds.
Find the distance travelled and the final speed.

5 A car brakes from $31\,\mathrm{m\,s^{-1}}$ to $10\,\mathrm{m\,s^{-1}}$ under constant deceleration while travelling $250\,\mathrm{m}$. Find the deceleration and the time taken to slow down.

6 The motion of an object moving in a straight line with constant acceleration a is shown in this velocity–time graph. The area under the graph represents the displacement of the object.

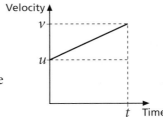

(a) By splitting the area into a rectangle and a triangle as shown, show that $s = ut + \frac{1}{2}at^2$.

(b) Use the graph to show that $s = vt - \frac{1}{2}at^2$.

7 A motorcyclist travelling at $24\,\mathrm{m\,s^{-1}}$ accelerates uniformly for 30 seconds over a distance of 900 metres.

(a) Calculate the acceleration of the motorcyclist.

(b) What is his final velocity?

8 A train travels with constant acceleration along a straight horizontal track.
It passes point O with speed $5\,\mathrm{m\,s^{-1}}$.
It passes point A 25 seconds later with speed $18\,\mathrm{m\,s^{-1}}$.

(a) Show that the acceleration of the train is $0.52\,\mathrm{m\,s^{-2}}$.

(b) Find the distance OA.

(c) The point B is the mid-point of OA.
Find, to three significant figures, the speed of the train when it passes B.

9 A train travelling at $9\,\mathrm{m\,s^{-1}}$ enters a straight stretch of track of length $1000\,\mathrm{m}$. It immediately accelerates at $0.24\,\mathrm{m\,s^{-2}}$ and maintains this acceleration until the end of the straight stretch.
Find the time taken for the train to cover this distance.

10 (a) A snooker ball hit at $1.8\,\mathrm{m\,s^{-1}}$ stops after travelling $3.2\,\mathrm{m}$ with constant retardation. Find the speed with which the ball would have hit a second ball $1.6\,\mathrm{m}$ from the starting point if it had been in the way.

(b) A ball is struck at $u\,\mathrm{m\,s^{-1}}$ and travels with constant retardation, stopping after s metres.
What was its velocity after going $\frac{1}{2}s$ metres?

Key points

- Average speed $= \dfrac{\text{total distance travelled}}{\text{time taken}}$

  Average velocity $= \dfrac{\text{displacement from starting point}}{\text{time taken}}$ (p 8)

- The gradient of a displacement–time graph gives the velocity. (p 8)

- The gradient of a velocity–time graph gives the acceleration. (p 12)

- The area under a velocity–time graph gives the displacement. (p 15)

- The constant acceleration equations for motion in one dimension are

  $v = u + at$

  $s = \frac{1}{2}(u + v)t$

  $s = ut + \frac{1}{2}at^2$

  $s = vt - \frac{1}{2}at^2$

  $v^2 = u^2 + 2as$ (pp 18–19, 21)

Mixed questions (answers p 142)

1 A car travels along a straight horizontal road on which there are some roadworks with a speed restriction in force. The brakes are applied for 5 seconds on the approach to the roadworks, reducing the car's speed from $28\,\text{m s}^{-1}$ to $22\,\text{m s}^{-1}$. The brakes are released and the car continues at a constant speed of $22\,\text{m s}^{-1}$ for a further 10 seconds.

The velocity–time graph for this motion is shown.

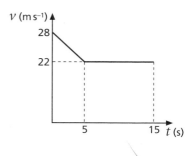

(a) Explain how the velocity–time graph shows that when the brakes are applied the car undergoes constant deceleration.

(b) Calculate the car's deceleration in the first 5 seconds of the motion.

(c) Find the total distance covered by the car during the 15 seconds.

(d) What is the car's average speed during the 15 seconds?

2 A tram moves with constant acceleration along a straight horizontal track. It passes point A with speed $4\,\text{m s}^{-1}$ and 10 seconds later passes point B where $AB = 80\,\text{m}$.

(a) Find the acceleration of the tram.

(b) When the tram passes point C its speed is $16\,\text{m s}^{-1}$. Find the distance AC.

3 A lift can travel at a maximum speed of $1.6 \, \mathrm{m\,s^{-1}}$.

The lift accelerates at a constant rate from rest and reaches its maximum velocity after 10 seconds. It continues at this constant velocity then finally decelerates at a constant rate for 12 seconds before coming to rest.

The lift has travelled a total distance of 40 metres.

(a) Find the initial acceleration of the lift.

(b) Find the deceleration of the lift.

(c) Find the time taken for the lift to travel 40 m.

4 A toy rocket is fired vertically upwards using a catapult. A student attempts to model the motion of the rocket using the velocity–time graph shown below.

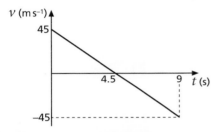

(a) At what time is the velocity of the rocket zero?

(b) Find the acceleration of the rocket.

(c) Find the total distance travelled by the rocket during its flight.

5 A truck and a car are at rest and level with each other at a set of traffic lights on a straight road. When the lights change they move off at the same time.

The truck accelerates with constant acceleration until it reaches a top speed of $15 \, \mathrm{m\,s^{-1}}$. It then continues at this constant speed.

The car accelerates with constant acceleration for 20 seconds until it reaches a top speed $V \, \mathrm{m\,s^{-1}}$, where $V > 15 \, \mathrm{m\,s^{-1}}$. It then continues at this constant speed. The car draws level with the truck when the truck has been travelling for 30 seconds at its top speed.

The distance travelled by each vehicle is then 525 m.

(a) Find the time for which the truck is accelerating.

(b) On the same diagram sketch velocity–time graphs to illustrate the motion of the two vehicles from the time they start to the time when the car overtakes the truck.

(c) Find the top speed of the car.

6 The velocity–time graph shows the motion of a particle P moving with constant acceleration.

At times $t = 2$ and $t = 5$, P has velocities $3U$ and $5U$ respectively.

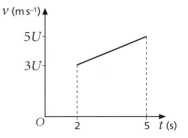

(a) (i) Find, in terms of U, the acceleration of P.

  (ii) Find, in terms of U, the distance travelled by P between the times $t = 2$ and $t = 5$.

(b) When $t = 5$, the motion of P changes and subsequently P moves with constant retardation.
The particle P comes to rest after travelling a **further** 20 metres in the next 4 seconds.
Find the value of U.

AQA 2003

*7 A lorry of length 16 m is travelling at a constant speed of $12\,\mathrm{m\,s^{-1}}$ in the inside lane of a straight road. A car of length 4 m is initially travelling in the outside lane in the same direction as the lorry and at the same speed. The gap between the two vehicles is 50 m.

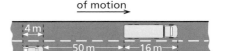

The car accelerates at $2\,\mathrm{m\,s^{-2}}$ for 5 seconds, then travels at constant speed for a time and finally decelerates at $2\,\mathrm{m\,s^{-2}}$ for 5 seconds. Now the car is travelling at the same speed as before, but in front of the lorry and the gap is the same as it was before.

How long did the car take to get from its initial to its final position? How far did the car travel in this time?

Test yourself (answers p 143)

1 The graph shows how the velocity, $v\,\mathrm{m\,s^{-1}}$, of a car varies with time, t seconds, as it moves along a straight horizontal road.

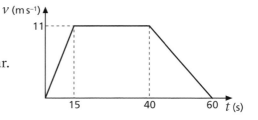

(a) Calculate the total distance travelled by the car.

(b) Find the acceleration of the car between

  (i) $t = 0$ and $t = 15$ (ii) $t = 15$ and $t = 40$

  (iii) $t = 40$ and $t = 60$

2 A sprinter starts from rest, and accelerates at $2\,\mathrm{m\,s^{-2}}$ for the first 4 seconds of a race. Assume that the sprinter moves along a straight line.

   (a) Find the distance travelled by the sprinter in the first 4 seconds.

   (b) Find the speed of the sprinter at the end of the first 4 seconds.

   (c) The sprinter then travels at this speed for the remainder of the race.
   He travels a total distance of 100 metres.
   Find the total time that he takes to complete the race.

AQA 2003

3 A cyclist sets off from rest and moves along a straight horizontal road until she again comes to rest.
The motion of the cyclist can be modelled as **three** separate stages.

   In the first stage she accelerates uniformly from rest for 5 seconds until she reaches a velocity $V\,\mathrm{m\,s^{-1}}$.
   She then moves with constant velocity $V\,\mathrm{m\,s^{-1}}$ for 55 seconds.
   Finally she moves with a constant retardation for 10 seconds until coming to rest.

   (a) Sketch a velocity–time graph to show the motion of the cyclist.

   (b) Given that the total length of the journey is 300 metres, find the value of V.

AQA 2002

4 A cyclist is travelling along a straight horizontal road.
As she passes a bus stop she sees a red traffic light ahead of her.
She continues to travel with a constant speed of $3\,\mathrm{m\,s^{-1}}$ for 20 seconds and then decelerates at a constant rate of $0.2\,\mathrm{m\,s^{-2}}$ until coming to rest at the traffic light.

   (a) Calculate the distance between the bus stop and the traffic light.

   (b) Calculate the time the cyclist takes to travel from the bus stop to the traffic light.

   (c) Calculate the average speed of the cyclist between the bus stop and the traffic light.

AQA 2002

5 The velocity–time graphs below show the motion of a car and a bicycle as they travel along a straight horizontal road.
When $t = 0$, the car and bicycle pass a traffic light on the road.
At the traffic light, the bicycle is travelling at a constant velocity of $5\,\mathrm{m\,s^{-1}}$, but the car is travelling at $3\,\mathrm{m\,s^{-1}}$ and accelerating.

   (a) (i) Explain how the graph indicates that the acceleration of the car is constant.

   (ii) Find the acceleration of the car.

   (b) When $t = T$, the car has travelled twice as far from the traffic light as the bicycle.
   Find the value of T.

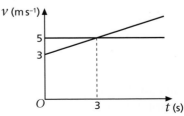

AQA 2001

2 Kinematics in two dimensions

In this chapter you will learn how to
- use vectors to represent position, velocity and acceleration
- use the unit vectors **i** and **j**
- find the magnitude and direction of a vector
- solve problems involving resultant velocities
- use the constant acceleration equations in two dimensions

A Displacement (answers p 143)

A1 Alexia is standing in the centre of a large field.
She walks in a straight line for a distance of 50 metres.
Sketch her possible finishing points.

From the information given above it is not possible to find a single finishing point for Alexia. The distance she covers has been given, but in order to decide where she finishes you need to know in which direction she has walked.

If you know that Alexia has walked 50 m north-east, then her finishing point is fully defined.

This vector represents her walk.

> K
>
> The quantity that includes both distance and direction is the **displacement**.
>
> The **magnitude** or size of the displacement is the distance.
>
> Displacement is a **vector** quantity, a quantity that has both magnitude and direction.
>
> Distance is a **scalar** quantity; it has magnitude but not direction.

Displacement can be given as a distance and a direction – for example, Alexia's displacement can be defined by giving a distance (50 m) and a direction (NE) – but it can also be represented as a column vector.

Alexia's displacement can also be described using the distance she could have walked east followed by the distance she could have walked north to give the same total displacement.

$a = 50 \cos 45° = 35.4$ to 1 d.p.
$b = 50 \sin 45° = 35.4$ to 1 d.p.

So Alexia could have walked 35.4 m east followed by 35.4 m north to give the same total displacement.

These distances are the **components** of her displacement in the east and north directions.

If east is taken as the *x*-direction and north as the *y*-direction, then a displacement can be described as a column vector using the *x*- and *y*-**components** of the displacement.

Alexia's displacement can be written $\begin{bmatrix} 35.4 \\ 35.4 \end{bmatrix}$ m.

K If a vector is given as a magnitude and direction, expressing it as a pair of components in two perpendicular directions is called **resolving** the vector into components.

A2 A model plane flies 36 m on a bearing of 030°.

(a) Resolve the displacement into *x*- and *y*-components.

(b) Write the displacement as a column vector.

Instead of using a column vector, a vector can be written in terms of **i** and **j**, where **i** is the unit vector in the *x*-direction and **j** is the unit vector in the *y*-direction.

$$\mathbf{i} = \begin{bmatrix} 1 \\ 0 \end{bmatrix}, \mathbf{j} = \begin{bmatrix} 0 \\ 1 \end{bmatrix}$$

The vector shown on the grid can be written

$$3\begin{bmatrix} 1 \\ 0 \end{bmatrix} + 2\begin{bmatrix} 0 \\ 1 \end{bmatrix} \quad \text{or} \quad 3\mathbf{i} + 2\mathbf{j}.$$

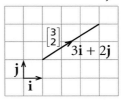

Using this notation the vector $\begin{bmatrix} 20 \\ -30 \end{bmatrix}$ is equivalent to $20\begin{bmatrix} 1 \\ 0 \end{bmatrix} - 30\begin{bmatrix} 0 \\ 1 \end{bmatrix}$ or $20\mathbf{i} - 30\mathbf{j}$.

Note that vector quantities are represented by bold type in this book.

In written work underlining can be used, for example i̲ and j̲, or ḭ and j̰.

A displacement given as a column vector or in terms of **i** and **j** can be converted into distance and direction form.

Example 1

The displacement of a model boat is given by $(-10\mathbf{i} + 15\mathbf{j})$ m.
Write the displacement in distance and direction form.

Solution

Sketch the vector.

Use Pythagoras's theorem to calculate the magnitude, d, of the displacement.

$$d = \sqrt{15^2 + 10^2} = \sqrt{325} = 18.0 \text{ to 1 d.p.}$$

The vector makes an angle θ° with the negative x-direction.

$$\tan\theta = \frac{15}{10} = 1.5, \text{ from which } \theta = 56.3° \text{ to 1 d.p.}$$

The displacement is 18.0 m at 56.3° to the negative *x*-direction.

A3 Gina walks in a straight line. Her final displacement is $(60\mathbf{i} + 80\mathbf{j})\,\text{m}$.

    (a) Sketch a vector to represent her walk.

    (b) Use Pythagoras's theorem to calculate the distance she walks.

    (c) Use trigonometry to calculate the angle the vector makes with the x-direction.

Mike walks 30 m on a bearing of 110°.

The sketch shows his displacement.

The dotted lines show the components of his displacement in the x- and y-directions.

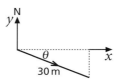

In order to write the displacement in terms of $\mathbf{i}$ and $\mathbf{j}$ or as a column vector these components need to be calculated.

In this case the displacement is positive in the x-direction and negative in the y-direction.

    A4 (a) Find angle θ.

    (b) Calculate the x- and y-components of this displacement.

    (c) Write the displacement in terms of $\mathbf{i}$ and $\mathbf{j}$.

K Displacement can be

    (1) given as a magnitude and direction, or

    (2) resolved into two components at right angles to each other and represented as either a column vector $\begin{bmatrix} a \\ b \end{bmatrix}$ or in the form $a\mathbf{i} + b\mathbf{j}$, where $\mathbf{i}$ and $\mathbf{j}$ are unit vectors at right angles to each other.

Example 2

Keith walks 75 m on a bearing of 040°.
Taking $\mathbf{i}$ and $\mathbf{j}$ as the unit vectors in the directions east and north respectively, find his displacement in terms of $\mathbf{i}$ and $\mathbf{j}$.

Solution

Sketch the vector.

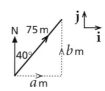

The displacement is $a\mathbf{i} + b\mathbf{j}$.

Use trigonometry to find a and b.

    $a = 75 \sin 40° = 48.2$ to 1 d.p.

    $b = 75 \cos 40° = 57.5$ to 1 d.p.

    Keith's displacement is $(48.2\mathbf{i} + 57.5\mathbf{j})\,\text{m}$.

Exercise A (answers p 143)

1 Taking east as the x-direction and north as the y-direction, write each of the following displacements

      (i) as a column vector **(ii)** in terms of $\mathbf{i}$ and $\mathbf{j}$

  (a) 20 km east and 15 km north   **(b)** 20 km west

  (c) 18 km east and 6 km south   **(d)** 5 km west and 10 km north

2 (a) Sketch the vector $\begin{bmatrix} 8 \\ 3 \end{bmatrix}$.

  (b) Find its magnitude and direction.

3 Darren walks in a straight line, so that his displacement is $(15\mathbf{i} - 12\mathbf{j})$ m.

  (a) How far does he walk?

  (b) What angle does his displacement make with the vector $\mathbf{i}$?

4 Fran walks 100 m on a bearing of 070°. Taking $\mathbf{i}$ and $\mathbf{j}$ as the unit vectors in the directions east and north respectively, find her displacement in terms of $\mathbf{i}$ and $\mathbf{j}$.

5 A model plane flies 50 m south-east. Taking east as the x-direction and north as the y-direction, write its displacement as a column vector.

6 A ship moves so that its displacement is given by $(-15\mathbf{i} + 20\mathbf{j})$ m. Find the distance and bearing from its starting point.

B Resultant displacement (answers p 144)

Vic has a model car. He drives it from point A, around a marker at B, to point C.

The displacement from A to B is $(6\mathbf{i} + 4\mathbf{j})$ m.

The displacement from B to C is $(\mathbf{i} - 5\mathbf{j})$ m.

The **resultant** displacement is from A to C.

The resultant can be found by adding the vectors $\overrightarrow{AB}$ and $\overrightarrow{BC}$. This is the **vector sum** or just sum of $\overrightarrow{AB}$ and $\overrightarrow{BC}$.

These vectors can be added 'tail to head' using a 'triangle rule'.

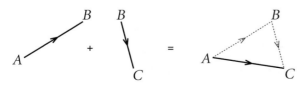

B1 Draw the triangle ABC on squared paper.
Write down the resultant displacement from A to C.

Vectors given in component form can be added by adding the x-components and adding the y-components.

B2 (a) Add together the vectors $(6\mathbf{i} + 4\mathbf{j})$ and $(\mathbf{i} - 5\mathbf{j})$.
Check that your answer is the same as for B1.

(b) Use a vector diagram to explain why this method works.

D

B3 (a) Calculate the magnitude of the displacement from A to C.

(b) Calculate the distance the car has travelled to get from point A to point C.

Example 3

A yacht sails from P, around a buoy at Q, to a buoy at R.

The displacement from P to Q is $\begin{bmatrix} 8 \\ -2 \end{bmatrix}$. The displacement from Q to R is $\begin{bmatrix} 4 \\ 4 \end{bmatrix}$.

Find the displacement of R from P.

Solution

Add x-components; add y-components.
$$\begin{bmatrix} 8 \\ -2 \end{bmatrix} + \begin{bmatrix} 4 \\ 4 \end{bmatrix} = \begin{bmatrix} 12 \\ 2 \end{bmatrix}$$

Example 4

A displacement of $(3\mathbf{i} + 2\mathbf{j})$ m is followed by a displacement of $(7\mathbf{i} - 6\mathbf{j})$ m.
Find the magnitude and direction of the resultant displacement.

Solution

Find the resultant displacement by adding.   Resultant $= (3\mathbf{i} + 2\mathbf{j}) + (7\mathbf{i} - 6\mathbf{j})$

Rearrange to separate the terms in $\mathbf{i}$ and $\mathbf{j}$. $= (3 + 7)\mathbf{i} + (2 - 6)\mathbf{j}$

$= 10\mathbf{i} - 4\mathbf{j}$

Sketch the resultant vector.

Use Pythagoras to find the magnitude. $\sqrt{10^2 + 4^2} = \sqrt{116} = 10.8$ m to 1 d.p.

Use trigonometry to find the direction. $\tan\theta = \frac{4}{10} = 0.4$

$\theta = 21.8°$ to 1 d.p.

The resultant is a displacement of 10.8 m at 21.8° below the vector $\mathbf{i}$.

Exercise B (answers p 144)

1 A displacement of $\begin{bmatrix} 30 \\ 40 \end{bmatrix}$ is followed by a displacement of $\begin{bmatrix} 120 \\ -70 \end{bmatrix}$.

Find the resultant displacement.

2 A displacement of $6\mathbf{i} - 2\mathbf{j}$ is followed by a displacement of $-4\mathbf{i} + 4\mathbf{j}$.

(a) Find the resultant displacement.

(b) Find the magnitude and direction of the resultant displacement.

3 Four displacement vectors have a resultant of $10\mathbf{i} - 2\mathbf{j}$.
Given that three of them are $-2\mathbf{i} - 3\mathbf{j}$, $5\mathbf{i} - 7\mathbf{j}$ and $16\mathbf{i} + 4\mathbf{j}$, find the fourth vector.

4 A model car drives from point A to point B with a displacement of $(8\mathbf{i} - 2\mathbf{j})$ m.
It then drives from point B to point C with a displacement of $(-3\mathbf{i} + 10\mathbf{j})$ m.

(a) Find its resultant displacement.

(b) Calculate the direct distance from point A to point C.

(c) Calculate the total distance travelled by the car.

5 A hiker walks from marker post P to post Q and then to post R.
The displacement from P to Q is $(30\mathbf{i} + 20\mathbf{j})$ m, the displacement from Q to R
is $(50\mathbf{i} - 10\mathbf{j})$ m, where $\mathbf{i}$ and $\mathbf{j}$ are unit vectors in the directions east and north
respectively.

Find the magnitude of the displacement from P to R and the direction this
displacement makes with the vector $\mathbf{i}$.

C **Position vector** (answers p 144)

The displacement of an object is the distance moved in a certain direction.

The position of an object is defined by its displacement from a fixed origin.
This displacement is called the **position vector** of the object.

Notation: the letter $\mathbf{r}$ is used for position vector;
the letter $\mathbf{s}$ is used for displacement.
The unit vectors $\mathbf{i}$ and $\mathbf{j}$ are at right angles to each other.

The position vector of the point A with respect to the origin O
is given by $\mathbf{r}_A = 4\mathbf{i} + 2\mathbf{j}$.

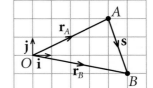

C1 Write down the position vector of point B.

C2 An object moves from A to B.
Write down its displacement, $\mathbf{s}$.

If the original position vector of an object and its displacement are known,
its final position vector can be found by adding the two vectors.

$$\mathbf{r}_A + \mathbf{s} = \mathbf{r}_B$$

C3 An object with position vector $(6\mathbf{i} - 2\mathbf{j})$ is displaced by $(-3\mathbf{i} + \mathbf{j})$.
What is its final position vector?

C4 (a) Write down the position vectors of points C and D.

    (b) Write down the displacement from C to D.

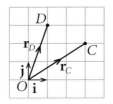

The displacement of the object is the difference between
the position vector of D and the position vector of C.

Vectors given in component form can be subtracted by subtracting
the x-components and subtracting the y-components.

C5 Find $\mathbf{r}_D - \mathbf{r}_C$. Check that your answer is the same as in C4(b).

C6 An object moves from the point $(-2\mathbf{i} + 5\mathbf{j})$ to the point $(4\mathbf{i} + 3\mathbf{j})$.
What is its displacement?

K The final position vector of an object is the sum of its
initial position vector and its displacement.

$$\mathbf{r}_B = \mathbf{r}_A + \mathbf{s}$$

To find the displacement of an object, subtract
the initial position vector from the final position vector.

$$\mathbf{s} = \mathbf{r}_B - \mathbf{r}_A$$

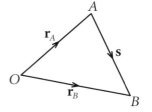

C7 The position vector, in metres, of a speedboat at time t seconds relative to a
fixed point O is given by $\mathbf{r} = 30t\mathbf{i} + (20 - 4t)\mathbf{j}$, where $\mathbf{i}$ and $\mathbf{j}$ are unit vectors
in the directions east and north respectively.

    (a) Find the position vectors of the ship when $t = 0$ and $t = 10$.
Plot these positions on a grid.

    (b) Find the displacement of the speedboat between $t = 0$ and $t = 10$.

    (c) What distance has the speedboat travelled between $t = 0$ and $t = 10$?

    (d) At what time is the speedboat due east of its starting point?

Example 5

The position vector, in metres, of an object at time t seconds is given by
$\mathbf{r} = t^2\mathbf{i} + (4 - 5t)\mathbf{j}$.
Find its displacement between $t = 5$ and $t = 10$.

Solution

Find the position vectors at the two times.	When $t = 5$	$\mathbf{r} = 5^2\mathbf{i} + (4 - 5\times5)\mathbf{j} = 25\mathbf{i} - 21\mathbf{j}$
	When $t = 10$	$\mathbf{r} = 10^2\mathbf{i} + (4 - 5\times10)\mathbf{j} = 100\mathbf{i} - 46\mathbf{j}$
Subtract to find the displacement.		$\mathbf{s} = (100\mathbf{i} - 46\mathbf{j}) - (25\mathbf{i} - 21\mathbf{j})$
		$\mathbf{s} = 75\mathbf{i} - 25\mathbf{j}$

Example 6

An object moves so that its position vector, in metres, relative to the origin O at time t seconds ($t \geq 0$) is given by $\mathbf{r} = (200 + 10t)\mathbf{i} + t^2\mathbf{j}$, where $\mathbf{i}$ and $\mathbf{j}$ are unit vectors in the directions east and north respectively.
At what time is the object north-east of the origin?

Solution

The object is north-east of the origin when the $\mathbf{i}$- and $\mathbf{j}$-components of the position vector are equal and both positive.

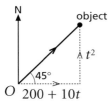

$$200 + 10t = t^2$$

$$t^2 - 10t - 200 = 0$$

$$(t + 10)(t - 20) = 0$$

$$t = -10 \text{ or } 20$$

Take the positive value for the time.   The object is north-east of the origin when $t = 20$.

Exercise C (answers p 144)

1 An object with position vector $\begin{bmatrix} 4 \\ 2 \end{bmatrix}$ is displaced by $\begin{bmatrix} 8 \\ -3 \end{bmatrix}$.

What is its new position vector?

2 A hot air balloon has position vector $(6\mathbf{i} - \mathbf{j})$ km relative to its launch site. It moves by $(-2\mathbf{i} + 3\mathbf{j})$ km. The unit vectors $\mathbf{i}$ and $\mathbf{j}$ are directed east and north respectively.

(a) What is its new position vector?

(b) What distance is the balloon from its launch site?

3 An object moves from A with position vector $\begin{bmatrix} -3 \\ 6 \end{bmatrix}$ to B with position vector $\begin{bmatrix} 4 \\ -2 \end{bmatrix}$.

Find the displacement from A to B.

4 A yacht is at the point with position vector $(25\mathbf{i} - 40\mathbf{j})$ m.
A lifeboat is at the point with position vector $(40\mathbf{i} - 30\mathbf{j})$ m.
Find the displacement of the yacht from the lifeboat.

5 The position vector, in metres, of an object at time t seconds is given by $\mathbf{r} = 3t^2\mathbf{i} + (4t - 2)\mathbf{j}$.

(a) Find the position vector of the object at $t = 0$.

(b) Find the position vector of the object at $t = 10$.

(c) Sketch a diagram to show the positions of the object at $t = 0$ and $t = 10$.

(d) What is the displacement of the object between $t = 0$ and $t = 10$?

6 A ball is kicked so that its position vector, in metres, after time t seconds is given by $\mathbf{r} = 18t\mathbf{i} + (8t - 4.9t^2)\mathbf{j}$, where $\mathbf{i}$ and $\mathbf{j}$ are horizontal and vertical unit vectors respectively.

   (a) Find the position of the ball when $t = 1$.

   (b) Find the time when the ball hits the ground.

   (c) What horizontal distance has the ball covered in this time?

7 The position vector, in metres, of a particle relative to the origin at time t seconds is given by $\mathbf{r} = (2t - 10)\mathbf{i} + (t^2 + 6)\mathbf{j}$, where $\mathbf{i}$ and $\mathbf{j}$ are unit vectors in the directions east and north respectively.

   (a) At what time is the particle due north of the origin?

   (b) How far is the particle from its starting point at this time?

8 The position vector, in km, of an object relative to the origin at time t hours is given by $\mathbf{r} = (8t - 12)\mathbf{i} + (t^2 - 8)\mathbf{j}$, where $\mathbf{i}$ and $\mathbf{j}$ are unit vectors in the directions east and north respectively.

   (a) At what time is the object south-east of the origin?

   (b) What distance is the object from the origin at this time?

D Velocity (answers p 145)

In the previous chapter we dealt with objects moving in one dimension.
Here we will consider objects moving in two dimensions.

> Velocity is a vector quantity, a quantity with both magnitude and direction.
>
> The magnitude of the velocity is the speed.
>
> Speed is a scalar quantity; it has magnitude but not direction.

A ship moves with constant velocity $(4\mathbf{i} + 2\mathbf{j})\,\text{m s}^{-1}$.

This velocity can also be written as $\begin{bmatrix} 4 \\ 2 \end{bmatrix}\text{m s}^{-1}$.

Velocity is the increase in displacement per second, so a velocity of $(4\mathbf{i} + 2\mathbf{j})\,\text{m s}^{-1}$ means that the displacement of the ship increases by $(4\mathbf{i} + 2\mathbf{j})\,\text{m}$ each second.

The position of the ship will be as shown in the diagram.

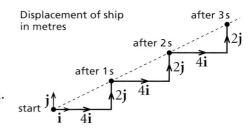

D1 The ship starts from the origin O when $t = 0$.

   (a) Write down the position vector of the ship when $t = 1$.

   (b) Write down the position vector of the ship when $t = 5$.

   (c) Write down the position vector of the ship when $t = 2.5$.

D2 The diagram shows the velocity vector for the ship.

(a) What is the magnitude of the velocity?

(b) Find θ, the angle that the velocity makes with the vector **i**.

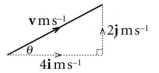

D3 A helicopter flies south-east at a constant speed of $55\,\text{m s}^{-1}$.
Take **i** and **j** as the unit vectors directed east and north respectively.

(a) Sketch the velocity vector for the helicopter.

(b) What angle does the velocity make with the vector **i**?

(c) Use trigonometry to work out the components of the velocity in the **i**- and **j**-directions.

(d) Write the velocity of the helicopter in terms of **i** and **j**.

In one-dimensional motion the **average velocity** was defined as the constant velocity at which a journey of the same overall displacement could have been completed in the same total time. This also applies to two-dimensional motion.

$$\text{Average velocity} = \frac{\text{displacement from starting point}}{\text{time taken}}$$

If the position vector of an object at two different times is known, then the displacement is the change in position vector.

$$\text{Average velocity} = \frac{\text{change in position vector}}{\text{time taken}}$$

D4 The position vector of a ship is $(7\mathbf{i} - 8\mathbf{j})\,\text{m}$.
Five seconds later it is at point B with position vector $(22\mathbf{i} + 17\mathbf{j})\,\text{m}$.

(a) Write down the displacement of the ship.

(b) What is the average velocity of the ship?

D5 The position vector, in metres, of a model plane at time t seconds is given by $\mathbf{r} = (2t + 3)\mathbf{i} + 8t\mathbf{j}$, where **i** and **j** are unit vectors in the directions east and north respectively.

(a) Write down the plane's position when $t = 0$.

(b) Write down its position when $t = 30$.

(c) Find the displacement of the plane in the first 30 seconds of the flight.

(d) What is the average velocity of the plane for the first 30 seconds?

Exercise D (answers p 145)

1 Write these velocities in terms of **i** and **j**, where **i** and **j** are unit vectors in the directions east and north respectively.

(a) $20\,\text{m s}^{-1}$ due north

(b) $5\,\text{m s}^{-1}$ due west

2 A model plane moves with constant velocity $\begin{bmatrix} 3 \\ 1 \end{bmatrix}$ m s^{-1}, where east is the x-direction and north is the y-direction.

(a) Write down its displacement after 1 second.

(b) Write down its displacement after 10 seconds.

3 A ship moves with velocity $(12\mathbf{i} - 8\mathbf{j})$ m s^{-1}.

(a) Find the magnitude of the velocity.

(b) Find the angle that the motion makes with the vector $\mathbf{i}$.

4 A ship moves at 20 m s^{-1} on a bearing of $065°$.
Taking x and y as east and north respectively, find the velocity as a column vector.

5 A golf ball is hit so that it moves off at a speed of 15 m s^{-1} at an angle of $30°$ to the horizontal.
Find the initial velocity of the golf ball in terms of $\mathbf{i}$ and $\mathbf{j}$, where $\mathbf{i}$ and $\mathbf{j}$ are horizontal and vertical unit vectors respectively.

6 The position vector of a helicopter is $(70\mathbf{i} + 30\mathbf{j})$ m, where $\mathbf{i}$ and $\mathbf{j}$ are unit vectors in the directions east and north respectively.
After 60 seconds it is at the point with position vector $(40\mathbf{i} + 270\mathbf{j})$ m.

(a) Find the displacement of the helicopter.

(b) What is the average velocity of the helicopter for the 60 seconds?

7 The position vector, in metres, of a ship at time t seconds is given by
$\mathbf{r} = (10 - 3t)\mathbf{i} + (5t + 1)\mathbf{j}$.
Find the average velocity of the ship in the first 30 seconds of its motion.

8 The position vector, in metres, of a particle at time t seconds is given by
$\mathbf{r} = 2t^2\mathbf{i} + (8 - 3t)\mathbf{j}$.

(a) Find the position of the particle when $t = 10$.

(b) Find the position of the particle when $t = 20$.

(c) Find the average velocity of the particle between $t = 10$ and $t = 20$.

9 The initial position vector of a ship, in metres, is $(20\mathbf{i} + 30\mathbf{j})$, where $\mathbf{i}$ and $\mathbf{j}$ are unit vectors in the directions east and north respectively.
The ship moves with a constant velocity $(4\mathbf{i} - 3\mathbf{j})$ m s^{-1} for t seconds.

(a) Find an expression for the displacement, $\mathbf{s}$, of the ship after t seconds.

(b) Find an expression for the position vector, $\mathbf{r}$, of the ship after t seconds.

(c) What is the position vector of the ship when $t = 60$?

10 An object moves with velocity $(10\mathbf{i} - 3\mathbf{j})$ m s^{-1}.
Initially it is at the point with position vector $(-30\mathbf{i} + 12\mathbf{j})$ m.
Find its position vector after 20 seconds.

E Resultant velocity (answers p 145)

A motorised toy duck walks at a speed of $0.3\,\mathrm{m\,s^{-1}}$. It walks on a tray, as shown in this diagram.

↑0.3 m s⁻¹

As the duck walks on the tray, the tray itself is moved in the same direction as the duck and at a speed of $0.2\,\mathrm{m\,s^{-1}}$.

The **resultant velocity** of the duck is the sum of its velocity on the tray and the velocity of the tray itself, that is $0.5\,\mathrm{m\,s^{-1}}$.

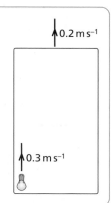

E1 Suppose that the tray moves at $0.2\,\mathrm{m\,s^{-1}}$ but in the opposite direction to the duck. What is the resultant velocity of the duck?

Suppose the tray moves at $0.2\,\mathrm{m\,s^{-1}}$ but at right angles to the direction in which the duck walks on the tray.

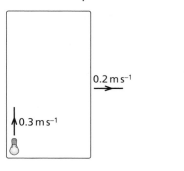

As the duck moves on the tray, so the tray moves it sideways. This diagram shows how the duck moves.

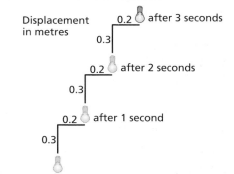

The duck's resultant velocity is found by adding the velocity vectors 'tail to head' using a vector triangle.

The resultant velocity is denoted by a double-headed arrow.

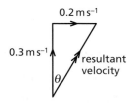

> Resultant velocity = velocity of duck on tray + velocity of tray

E2 (a) Find the magnitude of the resultant velocity.

(b) Find the angle, θ, this velocity makes with the edge of the tray.

The resultant velocity of an object can be found by adding its separate velocities using a vector triangle.

E3 Suppose the duck walks on the tray at 0.3 m s⁻¹ at an angle of 45° to the edges of the tray, while the tray moves at 0.2 m s⁻¹ as shown here.

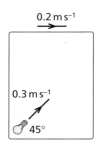

    (a) Sketch a vector triangle for finding the resultant velocity of the duck.

    (b) Draw the vector triangle to scale and use your scale drawing to find the resultant speed and direction of the duck.

Rowing (or driving) a boat on water that is itself moving is essentially the same as moving across a tray that is itself moving. The resultant velocity of the boat (as seen, for example, by someone looking down from above) is the vector sum of the velocity of the boat **relative** to the water and the velocity of the water itself.

Fraser can row his boat at a speed of 2 m s⁻¹ in still water.
He is rowing in a river which is flowing parallel to its banks at a constant 1 m s⁻¹.
The speed of his boat relative to the water is 2 m s⁻¹.

E4 Fraser directs his boat downstream, that is in the direction of the current, as shown in the diagram.
What is his resultant velocity?

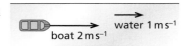

E5 He now directs his boat upstream, that is in the opposite direction to the current.

    (a) Sketch a diagram to show the velocities of the boat and the river.

    (b) What is the resultant velocity?

Fraser now attempts to row his boat across the river, perpendicular to the river bank.

The velocity vectors are as shown.

As Fraser rows across the river, the current moves his boat downstream. He directs the boat across the river, but the resultant velocity is at an angle θ to the bank.

This velocity triangle shows the resultant velocity of the boat.

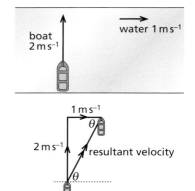

Resultant velocity = velocity of boat relative to the water + velocity of water

E6 **(a)** Find the magnitude of the resultant velocity.

    (b) Find the angle this velocity makes with the bank of the river.

E7 Fraser reduces his velocity to 1 m s⁻¹ perpendicular to the river bank. The velocity of the river remains constant at 1 m s⁻¹.

    (a) Sketch a velocity triangle showing his resultant velocity.

    (b) Find the magnitude and direction of the resultant velocity.

E8 Fraser rows at $1.5\,\mathrm{m\,s^{-1}}$ across the river flowing at $1\,\mathrm{m\,s^{-1}}$.
Find the magnitude and direction of his resultant velocity.

K When the speed of a boat is given, this is the speed that the boat would
travel at in still water, or the speed relative to the water.
The resultant velocity of the boat is the vector sum of the velocity of the boat
relative to the water and the velocity of the water.

Example 7

A model plane is flying with a constant velocity of $(5\mathbf{i} - \mathbf{j})\,\mathrm{m\,s^{-1}}$ relative to the air.
A wind with velocity $(-\mathbf{i} + 2\mathbf{j})\,\mathrm{m\,s^{-1}}$ is blowing.
Find the magnitude of the resultant velocity and the angle it makes with the vector $\mathbf{i}$.

Solution

Add the velocities to find the resultant. $\mathbf{v} = (5\mathbf{i} - \mathbf{j}) + (-\mathbf{i} + 2\mathbf{j}) = 4\mathbf{i} + \mathbf{j}$

Sketch the resultant velocity.

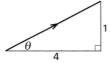

Use Pythagoras to find the magnitude. $v = \sqrt{4^2 + 1^2}$
$$= \sqrt{17} = 4.1\,\mathrm{m\,s^{-1}} \text{ to 1 d.p.}$$

Use trigonometry to find the angle. $\tan\theta = \frac{1}{4}$

$\theta = 14°$ to the nearest degree

The resultant velocity is $4.1\,\mathrm{m\,s^{-1}}$ at $14°$ to the $\mathbf{i}$-direction.

Exercise E (answers p 146)

1 A plane is flying at a velocity of $50\mathbf{i}\,\mathrm{m\,s^{-1}}$ relative to the air.
The wind is blowing with a velocity of $5\mathbf{j}\,\mathrm{m\,s^{-1}}$.
Find the resultant velocity of the plane.

2 A boat is propelled with velocity $\begin{bmatrix} -3 \\ 2 \end{bmatrix}\mathrm{km\,h^{-1}}$ across a river running at $\begin{bmatrix} 2 \\ -1 \end{bmatrix}\mathrm{km\,h^{-1}}$.
Find the resultant velocity of the boat.

3 Naomi can swim at a speed of $1\,\mathrm{m\,s^{-1}}$ in still water.
She swims across a river which flows parallel to its banks at $1.5\,\mathrm{m\,s^{-1}}$.
Assume that Naomi's speed relative to the water is $1\,\mathrm{m\,s^{-1}}$ and
the velocity of the water is constant across the width of the river.

(a) Sketch a velocity triangle showing Naomi's resultant velocity if she heads
directly across the river.

(b) Find the magnitude of her resultant velocity.

(c) Find the angle the resultant velocity makes with the bank.

4 A boat has a velocity of $(2\mathbf{i} + 5\mathbf{j})\,\mathrm{m\,s^{-1}}$ relative to the water.
The velocity of the water is $(-\mathbf{i} + \mathbf{j})\,\mathrm{m\,s^{-1}}$.

(a) Find the resultant velocity of the boat.

(b) Find the magnitude of the resultant velocity.

(c) Find the angle the resultant velocity makes with the vector $\mathbf{i}$.

5 Greg can row at a speed of $2.5\,\mathrm{m\,s^{-1}}$ in still water.
He rows across a river perpendicular to the bank.
The river is flowing at a speed of $2\,\mathrm{m\,s^{-1}}$ parallel to its banks.

(a) Find the magnitude and direction of Greg's resultant velocity.

(b) If the speed of the river increased to $3\,\mathrm{m\,s^{-1}}$, what would be the magnitude
and direction of his resultant velocity?

F Resultant velocity problems (answers p 146)

Fraser can row his boat at $2\,\mathrm{m\,s^{-1}}$ and wants to end up on
the other side of the river perpendicular to his starting point.

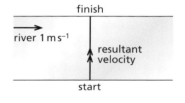

In this case the magnitude of the velocity of the boat
is known, but not the direction in which it should head.

Fraser's finishing point is known and this defines the direction
of the resultant velocity.

Fraser will need to direct his boat upstream in order to reach his desired
finishing point.

This is a vector triangle for the motion, where θ is the angle his boat
should make with the river bank and $\mathbf{v}$ is the resultant velocity.

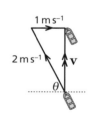

F1 (a) Calculate the magnitude of the resultant velocity.

(b) Calculate the angle the boat's velocity makes with the river bank.

F2 Fraser actually rows at $1.8\,\mathrm{m\,s^{-1}}$ and finishes on the other side of the river
perpendicular to his starting point.

(a) Sketch a velocity triangle for his motion.

(b) Calculate the magnitude of the resultant velocity.

(c) Calculate the angle the boat's velocity makes with the river bank.

Liz wants to fly her model plane from A to B, where B is due south of A.
The plane can fly at $10\,\mathrm{m\,s^{-1}}$ in still air.
A wind is blowing at $4\,\mathrm{m\,s^{-1}}$ at an angle of $40°$ to AB.

The resultant velocity of the plane needs to be directed along AB, so Liz
needs to work out the direction in which she needs to steer the plane.

If Liz heads the plane in the direction AB, the wind will blow it off course.
If she heads it at a suitable angle $\theta°$ to AB the wind will direct the plane
on to the required course.

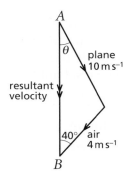

Resultant velocity = velocity of plane in still air + velocity of air

The velocity triangle is as shown.

The velocity of the plane and the velocity of the air can be resolved
into components parallel and perpendicular to AB.

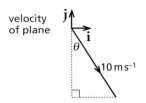

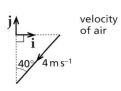

The velocity of the plane has component $10\sin\theta$ in the **i**-direction and
$-10\cos\theta$ in the **j**-direction.

Velocity of plane $= 10\sin\theta\,\mathbf{i} - 10\cos\theta\,\mathbf{j}$

F3 Write the velocity of the air in terms of **i** and **j**.

The resultant velocity is the sum of these two velocities.
As the resultant is directed in the negative **j**-direction, the sum of the **i** components
must be zero.

F4 (a) Show that $10\sin\theta = 4\sin40°$.

(b) Find the value of θ.

(c) Find the resultant velocity of the plane.

F5 An alternative method of solution for this problem
is to use the sine rule.

(a) Use the sine rule to find the value of θ.

(b) Find the third angle in the velocity triangle
and hence use the sine rule to find the magnitude
of the resultant velocity.

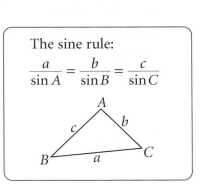

The sine rule:

$$\frac{a}{\sin A} = \frac{b}{\sin B} = \frac{c}{\sin C}$$

Example 8

A canoe travels in a straight line from point A to point B.
Relative to the water, the velocity of the canoe is $4\,\text{m s}^{-1}$
and directed at an angle of $30°$ to AB.
The current is at an angle of $45°$ to AB as shown in the
velocity triangle.

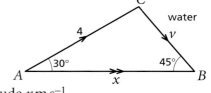

The resultant velocity is directed along AB and is of magnitude $x\,\text{m s}^{-1}$.

Find the value of x.

Solution

Resolve the velocities into components parallel and perpendicular to AB.

The resultant is along AB so the perpendicular component is zero. $4\sin 30° = v\sin 45°$

$$v = \frac{4\sin 30°}{\sin 45°} = 2.828\ldots\,\text{m s}^{-1}$$

Find the sum of the parallel components. $x = 4\cos 30° + 2.828\ldots\cos 45°$

$$x = 5.46 \text{ to 2 d.p.}$$

An alternative method using the sine rule is as follows.

Find the third angle in the triangle. $C = 180° - 30° - 45° = 105°$

Use the sine rule to find x.

$$\frac{x}{\sin 105°} = \frac{4}{\sin 45°}$$

$$x = \frac{4\sin 105°}{\sin 45°} = 5.46 \text{ to 2 d.p.}$$

Exercise F (answers p 146)

1 A girl wants to paddle her canoe across the river to the nearest point on the
   opposite bank. She paddles at $1.5\,\text{m s}^{-1}$ relative to the water.
   The river is running at $1\,\text{m s}^{-1}$.

   (a) Sketch a velocity triangle for this motion.

   (b) Find the angle that the velocity of the canoe relative to the water makes
        with the bank.

   (c) What is the magnitude of the resultant velocity?

   (d) If the river is $50\,\text{m}$ wide, how long does it take the girl to cross the river?

   (e) What modelling assumptions have you made in answering this question?

2 Suppose the girl in the previous question had pointed her canoe directly across the river.

    (a) How long would it have taken her to cross the river?

    (b) How far downstream would she end up?

3 A model plane is flying with a velocity of $(3\mathbf{i} + 2\mathbf{j})\,\mathrm{m\,s^{-1}}$ in still air.
A wind starts to blow causing the plane to fly with resultant velocity $(\mathbf{i} + 3\mathbf{j})\,\mathrm{m\,s^{-1}}$.

    (a) Find the magnitude of the velocity of the wind.

    (b) Find the angle the velocity of the wind makes with the unit vector $\mathbf{i}$.

4 A plane with an airspeed of $250\,\mathrm{km\,h^{-1}}$ has to fly from town A to town B, $100\,\mathrm{km}$ due west of town A. A wind is blowing from $030°$ at $50\,\mathrm{km\,h^{-1}}$, as shown in the velocity triangle.

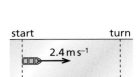

    (a) Find the direction the plane must be headed.

    (b) How long will it take the plane to travel from A to B?

5 Razia is sailing her model boat in a river which is flowing parallel to its banks at $0.8\,\mathrm{m\,s^{-1}}$.
The boat sails at $4\,\mathrm{m\,s^{-1}}$ relative to the water.
The resultant velocity of the boat is at an angle of $80°$ to the bank.

    (a) Sketch a velocity triangle for the motion.

    (b) At what angle to the bank did Razia direct the boat?

    (c) Find the magnitude of the resultant velocity.

*6 Steve rows in a river at a constant speed of $2.4\,\mathrm{m\,s^{-1}}$ relative to the water. He rows $50\,\mathrm{m}$ downstream then turns and rows back to his starting point. This takes a total of 75 seconds. Assuming that he can maintain the same speed relative to the water for the whole 75 seconds, find the speed of the water.

G Acceleration (answers p 147)

Acceleration is a vector quantity, with both magnitude and direction.

For an object moving with constant acceleration:

$$\text{Acceleration} = \frac{\text{change in velocity}}{\text{time taken}}$$

A boat moves from rest with constant acceleration of $(2\mathbf{i} + \mathbf{j})\,\mathrm{m\,s^{-2}}$.

Acceleration is the change in velocity per second, so an acceleration of $(2\mathbf{i} + \mathbf{j})\,\mathrm{m\,s^{-2}}$ means that the velocity of the boat changes by $(2\mathbf{i} + \mathbf{j})\,\mathrm{m\,s^{-1}}$ each second.

    G1 Write down the velocity of the boat after

        (a) 1 second   **(b)** 2 seconds   **(c)** 5 seconds

G2 An object moves with constant acceleration $(-2\mathbf{i} + 5\mathbf{j})\,\mathrm{m\,s}^{-2}$.

(a) Sketch the acceleration vector for the object.

(b) What is the magnitude of the acceleration?

(c) What angle does the acceleration make with the vector $\mathbf{i}$?

An object has an initial velocity of $(\mathbf{i} - 3\mathbf{j})\,\mathrm{m\,s}^{-1}$.
It undergoes a constant acceleration of $(\mathbf{i} + \mathbf{j})\,\mathrm{m\,s}^{-2}$.

Acceleration is the change in velocity per second, so the velocity of the object
will change by $(\mathbf{i} + \mathbf{j})\,\mathrm{m\,s}^{-1}$ each second.

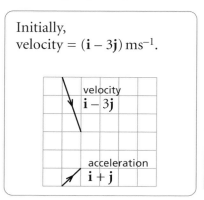

Initially,
velocity $= (\mathbf{i} - 3\mathbf{j})\,\mathrm{ms}^{-1}$.

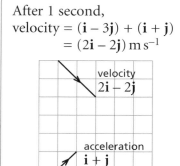

After 1 second,
velocity $= (\mathbf{i} - 3\mathbf{j}) + (\mathbf{i} + \mathbf{j})$
$= (2\mathbf{i} - 2\mathbf{j})\,\mathrm{m\,s}^{-1}$

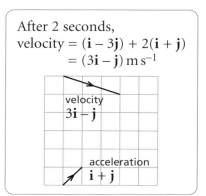

After 2 seconds,
velocity $= (\mathbf{i} - 3\mathbf{j}) + 2(\mathbf{i} + \mathbf{j})$
$= (3\mathbf{i} - \mathbf{j})\,\mathrm{m\,s}^{-1}$

The acceleration causes the direction, as well as the magnitude, of the velocity to change.

G3 These are the velocity vectors at one-second intervals for a particle undergoing
constant acceleration.

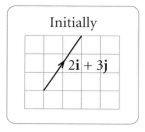

Initially

2i + 3j

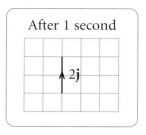

After 1 second

2j

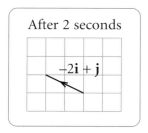

After 2 seconds

−2i + j

What is the vector for the acceleration?

G4 A plane is moving with constant acceleration.
Its velocity as it flies over a tower is $(70\mathbf{i} - 20\mathbf{j})\,\mathrm{m\,s}^{-1}$.
20 seconds later its velocity has become $(50\mathbf{i} + 10\mathbf{j})\,\mathrm{m\,s}^{-1}$.

(a) Find the change in velocity of the plane.

(b) What is the acceleration of the plane?
Sketch the acceleration vector.

Exercise G (answers p 147)

1 An object moves from rest with acceleration $\begin{bmatrix} 1 \\ -1 \end{bmatrix}$ m s^{-2}.

Find the velocity of the object after

(a) 1 second   (b) 5 seconds

2 An object moves with constant acceleration $(2\mathbf{i} - \mathbf{j})$ m s^{-2}.
Its initial velocity is $(-\mathbf{i} + \mathbf{j})$ m s^{-1}.
What is the velocity of the object after 3 seconds?

3 A model car is initially moving with velocity $(\mathbf{i} - 4\mathbf{j})$ m s^{-1}.
After 10 seconds of constant acceleration it is moving with velocity $(3\mathbf{i} + 2\mathbf{j})$ m s^{-1}.

(a) Find the change in velocity of the car.

(b) What is the constant acceleration?

4 An object moves with constant acceleration so that its velocity changes from
$(16\mathbf{i} + 3\mathbf{j})$ m s^{-1} to $(6\mathbf{i} - 2\mathbf{j})$ m s^{-1} in 5 seconds.
Find the acceleration of the object.

5 A ship moves with constant acceleration $(\mathbf{i} - 2\mathbf{j})$ m s^{-2}, where $\mathbf{i}$ and $\mathbf{j}$
are unit vectors in the directions east and north respectively.
Find the magnitude and direction of the acceleration.

6 A particle starts from rest and moves with constant acceleration.

After 4 seconds its velocity is $\begin{bmatrix} 4 \\ 2 \end{bmatrix}$ m s^{-1}.

Find the acceleration of the particle.

H Constant acceleration equations in two dimensions

Some of the constant acceleration equations derived in the previous chapter
can be applied to motion in two dimensions.

In the vector form of the equations,

$\mathbf{u}$ m s^{-1} is the initial velocity of the object
$\mathbf{v}$ m s^{-1} is the final velocity
$\mathbf{a}$ m s^{-2} is the constant acceleration
t s is the time for which the object is accelerating
$\mathbf{s}$ m is the displacement during the time the object is accelerating

K   The constant acceleration equations in vector form are

$\mathbf{v} = \mathbf{u} + \mathbf{a}t$

$\mathbf{s} = \frac{1}{2}(\mathbf{u} + \mathbf{v})t$

$\mathbf{s} = \mathbf{u}t + \frac{1}{2}\mathbf{a}t^2$

$\mathbf{s} = \mathbf{v}t - \frac{1}{2}\mathbf{a}t^2$

Notice that $v^2 = u^2 + 2as$ is not represented here as it would involve multiplying vectors together.

Example 9

A ship, moving with constant acceleration, is travelling due east at a speed of $10\,\mathrm{m\,s^{-1}}$.
After 20 seconds it is travelling due south at $5\,\mathrm{m\,s^{-1}}$.
Find the displacement from its initial position after 20 seconds.

Solution

Take $\mathbf{i}$ as due east and $\mathbf{j}$ as due north.
List the known values and the unknown, writing the velocities in terms of $\mathbf{i}$ and $\mathbf{j}$.

$$\mathbf{u} = 10\mathbf{i}, \ \mathbf{v} = -5\mathbf{j}, \ t = 20, \ \mathbf{s} = \,?$$

Substitute the known values into $\mathbf{s} = \frac{1}{2}(\mathbf{u} + \mathbf{v})t$.

$$\mathbf{s} = \tfrac{1}{2}(10\mathbf{i} - 5\mathbf{j}) \times 20$$

$$\mathbf{s} = 100\mathbf{i} - 50\mathbf{j}$$

The displacement is $(100\mathbf{i} - 50\mathbf{j})\,\mathrm{m}$.

Example 10

An object is moving with constant acceleration. Initially it is moving with velocity
$\begin{bmatrix} 8 \\ 1 \end{bmatrix} \mathrm{m\,s^{-1}}$ and after 10 seconds it is moving with velocity $\begin{bmatrix} -2 \\ 4 \end{bmatrix} \mathrm{m\,s^{-1}}$.
Find its acceleration.

Solution

First list the known values and the unknown.

$$\mathbf{u} = \begin{bmatrix} 8 \\ 1 \end{bmatrix}, \ \mathbf{v} = \begin{bmatrix} -2 \\ 4 \end{bmatrix}, \ t = 10, \ \mathbf{a} = \,?$$

Substitute the known values into $\mathbf{v} = \mathbf{u} + \mathbf{a}t$.

$$\begin{bmatrix} -2 \\ 4 \end{bmatrix} = \begin{bmatrix} 8 \\ 1 \end{bmatrix} + 10\mathbf{a}$$

Rearrange to find $\mathbf{a}$. Note that the components are dealt with separately.

$$10\mathbf{a} = \begin{bmatrix} -2 - 8 \\ 4 - 1 \end{bmatrix} = \begin{bmatrix} -10 \\ 3 \end{bmatrix}$$

$$\mathbf{a} = \begin{bmatrix} -1 \\ 0.3 \end{bmatrix}$$

The acceleration is $\begin{bmatrix} -1 \\ 0.3 \end{bmatrix} \mathrm{m\,s^{-2}}$

Example 11

An object is initially at the origin moving with velocity $(\mathbf{i} + 3\mathbf{j})\,\mathrm{m\,s^{-1}}$.
It has a constant acceleration of $(2\mathbf{i} - \mathbf{j})\,\mathrm{m\,s^{-2}}$.

Find the position vector of the object at time t, and the distance it is
from the origin after 20 seconds.

Solution

First list the known values and the unknown. $\quad \mathbf{u} = \mathbf{i} + 3\mathbf{j}, \ \mathbf{a} = 2\mathbf{i} - \mathbf{j}, \ \mathbf{s} = ?$

Substitute the known values into $\mathbf{s} = \mathbf{u}t + \frac{1}{2}\mathbf{a}t^2$. $\quad \mathbf{s} = (\mathbf{i} + 3\mathbf{j})t + \frac{1}{2}(2\mathbf{i} - \mathbf{j})t^2$

$$\mathbf{s} = (t\mathbf{i} + 3t\mathbf{j}) + (t^2\mathbf{i} - \tfrac{1}{2}t^2\mathbf{j})$$

Rearrange to separate the terms in $\mathbf{i}$ *and* $\mathbf{j}$. $\quad \mathbf{s} = (t + t^2)\mathbf{i} + (3t - \tfrac{1}{2}t^2)\mathbf{j}$

The object was initially at the origin, so its position vector is its displacement at time t.

$$\text{Position vector } \mathbf{r} = (t + t^2)\mathbf{i} + (3t - \tfrac{1}{2}t^2)\mathbf{j}$$

Substitute $t = 20$. $\quad$ After $20\,\mathrm{s}$, $\mathbf{r} = (20 + 20^2)\mathbf{i} + (3 \times 20 - \frac{1}{2} \times 20^2)\mathbf{j}$

$$\mathbf{r} = 420\mathbf{i} - 140\mathbf{j}$$

The distance is the magnitude of the displacement. $\quad$ Distance $= \sqrt{420^2 + 140^2}$

$$= 443\,\mathrm{m} \text{ to 3 s.f.}$$

Exercise H (answers p 147)

1 An object is initially moving at $(8\mathbf{i} + \mathbf{j})\,\mathrm{m\,s^{-1}}$.
  It has a constant acceleration of $(3\mathbf{i} - 2\mathbf{j})\,\mathrm{m\,s^{-2}}$.
  Find its velocity after 10 seconds.

2 A boat is moving with constant acceleration.
  Initially its velocity is $\begin{bmatrix} 4 \\ -1 \end{bmatrix}\mathrm{m\,s^{-1}}$. After 20 seconds its velocity is $\begin{bmatrix} 3 \\ 2 \end{bmatrix}\mathrm{m\,s^{-1}}$.
  Find its displacement during the 20 seconds.

3 A model boat moves from rest with a constant acceleration of $(0.2\mathbf{i} + 0.1\mathbf{j})\,\mathrm{m\,s^{-2}}$.
  Find its displacement after 5 seconds.

4 An object is moving with a constant acceleration of $(-\mathbf{i} + 3\mathbf{j})\,\mathrm{m\,s^{-2}}$.
  After 30 seconds its velocity is $(4\mathbf{i} + 12\mathbf{j})\,\mathrm{m\,s^{-1}}$.
  Find its displacement during the 30 seconds.

5 A plane is moving with constant acceleration. After $10\,\mathrm{s}$ its displacement
  is $(100\mathbf{i} + 80\mathbf{j})\,\mathrm{m}$ and it is moving with velocity $(25\mathbf{i} + 15\mathbf{j})\,\mathrm{m\,s^{-1}}$.
  Find the initial velocity of the plane.

6 A model boat has initial velocity $\begin{bmatrix} -1 \\ 1 \end{bmatrix}$ m s^{-1} and 20 s later has velocity $\begin{bmatrix} 3 \\ 0 \end{bmatrix}$ m s^{-1}.
The boat moves with constant acceleration.

(a) Find the displacement of the boat during the 20 s.

(b) Find the acceleration of the boat.

7 An object is moving with a constant acceleration of $(-\mathbf{i} + 2\mathbf{j})$ m s^{-2}.
Its displacement after 8 seconds is $(8\mathbf{i} + 12\mathbf{j})$ m.
Find its velocity after 8 seconds.

8 An object moves with a constant acceleration of $(4\mathbf{i} - \mathbf{j})$ m s^{-2}.
After 3 seconds its velocity is $(12\mathbf{i} + 2\mathbf{j})$ m s^{-1}.
Find its initial velocity.

9 A particle moves with a constant acceleration of $\begin{bmatrix} 0.5 \\ -0.5 \end{bmatrix}$ m s^{-2}.

After 10 seconds its displacement is $\begin{bmatrix} 10 \\ 5 \end{bmatrix}$ m.

Find its initial velocity.

10 A particle is moving with constant acceleration of $(-2\mathbf{i} + \mathbf{j})$ m s^{-2}.
At time $t = 0$ it is moving with velocity $(3\mathbf{i} + \mathbf{j})$ m s^{-1}.

(a) Find an expression for the velocity of the particle at time t.

(b) Find the speed of the particle when $t = 5$.

11 At time $t = 0$ a particle is at the origin and moving with velocity $(6\mathbf{i} - 2\mathbf{j})$ m s^{-1}.
When $t = 10$ the position vector of the particle is $(20\mathbf{i} + 35\mathbf{j})$ m.
The particle is moving with constant acceleration.

(a) Find the acceleration of the particle.

(b) Find the position vector of the particle at time t.

12 A particle is moving with a constant acceleration of $(2\mathbf{i} - 4\mathbf{j})$ m s^{-2}.
Initially it is at the origin with velocity $(5\mathbf{i} + \mathbf{j})$ m s^{-1}.

(a) Find the velocity of the particle after 3 seconds.

(b) Find the distance of the particle from the origin after 10 seconds.

(c) Find the speed of the particle after 10 seconds.

13 A particle is moving horizontally with constant acceleration.
Initially the particle is at the point with position vector $(4\mathbf{i} + 2\mathbf{j})$ m and has velocity $12\mathbf{j}$ m s^{-1}.
After accelerating for 5 seconds its velocity is $(5\mathbf{i} - 3\mathbf{j})$ m s^{-1}.

(a) Find the acceleration of the particle.

(b) Find the position vector of the particle when $t = 10$.

Key points

- A vector is a quantity that has both magnitude and direction.
  A vector can be resolved into two components at right angles to each other
  and represented as a column vector or in terms of the unit vectors **i** and **j**.   (pp 28–30)

- Displacement, velocity and acceleration are vector quantities.
  Distance and speed are scalar quantities.
  The magnitude of the displacement is the distance.
  The magnitude of the velocity is the speed.   (pp 28, 36, 45)

- The position vector, **r**, of an object is its displacement from a fixed origin.   (p 33)

- Average velocity $= \dfrac{\text{change in position vector}}{\text{time taken}}$ (p 37)

- The resultant velocity of an object can be found by adding its separate
  velocities or by using a vector triangle.   (pp 39–40)

- For constant acceleration, acceleration $= \dfrac{\text{change in velocity}}{\text{time taken}}$ (p 45)

- The constant acceleration equations in vector form are:

  $\mathbf{v} = \mathbf{u} + \mathbf{a}t$

  $\mathbf{s} = \frac{1}{2}(\mathbf{u} + \mathbf{v})t$

  $\mathbf{s} = \mathbf{u}t + \frac{1}{2}\mathbf{a}t^2$

  $\mathbf{s} = \mathbf{v}t - \frac{1}{2}\mathbf{a}t^2$ (p 47)

Mixed questions (answers p 148)

1 A boat moves, with constant acceleration, so that at time t its velocity is given by
  $$\mathbf{v} = 2(a - t)\mathbf{i} + 4(3 - t)\mathbf{j}$$
where a is constant and **i** and **j** are unit vectors directed east and north respectively.

(a) The boat is heading due north when $t = 2$. Find a.

(b) Find
  (i) the initial velocity of the boat
  (ii) the acceleration of the boat

(c) Find the distance between the initial position of the boat and its position
  when $t = 2$.   AQA 2002

2 A child is playing with a toy aeroplane.
The aeroplane is flying with velocity $(6\mathbf{i} + 2\mathbf{j})\,\mathrm{m\,s^{-1}}$.
A breeze begins to blow with velocity $0.5\mathbf{j}\,\mathrm{m\,s^{-1}}$ affecting
the motion of the aeroplane.

(a) Find the magnitude of the resultant velocity of the aeroplane.

(b) Find the angle this resultant velocity makes with the unit vector $\mathbf{i}$. AQA 2002

3 Ship A is moving with a constant velocity of $6\mathbf{i}\,\mathrm{km\,h^{-1}}$.
Ship B is moving with a constant velocity of $(4\mathbf{i} - \mathbf{j})\,\mathrm{km\,h^{-1}}$.
The unit vectors $\mathbf{i}$ and $\mathbf{j}$ are directed east and north respectively.
Initially, ship A is at the origin O and ship B is $5\,\mathrm{km}$ due north of O.

(a) Find, in terms of t, the position vectors $\mathbf{r}_A$ and $\mathbf{r}_B$ of the two ships
relative to O after t hours.

(b) Find the time when B is due west of A.

(c) After t hours the distance between A and B is $d\,\mathrm{km}$.
Show that $d^2 = 5t^2 - 10t + 25$.

(d) Initially the ships are $5\,\mathrm{km}$ apart.
After how many hours are they again $5\,\mathrm{km}$ apart?

4 A boat moves with a constant acceleration of $(0.2\mathbf{i} + 0.1\mathbf{j})\,\mathrm{m\,s^{-2}}$, where
the unit vectors $\mathbf{i}$ and $\mathbf{j}$ are directed east and north respectively.
Time t is measured in seconds.

At time $t = 10$, the boat is at the point A, which has position vector $(30\mathbf{i} - 35\mathbf{j})$ metres.
At time $t = 20$, the boat is at the point B, which has position vector $(70\mathbf{i} - 40\mathbf{j})$ metres.

(a) Find the vector $\overrightarrow{AB}$.

(b) Find the velocity of the boat when $t = 10$.

(c) Using your answer to part (b), find the velocity of the boat when $t = 0$.

(d) Find the position vector of the boat when $t = 0$. AQA 2003

5 A model aircraft flies on a bearing of $010°$ with a speed
of $50\,\mathrm{km\,h^{-1}}$ relative to the air. A strong wind is blowing
with a constant speed of $x\,\mathrm{km\,h^{-1}}$.
The resultant velocity of the aircraft is directed due north.
The wind is blowing at an angle of $50°$ to the resultant
velocity of the aircraft as shown in the diagram.

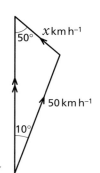

(a) Show that the value of x is approximately 11.3.

(b) (i) Find the northerly component of the $50\,\mathrm{km\,h^{-1}}$ velocity.

(ii) Hence, or otherwise, find the magnitude of the resultant velocity
of the aircraft. AQA 2002

Test yourself (answers p 148)

1 A ship moves so that its position vector, in metres, relative to a lighthouse at time t seconds is $\mathbf{r} = (80 - 0.4t)\mathbf{i} + (2t - 80)\mathbf{j}$, where $\mathbf{i}$ and $\mathbf{j}$ are unit vectors directed east and north respectively.

   (a) Find the distance of the ship from the lighthouse when $t = 60$.

   (b) Find the times when the ship is

      (i) due north of the lighthouse

      (ii) north-east of the lighthouse   AQA 2001

2 A girl swims across a river.
When she swims in still water, she swims at $1.25\,\mathrm{m\,s^{-1}}$.
The river flows parallel to its banks at $v\,\mathrm{m\,s^{-1}}$.

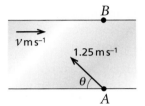

   The girl aims to swim upstream at an angle θ degrees to the river bank so that her resultant velocity, of magnitude $1\,\mathrm{m\,s^{-1}}$, is along AB, perpendicular to the river bank.

   (a) Sketch an appropriate triangle of velocities.

   (b) Find the value of v.

   (c) Find the value of θ.   AQA 2003

3 A particle moves with constant acceleration. Initially, the particle is travelling due north at $4\,\mathrm{m\,s^{-1}}$ and 10 seconds later it is travelling east at $6\,\mathrm{m\,s^{-1}}$.
The unit vectors $\mathbf{i}$ and $\mathbf{j}$ are directed east and north respectively.

   (a) Write down the initial velocity of the particle as a vector.

   (b) Show that the acceleration of the particle is $(0.6\mathbf{i} - 0.4\mathbf{j})\,\mathrm{m\,s^{-2}}$ and calculate its magnitude.

   (c) Assuming that the particle starts at the origin, find its position after 10 seconds.   AQA 2002

4 A particle is initially at rest at the origin O. It moves with constant acceleration and 4 seconds later is at the point A with position vector $(16\mathbf{i} - 12\mathbf{j})$ metres.

   (a) Find the acceleration of the particle.

   (b) Find the speed of the particle at A.

   (c) Verify that the particle passes through the point with position vector $(60\mathbf{i} - 45\mathbf{j})\,\mathrm{m}$.

3 Forces

In this chapter you will learn how to
- combine forces into a single resultant force
- resolve forces into components
- solve problems about forces in equilibrium, including weights, tensions, thrusts and friction forces

A Forces as vectors (answers p 149)

In this picture, Katy is being pulled by a dog.
The dog exerts a **force** on Katy. However, Katy manages to stand still.

Force is measured in **newtons** (N). The way in which a newton is defined will become clear in a later chapter. (To get an idea of what a force of 1 N feels like, hold a medium-sized apple in your hand. The weight of the apple is about 1 N.)

In the next picture, Katy is being pulled by two dogs, Spot and Pepi. Spot is stronger and pulls with a force of 10 N. Pepi pulls with a force of 6 N.

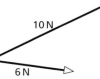

The two forces are in different directions. To specify a force you have to give not only its size, or **magnitude**, but its **direction** as well.

 Force is a vector quantity. A force can be represented by a line in the direction of the force whose length shows the magnitude of the force.

The forces exerted by the two dogs are shown in this vector diagram. An open arrowhead is used here to denote a force.

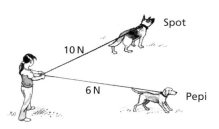

A1 Imagine that Katy weakens and can hold still no longer.
The dogs continue to pull with the same forces in the same directions.

In which of the following directions do you think Katy will start to move?

A   The direction in which Spot is pulling

B   The direction in which Pepi is pulling

C   The direction that exactly bisects the angle between Spot's and Pepi's forces

D   A direction between Spot's and Pepi's forces, but nearer to Spot's direction than Pepi's

E   A direction between Spot's and Pepi's forces, but nearer to Pepi's direction than Spot's

The two forces exerted by Spot and Pepi can be combined into a single force by the **parallelogram rule**.

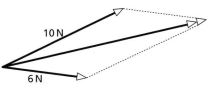

The two forces are represented, in magnitude and direction, by the adjacent sides of a parallelogram. The diagonal from the point where the forces are applied represents the single force equivalent to the two.

This single force (shown by the double arrow) is called the **resultant** of the two forces.

Notice that the direction of the resultant is closer to that of the larger force. (This explains why the correct answer to question A1 is D.)

A2 This diagram shows two forces that are of equal magnitude (10 N) with an angle of 60° between them.

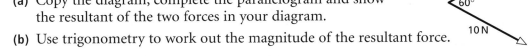

    (a) Copy the diagram, complete the parallelogram and show the resultant of the two forces in your diagram.

    (b) Use trigonometry to work out the magnitude of the resultant force.

A3 Repeat question A2, but for an angle of 90° between the two forces.

In earlier work on vectors, you added vectors 'tail to head' by a 'triangle rule':

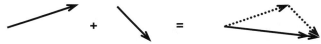

The resultant of two forces can also be found by the triangle rule. However, using a parallelogram rather than a triangle draws attention to the point where the forces are applied, and this can be extremely important in applications.

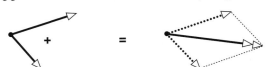

K   Two forces that exactly balance each other are said to be **in equilibrium**. One force is then equal and opposite to the other.

Three forces will be in equilibrium if the resultant of any two of them balances the third force.

The parallelogram rule can be verified experimentally by using 'newton meters' (which measure forces by stretching a spring).

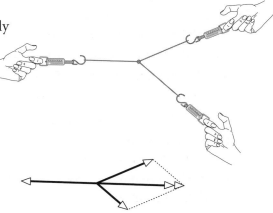

Three strings, each connected to a newton meter, are knotted at one point (or tied to a small ring). They are pulled tight in different directions.

The readings on the meters are used to draw vectors in the directions of the strings. When two of these vectors are combined by the parallelogram rule, the resultant will be found to be equal and opposite to the third force.

Mechanics is about forces and motion. In chapters 1 and 2 you looked at motion without considering forces. In this chapter you are looking at forces without considering motion. In later work, forces and motion will be brought together and you will learn how a force affects the motion of an object.

Exercise A (answers p 149)

1 An object is pulled by two forces of 8 N and 10 N with an angle of 45° between them.

By making a scale drawing, find

(a) the magnitude of the resultant force

(b) the angle between the resultant and the direction of the 10 N force

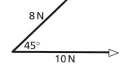

2 The following two forces act on an object:

- a force of 8 N acting in the direction east

- a force of 6 N acting in the direction north

(a) Sketch the parallelogram of forces.

(b) Use Pythagoras's theorem to calculate the magnitude of the resultant force.

(c) Use trigonometry to calculate the angle between the resultant and the direction east.

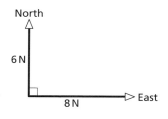

3 The three forces shown in this diagram are in equilibrium, so the force **F** exactly balances the resultant of the other two forces.

(a) Calculate the magnitude of the resultant of the 5 N and 3 N forces.

(b) Calculate the angle the resultant makes with the x-axis.

(c) Hence state the magnitude of **F** and the angle between **F** and the negative x-axis.

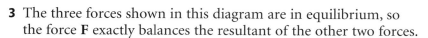

4 A ship is pulled by horizontal cables attached to two tugboats, as shown in this diagram.
Each cable makes an angle of 20° with the direction of motion of the ship. The force exerted on the ship by each tugboat is 4000 N.

(a) Calculate the magnitude of the resultant of the two forces.

(b) What is the direction of the resultant?

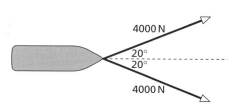

5 An object is pulled by two forces each of magnitude P newtons with an angle θ between them.

(a) Sketch the parallelogram of forces.

(b) Show that the resultant force has magnitude $2P\cos\left(\frac{1}{2}\theta\right)$ newtons.

B Resolving a force (answers p 149)

You have seen how two forces can be combined into a single force
using the parallelogram rule. In the special case where the two forces
are at right angles, the parallelogram is a rectangle. In this diagram
the two forces F_1 and F_2 combine to give the single force F.

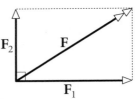

It is often useful to reverse this process and replace a single force by two
components at right angles to each other.
We say the single force is **resolved** into the two components.

In the diagram above, the force F has been resolved into the two components
F_1 and F_2.

The magnitude of F, in newtons, is denoted by F (not bold).

K In this diagram, the force with magnitude F is resolved into
components in the two perpendicular directions a and b.

Let θ be the angle between the force F and direction a.
From the shaded right-angled triangle, the components are

$\qquad F\cos\theta$ in direction a

and $\quad F\sin\theta$ in direction b

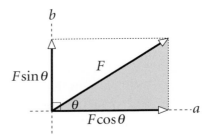

A force can be resolved in **any** two perpendicular directions.
In the diagram on the right, the force of magnitude 8 N has been
resolved into two components in the directions p and q.

B1 Calculate the component of this force in each of the
two directions p and q.

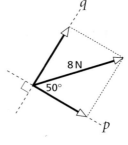

B2 A force of 20 N acts at an angle of 18° to a line l.
Calculate the component of the force

(a) in the direction l

(b) perpendicular to the direction l

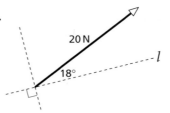

B3 The components of a force in two perpendicular directions
are 9 N and 4 N, as shown in this diagram.

Calculate

(a) the magnitude of the force

(b) the angle θ

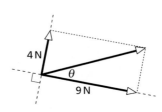

Components can be used to find a resultant of two or more forces.

B4 This diagram shows two forces acting at a point O.

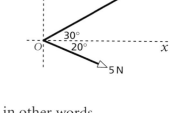

(a) Find the component of the 10 N force in the direction Ox.

(b) Find the component of the 5 N force in the direction Ox.

(c) Verify that the total of these two components is 13.359 N (to 3 d.p.).
This is the total component in the direction Ox, in other words the component of the resultant force in the direction Ox.

(d) Find the component of the 10 N force in the direction Oy.

(e) Find the component of the 5 N force in the direction Oy.

(f) Explain why the total of these two components is 3.290 N (to 3 d.p.).

(g) The resultant of the two forces has a component 13.359 N in the direction Ox, and a component 3.290 N in the direction Oy.

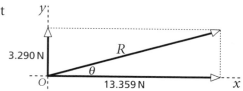

Calculate, to 3 s.f.,

(i) the magnitude R of the resultant force

(ii) the angle θ between the resultant and the direction Ox.

Example 1

Forces of 5 N, 3 N and 2 N act in the directions shown in the diagram.

Find the magnitude of the resultant force and the direction the resultant makes with Ox.

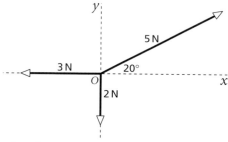

Solution

Resolve each force in the direction Ox.

The 5 N force has a component $5\cos 20°$ in the direction Ox.
The 3 N force has a component -3 in the direction Ox.
The 2 N force has no component in the direction Ox.

Total component in direction $Ox = (5\cos 20° - 3)\,\text{N} = 1.698\,\text{N}$ (to 3 d.p.)

Resolve each force in the direction Oy.

The 5 N force has a component $5\sin 20°$ in the direction Oy.
The 3 N force has no component in the direction Oy.
The 2 N force has a component -2 in the direction Oy.

Total component in direction $Oy = (5\sin 20° - 2)\,\text{N} = -0.290\,\text{N}$ (to 3 d.p.)

Sketch a diagram showing the components of the resultant force **R**.
The component –0.290 N *acts in the downward direction*.

$$R = \sqrt{1.698^2 + 0.290^2} = 1.72\,\text{N (to 2 d.p.)}$$

$$\tan\theta = \frac{0.290}{1.698} = 0.1707\ldots,\ \text{from which}\ \theta = 9.7°$$

So the resultant has magnitude 1.72 N and makes an angle 9.7° below *Ox*.

To avoid rounding errors, use more decimal places than are finally needed.

Exercise B (answers p 149)

1 A force of 20 N acts at angle of 60° to the direction *Ox*.
Find the component of the force

   (a) in the direction *Ox*

   (b) in the direction *Oy*

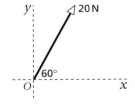

2 A force of 15 N acts at an angle of 40° to the direction *Oy*.
Find the component of the force

   (a) in the direction *Ox*

   (b) in the direction *Oy*

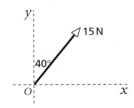

3 Forces **P** and **Q**, of magnitudes 6 N and 4 N, act in the
directions shown in the diagram.

   (a) Calculate the component of **P** in the direction *Ox*.

   (b) Calculate the component of **P** in the direction *Oy*.

   (c) Calculate the total of the components of **P** and **Q**
in the direction *Ox*.

   (d) Calculate the magnitude of the resultant of **P** and **Q**.

   (e) Calculate the angle the resultant makes with *Ox*.

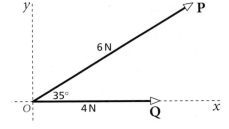

4 The vectors **i** and **j** shown here are perpendicular unit vectors.
The forces **P** and **Q**, in newtons, can be written as

either $\mathbf{P} = 2\mathbf{i} + 3\mathbf{j},\ \mathbf{Q} = 2\mathbf{i} - 2\mathbf{j}$ or as $\mathbf{P} = \begin{bmatrix} 2 \\ 3 \end{bmatrix},\ \mathbf{Q} = \begin{bmatrix} 2 \\ -2 \end{bmatrix}$.

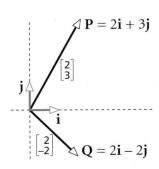

   (a) Find, both in terms of **i** and **j** and as a column vector,
the resultant force **P** + **Q**.

   (b) Find the magnitude of the resultant force and the angle
between the resultant and the vector **i**.

5 Two forces act at a point *O* as shown in the diagram. Find the magnitude of the resultant force and the angle the resultant makes with *Ox*.

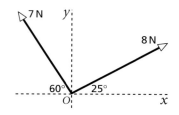

6 Find the magnitude of the resultant of the three forces shown in this diagram, and the angle the resultant makes with *Ox*.

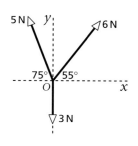

C Resolving coplanar forces in equilibrium (answers p 149)

Three or more forces that act in the same plane (for example, a horizontal plane or a vertical plane) are called **coplanar**. All sets of forces in this book will be coplanar.

The three forces *P*, *Q* and *R* in this diagram are acting on a stationary small object.
The object remains stationary, so the forces are in equilibrium.
The resultant of *P*, *Q* and *R* is zero.

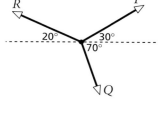

Because the resultant is zero, the components of *P*, *Q* and *R*, in any direction, add up to zero.

For example, resolving to the right along the dotted line, we get

$$P\cos 30° + Q\cos 70° - R\cos 20° = 0$$

Problems about forces in equilibrium can be tackled by resolving the forces and using the fact that the total component will always be zero.

C1 The three forces in this diagram are in equilibrium.

   (a) Write down an expression, in terms of *P*, for

      (i) the component of force *P* in the direction *Ox* (call this the *x*-component of force *P*)

      (ii) the *y*-component of force *P*

   (b) Explain why $P\cos 35° = 10\cos 75°$.

   (c) Explain why $P\sin 35° + 10\sin 75° = Q$.

   (d) From the equation in (b), find the value of *P*.

   (e) From the equation in (c), find the value of *Q*.

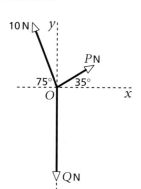

C2 The three forces in this diagram are in equilibrium.

(a) Explain why $U\cos 40° = V\cos 70°$.

(b) Write down expressions for the y-components of U and V.

(c) Explain why the total of the y-components of U and V must be 5 N.

(d) From parts (a) and (c) you will have two simultaneous equations for U and V. Solve the equations to find the values of U and V, correct to 3 s.f.

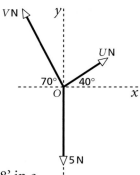

In future, all forces will be assumed to be in newtons. So a force labelled '8' in a diagram is a force of 8 newtons.

Example 2

The three forces shown here are in equilibrium. Find the values of P and Q.

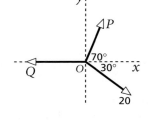

Solution

Resolve in the x-direction: $\qquad P\cos 70° + 20\cos 30° = Q$ (1)

Resolve in the y-direction: $\qquad P\sin 70° = 20\sin 30°$ (2)

From (2), $P = \dfrac{20\sin 30°}{\sin 70°} = 10.642$ (to 3 d.p.)

Substitute for P in (1): $\qquad 10.642\cos 70° + 20\cos 30° = Q$

$\Rightarrow \qquad Q = 20.960$

$P = 10.6$, $Q = 21.0$ (to 3 s.f.)

Exercise C (answers p 150)

1 The three forces shown in this diagram are in equilibrium.

(a) By resolving in the direction Ox, show that $P = Q$.

(b) Explain why $2P\sin 25° = 5$, and hence find the value of P, to 3 s.f.

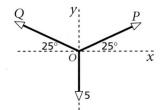

2 These three forces are in equilibrium.

(a) By resolving in the direction Oy, show that $P = 12.2$, to 3 s.f.

(b) Find the value of Q.

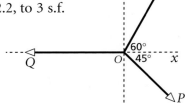

3 These three forces are in equilibrium.

(a) By resolving in the x-direction, find the value of θ.

(b) Find the value of P.

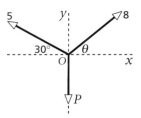

4 Three forces, of magnitudes 15, 12 and P newtons, act at a point in the directions shown in the diagram. The forces are in equilibrium. Find

(a) the value of θ (b) the value of P

The force of magnitude 12 newtons is now removed.

(c) Find the magnitude and direction of the resultant of the two remaining forces.

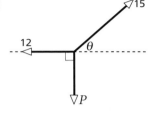

5 The three forces shown here are in equilibrium.

(a) Show that $P\cos\theta = 7$.

(b) Show that $P\sin\theta = 6\sin 60°$

(c) Use the fact that $\tan\theta = \dfrac{\sin\theta}{\cos\theta}$ to show that

$\tan\theta = \dfrac{6\sin 60°}{7}$, and hence find the value of θ.

(d) Find the value of P.

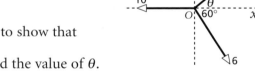

6 The three forces $p\mathbf{i} + 3\mathbf{j}$, $2\mathbf{i} - 4\mathbf{j}$ and $-7\mathbf{i} + q\mathbf{j}$ are in equilibrium. Find the values of p and q.

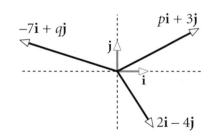

7 These three forces are in equilibrium. Find the values of P and Q, to 3 s.f.

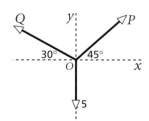

D Weight, tension and thrust (answers p 150)

These are some of the most common types of force occurring in mechanics.

Weight	Tension	Thrust
Objects are pulled vertically downwards by the force of gravity. This force acting on an object is its weight. 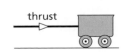	A tension is a pulling force, for example in a rope pulling on an object. 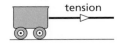	A thrust is a pushing force. 

In all the questions that follow, the object on which the forces act will be small in size (though not necessarily in weight). Such an object is called a **particle**.

The reason for working only with particles at this stage is that forces on a large object have different effects depending on exactly where they act.

For example, if a stationary box is pulled by two equal forces in line with each other, the forces will be in equilibrium and the box will not move.

But if the forces are still equal but not in line, the box will twist.

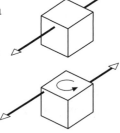

A particle can be treated as a point, so all forces acting on a particle act at the same point and the issue of twisting does not arise.

In practice, even a large object can be treated as a particle provided it can be assumed that all the forces on it act at the same point.

Force diagrams

The first step in solving a problem about forces on an object is to draw a diagram showing **all** the forces acting on the object.

This picture shows a stationary particle held in position by two light strings. Each string is attached to a ceiling.

This force diagram shows the three forces acting on the particle: the tensions in the two strings and the particle's weight.
The ceiling is not shown, because the purpose of this diagram is to show the forces acting on the particle.

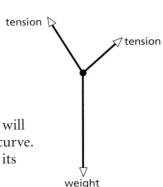

The particle is stationary, so the three forces are in equilibrium.

There is a reason for describing the strings as 'light'. A heavy string will not hang in a straight line – its own weight will cause it to form a curve. Of course, no real string can be weightless, but if it is light enough its weight can be ignored.

Treating the strings as weightless is an example of a **modelling assumption**. A model simplifies a real situation by leaving out things whose effects are so small they can be ignored.

D

D1 Sketch a diagram showing the forces acting on the particle in each case below. Label each force 'weight', 'tension', and so on.

   (a) A particle hanging from a vertical string

   (b) A particle supported by a vertical rod

D2 Two particles A and B are connected to each other by a light horizontal string.

Each particle is attached to a light string inclined at an angle to the horizontal. The other end of each string is attached to a ceiling.

   (a) Sketch a force diagram showing the forces acting on particle A.

   (b) Sketch a force diagram showing the forces acting on particle B.

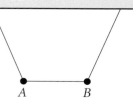

Example 3

A particle of weight 3 newtons is attached to the lower end of a light string, whose upper end is attached to a fixed point.
The string makes an angle of 25° to the vertical.
The particle is held in position by a light horizontal string.
Find the tension in each string.

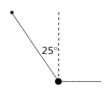

Solution

Always start by drawing a diagram showing all the forces acting on the object. There are three forces in this case, the weight and the two tensions. The diagram will explain the meaning of any new letters you introduce (in this case the two tensions T and S).

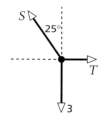

Choose directions in which to resolve the forces. Here the obvious directions are horizontal and vertical.

*Notice that the angle of S with the **vertical** is given, so the horizontal component of S is $S \sin 25°$.*

Resolve horizontally:	$T = S \sin 25°$	(1)
Resolve vertically:	$3 = S \cos 25°$	(2)
From equation (2),	$S = \dfrac{3}{\cos 25°} = 3.310$ (to 3 d.p.)	
So from equation (1),	$T = 3.310 \times \sin 25° = 1.399$	

To 3 s.f. the tensions are 1.40 N in the horizontal string and 3.31 N in the inclined string.

Exercise D (answers p 150)

1 A particle is is held in equilibrium by two light strings. One string is horizontal and the other is inclined at 25° to the horizontal. The tension in the inclined string is 15 N.

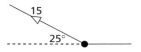

(a) Draw a diagram showing the forces acting on the particle.

(b) (i) Find the weight of the particle.

   (ii) Find the tension in the horizontal string.

2 A particle of weight 6 N is attached to one end of a light string. The other end of the string is attached to a fixed point O. The particle is held in equilibrium by a horizontal force P applied to it, with the string making an angle of 20° with the vertical.

Find

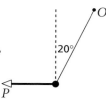

(a) the tension in the string

(b) the value of P

3 A particle P is attached to two points A and B by two light strings, as shown here. The particle hangs in equilibrium. The tension in string PA is 10 N.

Find

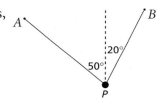

(a) the tension in string PB

(b) the weight of the particle

4 A particle of weight 20 N is held in equilibrium by two light strings. One is horizontal and the other is inclined at an angle α to the horizontal. The tension in the horizontal string is 12 N. Find

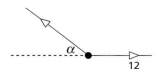

(a) the angle α   (b) the tension in the inclined string

5 A particle of weight W newtons is held in equilibrium by two light strings, each inclined at an angle α to the vertical.

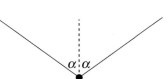

(a) Show that the tension in each string is $\dfrac{W}{2\cos\alpha}$ newtons.

(b) Does the tension in each string increase or decrease if the angle α is increased? Justify your answer.

(c) What happens as α approaches 90°?

6 A lantern of weight 10 N is attached to two fixed points A and B by two light ropes, as shown in the diagram.

Find the tension in each rope.

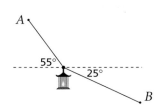

E Friction (answers p 150)

Imagine a horizontal sheet of ice on which objects can slide without any resistance at all. This kind of 'perfectly smooth' surface does not exist in reality, but is a useful idea.

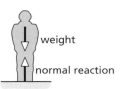

If the ice is strong enough, then an object standing on it will not fall through. This is because the ice surface exerts an upward force on the object, and this upward force counteracts the object's weight.

The force exerted on the object by the surface is called a **normal reaction**. (The word 'normal' means 'at right angles to the surface' – it doesn't mean normal in the sense of ordinary.)

If the ice is perfectly smooth, it can provide a normal reaction but can offer no resistance to a force pulling or pushing the object sideways.

Now imagine a rough horizontal surface with an object standing on it. As before, the surface exerts a normal reaction on the object counteracting the object's weight.

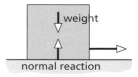

Imagine that the object is pulled sideways by a horizontal force.

> **E1** Suppose the pulling force is very small at first and is then gradually increased. What do you think will happen? Check by pulling a real object on a rough surface.

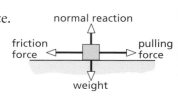

A rough surface is able to resist a horizontal pulling (or pushing) force. It does this by means of a force acting in the opposite direction to the pulling force. This force is called the **friction** force. As the pulling force increases, so does the friction force, and the object remains in equilibrium.

But the surface is able to resist only up to a certain limit. If the pulling force exceeds this limit, the object will move. When the force has just reached the limit, so that the object is just about to move, the object is in **limiting equilibrium**.

Experiments have shown that the maximum friction force F_{max} is proportional to the normal reaction R. The constant of proportionality is denoted by μ ('mu'), so $F_{max} = \mu R$.

μ is a measure of the roughness of the interface between the object and what it is in contact with: the larger the value of μ, the rougher the interface. Some approximate values of μ are given in this table.

Steel/steel	$\mu = 0.75$
Teflon/Teflon	$\mu = 0.04$
Wood/brick	$\mu = 0.6$

If an object on a rough surface is kept in equilibrium by a friction force of magnitude F, then $F \le \mu R$, where R is the magnitude of the normal reaction and μ is the coefficient of friction.
In limiting equilibrium, when the object is about to move, $F = \mu R$.

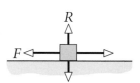

E2 A small box of weight 20 N is on a rough horizontal floor.
It is pulled by a horizontal force of 8 N and is in limiting equilibrium.

(a) Draw a diagram showing all the forces acting on the box.

(b) What is the magnitude of

   (i) the friction force acting on the box

   (ii) the normal reaction of the floor on the box

(c) Find the coefficient of friction between the box and the floor.

E3 An object of weight 12 N is on a rough horizontal floor.
The coefficient of friction between the object and the floor is 0.35.
The object is pulled by a light horizontal rope and is in limiting equilibrium.
Find the tension in the rope.

E4 An object of weight W N is on a rough horizontal surface.
The coefficient of friction between the object and the surface is 0.3.
The object is pulled by a horizontal force of 7.5 N and is in equilibrium
(but not necessarily limiting equilibrium).

(a) The normal reaction of the surface on the object is R N.
Explain why $R = W$.

(b) State the magnitude of the friction force F on the object.

(c) Use the inequality $F \leq \mu R$ to show that $W \geq 25$.

E5 A small object rests on a rough surface. It is pulled by a light rope inclined
at an angle to the horizontal and is in equilibrium.
Sketch a force diagram for the object, labelling each force.

E6 These two diagrams show the same object on the same
horizontal surface. In the first, the object rests on the
surface. In the second, it is pulled by an inclined force
and is in equilibrium.

For each situation, sketch a diagram showing all the forces acting on the object.
Explain why the normal reaction of the surface on the object is less in the
second case than in the first.

E7 A sledge of weight 40 N is on rough horizontal ground.
It is pulled by a force of 20 N inclined at 25° to the horizontal.
The sledge is in equilibrium.

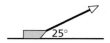

(a) Modelling the sledge as a particle, draw a diagram showing all
the forces acting on it.

(b) By resolving forces in a suitable direction, show that the normal
reaction R of the ground on the sledge is 31.5 N (to 3 s.f.).

(c) Show that the frictional force F on the sledge is 18.1 N (to 3 s.f.).

(d) The coefficient of friction between the sledge and the ground is μ.
By using the inequality $F \leq \mu R$, show that $\mu \geq 0.57$ (to 2 d.p.).

Example 4

A small object of weight $10\,\text{N}$ is standing on a rough horizontal surface. The object is pulled by a force of $6\,\text{N}$ acting at an angle of $30°$ to the horizontal. The object is in limiting equilibrium.

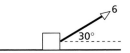

Find

(a)   the friction force

(b)   the normal reaction of the surface on the object

(c)   the coefficient of friction

Solution

*As usual, start by drawing a diagram showing **all** the forces acting on the object. To make the diagram clearer, leave out the surface itself (but of course include the forces it provides).*

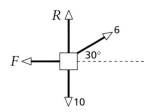

The friction force is labelled F.

Choose directions for resolving the forces.
Here the obvious directions are horizontal and vertical.

(It may help to draw a second diagram showing each component separately.)

(a)   Resolve horizontally: $F = 6\cos 30° = 5.196$ (to 4 s.f.)

(b)   Resolve vertically: $R + 6\sin 30° = 10$

So $R = 10 - 6\sin 30° = 7$

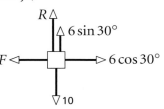

(c)   The object is in limiting equilibrium, so $F = \mu R$.

$$5.196 = \mu \times 7$$

$$\Rightarrow \quad \mu = \frac{5.196}{7} = 0.742 \text{ (to 3 s.f.)}$$

In the example above you are told that the object is in **limiting** equilibrium. If you were told only that it is in equilibrium, then you could use the inequality $F \le \mu R$ to find a range of possible values of μ, like this:

$$F \le \mu R$$

$$5.196 \le \mu \times 7$$

$$\Rightarrow \quad \mu \ge \frac{5.196}{7} = 0.742 \text{ (to 3 s.f.). So } \mu \ge 0.742$$

Example 5

A particle of weight $20\,\text{N}$ rests in equilibrium on a horizontal surface. The coefficient of friction between the particle and the surface is 0.3. A thrust of $P\,\text{N}$ acts on the particle at an angle of $20°$ to the horizontal.

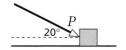

Show that $P \le 7.17$ (to 3 s.f.).

Solution

For clarity, the thrust P is shown as a 'pull'.

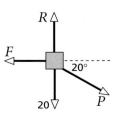

Resolve vertically: $\qquad R = 20 + P\sin 20° = 20 + 0.3420P$

Resolve horizontally: $\qquad F = P\cos 20° = 0.9397P$

Use $F \le \mu R$: $\qquad 0.9397P \le 0.3(20 + 0.3420P)$

$\qquad\qquad \Rightarrow \qquad 0.8371P \le 6$

$\qquad\qquad \Rightarrow \qquad P \le \dfrac{6}{0.8371} = 7.17 \text{ (to 3 s.f.)}$

Exercise E (answers p 151)

1 A small object of weight 15 N is on a rough horizontal surface.
It is pulled by a horizontal force of 12 N and is in limiting equilibrium.

(a) Sketch a diagram showing the forces acting on the object.

(b) Find the coefficient of friction.

2 An object of weight 8 N is on a rough horizontal surface.
The coefficient of friction between the object and the surface is 0.45.
The object is pulled by a horizontal force P N and is in limiting equilibrium.
Find the value of P.

3 An object of weight 10 N on a rough horizontal surface is in equilibrium
when pulled by a force of 4 N inclined at 30° to the horizontal.
The coefficient of friction between the object and the surface is μ.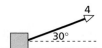

(a) Find the normal reaction of the surface on the object.

(b) Show that $\mu \ge 0.433$.

4 A particle on a rough horizontal surface is pulled by a force of 1.5 N
inclined at an angle of 40° the horizontal and is in limiting equilibrium.
The coefficient of friction between the particle and the surface is 0.4.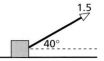

(a) Show that the friction force on the particle is 1.15 N.

(b) Find the normal reaction of the surface on the particle.

(c) Find the weight of the particle.

5 A particle of weight 7 N rests in equilibrium on a horizontal surface.
The coefficient of friction between the particle and the surface is 0.25.
The particle is pulled by a force of P newtons inclined at 45° to the
horizontal.

(a) Show that the normal reaction R is equal to $(7 - 0.707P)$ N.

(b) Show that $P \le 1.98$ (to 3 s.f.).

6 A particle of weight 6 N lies on a horizontal surface.
The coefficient of friction between the particle and the surface is μ.
The particle is pulled by a force of 3 N acting at 60° to the
horizontal and is in equilibrium.

   (a) Find the magnitude of the normal reaction between the surface
   and the particle.

   (b) Show that $\mu \geq 0.44$.

7 A particle of weight 10 N is in equilibrium on a horizontal plane.
The coefficient of friction between the particle and the plane is 0.2.

The particle is acted on by a horizontal force P N and a force of
6 N inclined at 45° to the horizontal, as shown in the diagram.

By considering separately the cases in which the friction force acts to the left
or to the right, show that $3.09 \leq P \leq 5.39$ (to 2 d.p.).

Key points

- Force is a vector quantity.
  The resultant of two forces is found by the parallelogram rule. (p 55)

- A force **F** of magnitude F can be resolved into
  components $F \cos \theta$ and $F \sin \theta$ in two directions
  at right angles to each other. 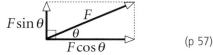 (p 57)

- A set of forces acting at a point is said to be in equilibrium if their resultant is zero.
  If the forces are in equilibrium, the total component in any direction is zero. (pp 55, 60–61)

- A particle is an object that can be treated as if it were a point, so that all forces
  acting on it act at the same point. (p 63)

- The normal reaction, of magnitude R, is the force at right angles to a surface which
  the surface exerts on an object in contact with it. (p 66)

- A rough surface can offer a friction force parallel to the surface. This friction
  force has a maximum magnitude given by $F_{max} = \mu R$, where μ is the coefficient
  of friction. (p 66)

- When the magnitude F of the friction force on an object is at its maximum, so that
  the object is about to move, the object is said to be in limiting equilibrium.
  If the object is in equilibrium but not limiting equilibrium, then $F < \mu R$. (pp 66, 68)

Mixed questions (answers p 151)

1 The forces **P** and **Q** shown here can be written, in newtons, as

either $\mathbf{P} = 5\mathbf{i} + 4\mathbf{j}$, $\mathbf{Q} = 3\mathbf{i} - 2\mathbf{j}$ or as $\mathbf{P} = \begin{bmatrix} 5 \\ 4 \end{bmatrix}$, $\mathbf{Q} = \begin{bmatrix} 3 \\ -2 \end{bmatrix}$.

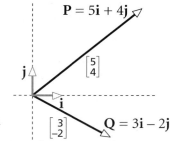

(a) Find, in terms of **i** and **j** and as a column vector, the resultant force **P** + **Q**.

(b) Find the magnitude of the resultant and the angle between it and the vector **i**.

2 Two forces, of magnitude 6 N and 3 N, act on a particle. The angle between the two forces is 120°. Find

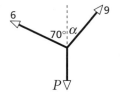

(a) the magnitude of the resultant of the two forces

(b) the angle the resultant makes with the direction of the 6 N force

3 A particle *P* lies on a smooth horizontal surface. It is acted on by two horizontal forces of magnitudes 25 N and 20 N. Relative to horizontal axes *Px* and *Py*, the directions of these two forces are as shown in the diagram. A third horizontal force **F** is required to keep *P* in equilibrium.

(a) Express the force of magnitude 25 N as a column vector, giving its components to one decimal place.

(b) Obtain **F** as a column vector, giving its components to one decimal place.

AQA 2002

4 The three forces shown in this diagram are in equilibrium. Find

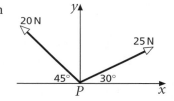

(a) the size of angle α

(b) the value of *P*

5 A particle of weight 8 N is attached to two light strings inclined at angles of 30° and 50° to the vertical, as shown here. The particle is in equilibrium. Find the tension in each string.

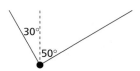

6 A small object of weight 5 N is on a rough horizontal surface. The coefficient of friction between the object and the plane is 0.5. The object is pulled by a string inclined at 30° to the horizontal and is in equilibrium. The tension in the string is of magnitude *T* N.

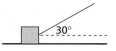

(a) Show that the normal reaction is of magnitude $(5 - 0.5T)$ N.

(b) Show that $T \le 2.24$.

Test yourself (answers p 152)

1 Two forces, $\mathbf{F}_1 = (3\mathbf{i} + 4\mathbf{j})$ N and $\mathbf{F}_2 = (6\mathbf{i} - 8\mathbf{j})$ N, act on a particle.
The resultant of these two forces is $\mathbf{F}$.
The unit vectors $\mathbf{i}$ and $\mathbf{j}$ are perpendicular.

(a) Find $\mathbf{F}$.

(b) Find the magnitude of $\mathbf{F}$.

(c) Find the acute angle between $\mathbf{F}$ and the unit vector $\mathbf{i}$.   AQA 2003

2 A particle is at a point O on a smooth horizontal surface.
It is acted on by three horizontal forces of magnitudes
6 N, 8 N and a N. Relative to horizontal axes Ox and Oy,
the directions of these forces are as shown in the diagram.
The resultant, $\mathbf{R}$, of these forces acts along the line Oy.

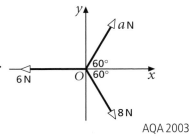

(a) Show that $a = 4$.

(b) Find the magnitude of $\mathbf{R}$.   AQA 2003

3 The three forces shown in this diagram are in equilibrium.
Find the values of P and Q.

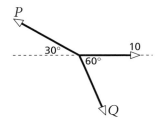

4 The diagram shows a small box resting on a rough horizontal
surface. The box is of weight W newtons. It is pushed with a
horizontal force of 12 newtons, and pulled with a force of
15 newtons at an angle of 30° to the horizontal.

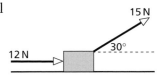

The box rests in limiting equilibrium.

(a) Draw a diagram to show all the forces acting on the box.

(b) Show that the frictional force acting on the box is approximately 25 newtons.

(c) The coefficient of friction between the box and the surface is $\frac{1}{3}$.
Find the normal reaction force between the box and the surface.

(d) Find the value of W.   AQA 2003

5 A sledge of weight 15 N rests on horizontal ground.
The coefficient of friction between the sledge and the
ground is 0.3. The sledge is pulled by a force of 4 N acting
at an angle of 30° to the horizontal. It is also pushed by a
horizontal force of P N. The sledge is in equilibrium and
can be modelled as a particle.

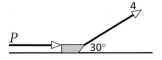

(a) Find the magnitude of the normal reaction of the ground on the sledge.

(b) Show that $P \leq 0.436$ (to 3 s.f.).

4 Momentum

In this chapter you will
- learn what momentum is
- solve problems involving the conservation of momentum

A Mass and momentum (answers p 152)

The **mass** of an object is measured in kilograms. It is the 'quantity of matter' in the object.

Mass is not the same as weight. Weight is the force of gravity acting downwards on an object and is measured in newtons. If the object is moved to the surface of the Moon, the force of gravity there is less than that of the Earth, so the object weighs less on the Moon. But the mass stays the same, wherever the object is.

A1 Imagine a light plastic ball and a heavy metal ball.
You kick the light ball and then give a kick of the same strength to the heavy ball.
Which ball will move faster?

The fundamental principles of mechanics were formulated by Isaac Newton (1642–1727). When Newton considered the situation just described, he started with the idea that the same 'amount of kick' should give the same 'amount of motion' to the two objects. He may have thought something like this:

Imagine that I have a 1 kg object. I give it a kick and it moves away at $10 \, \text{m s}^{-1}$. Now imagine that I have a 2 kg object and I give it the same amount of kick. The 2 kg object can be thought of as two 1 kg objects and the kick is shared equally between the two. Each 1 kg object gets half the amount of kick, and so moves at $5 \, \text{m s}^{-1}$. In other words, the whole 2 kg object moves at $5 \, \text{m s}^{-1}$.

Notice that the product mass×velocity is the same in both cases. Newton called this quantity **momentum**. The kick, when given to a 1 kg object, gives it a momentum of $1 \times 10 = 10 \, \text{kg m s}^{-1}$. (Notice the units.) The same kick given to a 2 kg object gives it the same momentum of $2 \times 5 = 10 \, \text{kg m s}^{-1}$.

Because velocity is a vector quantity, so is momentum. If objects are all moving along a straight line, momentum is positive in one direction and negative in the other.

$$2 \, \text{m s}^{-1} \qquad 3 \, \text{m s}^{-1}$$
$$\overrightarrow{\quad} \qquad \overleftarrow{\quad}$$
$$(7 \, \text{kg}) \qquad (5 \, \text{kg})$$

Momentum: $14 \, \text{kg m s}^{-1}$ $-15 \, \text{kg m s}^{-1}$

> The momentum of a moving object is the product mass×velocity.
> Momentum is a vector quantity.

A2 A footballer gives the same kick to two balls, one of mass 0.5 kg and the other of mass 1.5 kg. The first ball moves at $6 \, \text{m s}^{-1}$.
What is the velocity of the second?

A3 An object of mass 2.4 kg is kicked and moves with a velocity of $5 \, \text{m s}^{-1}$.
The same kick given to a second object causes it to move with a velocity of $3 \, \text{m s}^{-1}$.
What is the mass of the second object?

Momentum is a vector quantity. In two dimensions, the momentum of an object may be expressed either as a column vector or in the form $a\mathbf{i} + b\mathbf{j}$.

This diagram shows an object of mass 5 kg moving in two dimensions with a velocity of $\begin{bmatrix} 4 \\ 2 \end{bmatrix}$ or $(4\mathbf{i} + 2\mathbf{j})\,\mathrm{m\,s^{-1}}$.

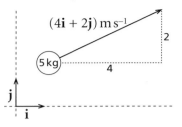

Its momentum, in $\mathrm{kg\,m\,s^{-1}}$, is mass × velocity

$$= 5(4\mathbf{i} + 2\mathbf{j}) = 20\mathbf{i} + 10\mathbf{j}$$

$$\text{or} \quad 5 \times \begin{bmatrix} 4 \\ 2 \end{bmatrix} = \begin{bmatrix} 20 \\ 10 \end{bmatrix}$$

Exercise A (answers p 152)

1 An object of mass 3.5 kg is moving at $4\,\mathrm{m\,s^{-1}}$ on a straight line. Find its momentum.

2 Two objects A and B are moving on a straight line. A has mass 7 kg and is moving forwards at $2.5\,\mathrm{m\,s^{-1}}$. B has mass 5 kg and is moving backwards at $1.5\,\mathrm{m\,s^{-1}}$.

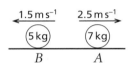

(a) Find the momentum of A.

(b) Explain why the momentum of B is not $7.5\,\mathrm{kg\,m\,s^{-1}}$ and write down the correct value.

3 Write down the momentum of each of these objects.

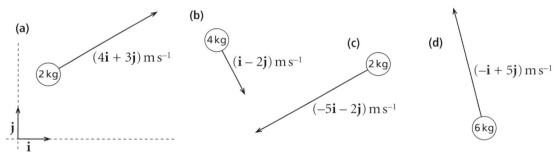

4 Write down, as a column vector, the momentum of each of these objects.

(a) An object of mass 5 kg moving with velocity $\begin{bmatrix} 3 \\ 5 \end{bmatrix}\mathrm{m\,s^{-1}}$

(b) An object of mass 3.5 kg moving with velocity $\begin{bmatrix} 6 \\ -4 \end{bmatrix}\mathrm{m\,s^{-1}}$

(c) An object of mass 0.8 kg moving with velocity $\begin{bmatrix} -4 \\ -5 \end{bmatrix}\mathrm{m\,s^{-1}}$

B Conservation of momentum

Imagine two objects A and B moving towards each other on a straight line.

A has a mass of $2\,\text{kg}$ and a velocity of $8\,\text{m}\,\text{s}^{-1}$.
B has a mass of $3\,\text{kg}$ and a velocity of $-4\,\text{m}\,\text{s}^{-1}$ (that is, $4\,\text{m}\,\text{s}^{-1}$ in the opposite direction).

The objects collide with each other.

When they collide, it is as if each object 'kicks' the other. Newton assumed that the two kicks are equal and opposite.

If the two objects are considered together, the total amount of kick on the pair is zero, because the two kicks are equal and opposite.

From this it follows that the total momentum of the two objects will be the same before and after the collision.

Suppose that, after the collision, A moves with velocity v_A and B with velocity v_B.

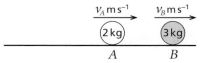

Before the collision, the momentum of A (in $\text{kg}\,\text{m}\,\text{s}^{-1}$) was $2 \times 8 = 16$, and the momentum of B was $3 \times -4 = -12$.

So the total momentum before the collision was $16 - 12 = 4$.

The total momentum afterwards is $2v_A + 3v_B$.

It follows that $2v_A + 3v_B = 4$.

This equation is not enough to find the values of v_A and v_B. But if one of the values is given, the other can be calculated.

> **K**
>
> If two objects moving on a straight line collide, the total momentum before the collision is equal to the total momentum after the collision.
>
> Suppose that an object with mass m_1 and velocity u_1 collides with an object with mass m_2 and velocity u_2. Afterwards m_1 moves with velocity v_1 and m_2 with velocity v_2. Then
>
> $$m_1 u_1 + m_2 u_2 = m_1 v_1 + m_2 v_2$$
>
> This is called the **principle of conservation of linear momentum**.

Here are some of the things that might happen when two objects, moving on a straight line, collide.

Before

Collision

After

| Both moving forwards before and after | 1st moving backwards after | 2nd stationary before; moving forwards after | 2nd stationary before; 1st stationary after | 2nd moving backwards before; forwards after |

There is one case that sometimes arises in problems. This is where the two objects stick together, or **coalesce**, after the collision. They become one combined object.

The mass of the combined object is, of course, the sum of the masses of the individual objects.

Objects coalescing after colliding

Whenever the velocity of an object, before or after the collision, is **backwards**, it must be entered as **negative** in the conservation of momentum equation.

Example 1

An object of mass 0.5 kg moving on a straight line with a speed of $6 \, \text{m s}^{-1}$ collides with an object of mass 2.5 kg moving in the same direction with a speed of $2 \, \text{m s}^{-1}$.

After the collision, the 0.5 kg object moves backwards at $0.4 \, \text{m s}^{-1}$. What are the speed and direction of the other object after the collision?

Solution

Sketch the situation before and after the collision.

Substitute the known values into $m_1 u_1 + m_2 u_2 = m_1 v_1 + m_2 v_2$.

Notice that v_1 *is negative (backwards), so* $v_1 = -0.4$.

From conservation of momentum: $0.5 \times 6 + 2.5 \times 2 = 0.5 \times -0.4 + 2.5 v_2$

$$\Rightarrow \qquad 8.2 = 2.5 v_2$$

$$\Rightarrow \qquad v_2 = 3.28$$

The 2.5 kg object moves at $3.28 \, \text{m s}^{-1}$ forwards.

Example 2

An object of mass 3 kg moving on a straight line with a speed of $8 \, \text{m s}^{-1}$ collides with a stationary object of mass 2 kg.

After the collision the two objects coalesce. Find the speed of the combined object after the collision.

Solution

Sketch the situation before and after the collision.
Notice that the speed of the second object before the collision is 0.
The final speed of the combined object has been called $v \, \text{m s}^{-1}$.

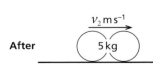

From conservation of momentum: $3 \times 8 + 2 \times 0 = 5 v$

$$\Rightarrow \qquad 24 = 5 v$$

$$\Rightarrow \qquad v = 4.8$$

The combined object moves at $4.8 \, \text{m s}^{-1}$ after the collision.

Exercise B (answers p 152)

1 An object of mass 5 kg moving on a straight line with a speed of $4\,\mathrm{m\,s^{-1}}$ collides with an object of mass 2 kg moving in the same direction with a speed of $3\,\mathrm{m\,s^{-1}}$.

Immediately after the collision, the 5 kg object moves forwards at $3.6\,\mathrm{m\,s^{-1}}$. What are the speed and direction of the other object after the collision?

2 An object of mass 3.5 kg moving on a straight line with a speed of $6\,\mathrm{m\,s^{-1}}$ collides with an object of mass 1.5 kg moving in the opposite direction with a speed of $2\,\mathrm{m\,s^{-1}}$.

Immediately after the collision, the 3.5 kg object moves forwards at $3\,\mathrm{m\,s^{-1}}$. What are the speed and direction of the other object after the collision?

3 A model railway truck of mass 0.6 kg is moving along a straight horizontal track with a speed of $0.5\,\mathrm{m\,s^{-1}}$ when it collides with a stationary truck of mass 0.9 kg.

On colliding, the two trucks are coupled and move together at the same speed. Find the speed of the trucks immediately after the collision.

4 Three trucks A, B, C, of masses 5 kg, 3 kg and 2 kg respectively, are on a straight horizontal track as shown in the diagram below.
A is moving towards B with a speed of $0.8\,\mathrm{m\,s^{-1}}$. B and C are stationary.

A collides with B and attaches itself to B. Then the pair collides with C and all three trucks are attached together and move with the same speed. Find this speed.

5 A particle of mass m kg is moving in a straight line with a velocity of $U\,\mathrm{m\,s^{-1}}$.
A second particle of mass $4m$ kg is moving in the same straight line, ahead of the first particle, with a velocity of $\frac{1}{2}U\,\mathrm{m\,s^{-1}}$.

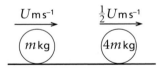

The particles collide and coalesce. Show that the velocity of the combined particle immediately after the collision is $\frac{3}{5}U\,\mathrm{m\,s^{-1}}$.

6 An object A of mass 3 kg, moving in a straight line with a speed of $0.2\,\mathrm{m\,s^{-1}}$, collides with an object B, of mass m kg, moving in the opposite direction with the same speed as A.

Immediately after the collision A is stationary and B moves with a speed of $0.3\,\mathrm{m\,s^{-1}}$. Find the value of m.

7 A particle, P, of mass 0.1 kg, is moving in a straight line with speed $3\,\mathrm{m\,s^{-1}}$ when it collides with a stationary particle, Q, of mass 0.5 kg. After the collision, P and Q move directly away from each other, each with speed $v\,\mathrm{m\,s^{-1}}$.

Find the value of v.

C Conservation of momentum in two dimensions (answers p 153)

A collision in two dimensions is more complicated than in one dimension.
It is easiest to see this if both objects are thought of as round, like snooker balls.

A snooker ball can give either a direct hit
or a 'glancing blow' to another stationary
ball. After a direct hit, the second ball
moves in the same straight line as the first,
so the situation is one-dimensional.

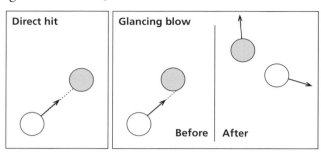

After a glancing blow, the balls move in
different directions.

If both balls are moving before they collide,
then both may change direction as a result
of the collision.

 The principle of conservation of momentum applies to motion in two (or three)
dimensions. In vector form, the equation is

$$m_1\mathbf{u}_1 + m_2\mathbf{u}_2 = m_1\mathbf{v}_1 + m_2\mathbf{v}_2$$

When applying conservation of momentum, you do not need to worry about
exactly what happens when the objects collide. Only the situations before and
after the collision are relevant.

C1 An object A of mass 3 kg has a velocity
of $(4\mathbf{i} + 4\mathbf{j})\,\mathrm{m\,s^{-1}}$.

It collides with an object B of mass 2 kg
travelling with velocity $(2\mathbf{i} - 3\mathbf{j})\,\mathrm{m\,s^{-1}}$.

Afterwards, A moves with velocity
$(2\mathbf{i} - \mathbf{j})\,\mathrm{m\,s^{-1}}$ and B with velocity $\mathbf{v}_2\,\mathrm{m\,s^{-1}}$
(unknown).

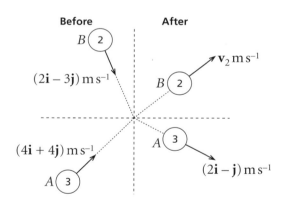

If the known quantities are substituted in the conservation of momentum
equation you get

$$3(4\mathbf{i} + 4\mathbf{j}) + 2(2\mathbf{i} - 3\mathbf{j}) = 3(2\mathbf{i} - \mathbf{j}) + 2\mathbf{v}_2$$

By solving this equation, show that $\mathbf{v}_2 = 5\mathbf{i} + 4.5\mathbf{j}$.

Question C1 can also be done using column vector notation. If the unknown

final velocity is called $\begin{bmatrix} a \\ b \end{bmatrix}$, the equation becomes $3\begin{bmatrix} 4 \\ 4 \end{bmatrix} + 2\begin{bmatrix} 2 \\ -3 \end{bmatrix} = 3\begin{bmatrix} 2 \\ -1 \end{bmatrix} + 2\begin{bmatrix} a \\ b \end{bmatrix}$

$$\Rightarrow \begin{bmatrix} 16 \\ 6 \end{bmatrix} = \begin{bmatrix} 6 + 2a \\ -3 + 2b \end{bmatrix} \quad \Rightarrow \quad a = 5,\ b = 4.5$$

C2 Suppose the situation before the collision is the same as in C1, but that the two objects coalesce and move together with velocity **v**.

Write down the equation of conservation of momentum in this case.

Solve the equation to find the value of **v**.

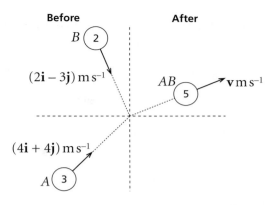

Example 3

An object of mass 8 kg, moving with velocity $(3\mathbf{i} + 2\mathbf{j})\,\mathrm{m\,s^{-1}}$, collides with a stationary object of mass 2 kg.

Immediately after the collision, the velocity of the 2 kg object is $(\mathbf{i} + \mathbf{j})\,\mathrm{m\,s^{-1}}$. Find the velocity after the collision of the 8 kg object.

Solution

As usual, sketch the situation before and after the collision.

From the conservation of momentum:

$$8(3\mathbf{i} + 2\mathbf{j}) = 8\mathbf{v} + 2(\mathbf{i} + \mathbf{j})$$

$\Rightarrow \qquad 24\mathbf{i} + 16\mathbf{j} = 8\mathbf{v} + 2\mathbf{i} + 2\mathbf{j}$

$\Rightarrow \qquad 22\mathbf{i} + 14\mathbf{j} = 8\mathbf{v}$

$\Rightarrow \qquad\qquad \mathbf{v} = 2.75\mathbf{i} + 1.75\mathbf{j}$

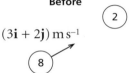
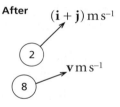

The velocity of the 8 kg object after the collision is $(2.75\mathbf{i} + 1.75\mathbf{j})\,\mathrm{m\,s^{-1}}$.

Exercise C (answers p 153)

1 An object of mass 3 kg, moving with velocity $(4\mathbf{i} + 3\mathbf{j})\,\mathrm{m\,s^{-1}}$, collides with an object of mass 2 kg, moving with a velocity of $(2\mathbf{i} + \mathbf{j})\,\mathrm{m\,s^{-1}}$.

Immediately after the collision, the velocity of the 3 kg object is $(3\mathbf{i} + 2\mathbf{j})\,\mathrm{m\,s^{-1}}$. Find the velocity after the collision of the 2 kg object.

2 An object of mass 4 kg, moving with velocity $\begin{bmatrix} -1 \\ 3 \end{bmatrix}\,\mathrm{m\,s^{-1}}$, collides with an object of mass 3 kg, moving with velocity $\begin{bmatrix} 2 \\ -1 \end{bmatrix}\,\mathrm{m\,s^{-1}}$.

Immediately after the collision, the 4 kg object moves with velocity $\begin{bmatrix} 2 \\ 0 \end{bmatrix}\,\mathrm{m\,s^{-1}}$. Find the velocity after the collision of the 3 kg object.

3 A particle of mass 0.35 kg travelling with velocity $(3\mathbf{i} - 5\mathbf{j})\,\mathrm{m\,s^{-1}}$ collides with a particle of mass 0.15 kg travelling with velocity $(\mathbf{i} - 2\mathbf{j})\,\mathrm{m\,s^{-1}}$. The two particles coalesce. Find the velocity of the pair of particles immediately after the collision.

4 A particle P of mass $0.03\,\text{kg}$, travelling with velocity $\mathbf{u}\,\text{m s}^{-1}$, collides with a stationary particle Q of mass $0.01\,\text{kg}$. Immediately after the collision, P moves with velocity $\begin{bmatrix} 4 \\ -1 \end{bmatrix}\text{m s}^{-1}$ and Q with velocity $\begin{bmatrix} 3 \\ 3 \end{bmatrix}\text{m s}^{-1}$. Find the value of $\mathbf{u}$.

5 A moving particle A collides with another moving particle B.
The mass of A is $1.5\,\text{kg}$ and its velocities before and after the collision are $(4\mathbf{i} + 2\mathbf{j})\,\text{m s}^{-1}$ and $(2\mathbf{i} - \mathbf{j})\,\text{m s}^{-1}$ respectively.

   (a) (i) Find the momentum lost by A as a result of the collision, giving the units.

      (ii) State the momentum gained by B as a result of the collision.

   (b) The mass of B is $0.5\,\text{kg}$. Immediately after the collision the velocity of B is $(\mathbf{i} + \mathbf{j})\,\text{m s}^{-1}$. Find the velocity of B immediately before the collision.

Key points

- The momentum of an object is defined as $\text{mass} \times \text{velocity}$.
  Momentum is a vector quantity. Its units are kg m s^{-1}. (p 73)

- If an object of mass m_1 travelling with velocity $\mathbf{u}_1$ collides with an object of mass m_2 travelling with velocity $\mathbf{u}_2$, and if $\mathbf{v}_1$ and $\mathbf{v}_2$ are the velocities of the objects immediately after the collision, then

  $$m_1\mathbf{u}_1 + m_2\mathbf{u}_2 = m_1\mathbf{v}_1 + m_2\mathbf{v}_2$$

  This is called the principle of conservation of momentum. (pp 75, 78)

Mixed questions (answers p 153)

1 Three trucks A, B and C, of masses $5\,\text{kg}$, $2\,\text{kg}$ and $8\,\text{kg}$ respectively, are situated on a smooth horizontal track as shown in the diagram. Initially A is moving at $4\,\text{m s}^{-1}$ towards B, and B and C are stationary.

   (a) After A collides with B, A's speed is reduced to $2\,\text{m s}^{-1}$.
Find the speed of B after this collision.

   (b) B then collides with C. B and C are coupled together in the collision.
Find the speed of the pair B, C after this collision.

   (c) Finally A collides with the pair B, C and all three trucks are coupled together.
Find the final speed of the three trucks.

2 A particle A of mass $m\,\text{kg}$, moving in a straight line with speed $u\,\text{m s}^{-1}$, collides with a second particle B, of mass $4m\,\text{kg}$, moving in the opposite direction with speed $u\,\text{m s}^{-1}$. As a result of the collision, the direction of A is reversed and A moves with speed $\frac{1}{2}u\,\text{m s}^{-1}$. Show that the speed of B after the collision is $\frac{5}{8}u\,\text{m s}^{-1}$.

3 A particle of mass 0.45 kg, moving with velocity $(-2\mathbf{i} + 4\mathbf{j})\,\mathrm{m\,s^{-1}}$, collides with a particle of mass 0.35 kg, moving with velocity $(2\mathbf{i} - 6\mathbf{j})\,\mathrm{m\,s^{-1}}$. In the collision the particles coalesce. Find, to 3 s.f., the **speed** of the particles after the collision.

4 A particle P has mass 5 kg. It is moving along a straight line with speed $4\,\mathrm{m\,s^{-1}}$, when it collides directly with another particle Q which is at rest. The mass of Q is m kg. After the collision P moves with a speed of $1.2\,\mathrm{m\,s^{-1}}$ and Q moves with a speed of $1.4\,\mathrm{m\,s^{-1}}$.

(a) If P and Q both move in the same direction after the collision, show that $m = 10$.

(b) If P and Q move in opposite directions after the collision, find m. AQA 2002

Test yourself (answers p 153)

1 A trolley, of mass 10 kg, is placed at rest on a set of straight horizontal rails. Large pellets, each of mass 0.5 kg, are fired at the trolley. When each pellet hits the trolley, the pellet is travelling horizontally and parallel to the rails at a speed of $20\,\mathrm{m\,s^{-1}}$. When the pellets hit the trolley, they stick to it and continue to move with the trolley. Assume that there is no resistance to the motion of the trolley.

(a) Show that the speed of the trolley after it has been hit by the first pellet is $\frac{20}{21}\,\mathrm{m\,s^{-1}}$.

(b) Find the speed of the trolley after it has been hit by the second pellet. AQA 2003

2 A stone, A, of mass 2 kg, is sliding across a smooth horizontal surface with velocity $\begin{bmatrix} 3 \\ 1 \end{bmatrix}\,\mathrm{m\,s^{-1}}$. It hits another stone, B, of mass 3 kg sliding across the same surface with velocity $\begin{bmatrix} -4 \\ -3 \end{bmatrix}\,\mathrm{m\,s^{-1}}$.

Stone A rebounds with velocity $\begin{bmatrix} -3 \\ -2 \end{bmatrix}\,\mathrm{m\,s^{-1}}$. Find the velocity of B after the collision.

3 A moving particle P collides with a particle Q, which is also moving. The particle P is of mass 0.25 kg, and its velocities immediately before and after the collision are $\begin{bmatrix} 3 \\ 6 \end{bmatrix}\,\mathrm{m\,s^{-1}}$ and $\begin{bmatrix} -1 \\ 4 \end{bmatrix}\,\mathrm{m\,s^{-1}}$ respectively.

(a) (i) Find the momentum lost by P due to the collision. State the units of your answer.

(ii) State the momentum gained by Q due to the collision.

(b) The mass of Q is 0.1 kg.
Immediately after the collision, Q moves with velocity $\begin{bmatrix} 5 \\ 2 \end{bmatrix}\,\mathrm{m\,s^{-1}}$.

Find the velocity of Q immediately before the collision. AQA 2003

5 Newton's laws of motion 1

In this chapter you will learn how to
- use Newton's first and second laws of motion
- solve problems involving inclined surfaces

A Force and momentum (answers p 154)

The most significant advances in mechanics were made by Isaac Newton.
From the time of the ancient Greeks it had been assumed that if an object
is moving, then there has to be an explanation – a cause of the motion.
It was thought that if this cause was removed, the object would stop moving.

Newton said, however, that if an object has a certain momentum, then it will
continue to have this momentum, unless a force acts on the object and changes
its momentum.

Imagine, for example, an object of mass 3 kg sliding in a straight line on perfectly
smooth horizontal ice with a velocity of $2\,\mathrm{m\,s^{-1}}$ (so that its momentum is $6\,\mathrm{kg\,m\,s^{-1}}$).
There is no horizontal force acting on the object, so it will continue to move with
the same velocity for ever unless a force acts on it to change its momentum.

In reality, of course, a horizontal force does act on the object, even on the
smoothest ice – the force of friction. It is this force that causes the object to lose
momentum and thus slow down. If there were no friction, the momentum,
and so the velocity, of the object would not change.

An object at rest is simply an object whose velocity is zero. If an object is at
rest and the resultant force acting on it is zero, then its momentum will not
change – in other words it stays at rest.

Newton's first law of motion

K An object at rest or moving in a straight line with constant velocity will
continue like that unless acted upon by a force.

In this section and sections B and C we shall assume that all motion is in
a horizontal straight line. Vertical forces (weight and normal reaction) balance
out and so do not need to be considered.

D **A1** Imagine an object that can slide on a perfectly
smooth horizontal surface. It is initially at rest.

(a) You blow on the object for a certain time
(say a few seconds).
What do you think will happen to the object

(i) while you are blowing   (ii) after you have stopped blowing

(b) What do you think will be the effect of

(i) blowing on the object (with the same force) but for twice the time

(ii) blowing twice as hard but for the same time as originally

A2 Now imagine that you have two objects, one heavier than the other, both on a smooth horizontal surface. You blow, with the same force and for the same time, on each of them.

What do you think will happen?

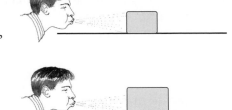

Newton said that the effect of a force on an object is to change its momentum. In fact, he said, we can measure a force by the amount of momentum it produces in a given time.

In metric units (which had not been invented in Newton's time), the unit of force is called a **newton**. A force of 1 newton is defined as a force that produces $1\,\text{kg m s}^{-1}$ of momentum when acting for 1 second.

So, for example, a force of 3 newtons acting for 8 seconds will produce a momentum of $24\,\text{kg m s}^{-1}$. This could be a 2 kg object moving at $12\,\text{m s}^{-1}$, or a 4 kg object moving at $6\,\text{m s}^{-1}$, and so on. The general rule is

force (newtons) × **time** (seconds) = **momentum produced** (kg m s^{-1})

A3 Jess blows with a force of 4 newtons on an object that is initially at rest. She blows for 10 seconds.

  (a) How much momentum will she produce in that time?

  (b) If the mass of the object is 5 kg, what will its velocity be when Jess has stopped blowing?

If a force acts on an object that is already moving, then what happens depends on the direction of the force.

A4 An object of mass 4 kg is moving initially at $5\,\text{m s}^{-1}$. Jess blows on the object with a force of 2 newtons for 3 seconds, in the same direction as the object is moving.

  (a) What was the object's momentum before Jess started blowing?

  (b) How much momentum does her blowing produce?

  (c) What is the object's momentum when Jess stops blowing?

  (d) Find the object's velocity when Jess stops blowing.

A5 Imagine that an object is sliding towards you on a smooth surface. You blow on the object for a time.

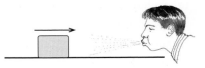

  (a) What will happen at first?

  (b) What will happen if you continue to blow on the object?

Force and momentum are both vector quantities, so direction is important. Applying a force in the opposite direction to an object's motion will produce negative momentum, so the object's momentum will be reduced.

Example 1

An object of mass 5 kg is moving with a velocity of $3\,\mathrm{m\,s^{-1}}$.
A force of 4 newtons acts on the object for 2 seconds.
Find the final velocity of the object

(a) if the force acts in the same direction as the object's motion

(b) if the force acts in the opposite direction to the object's motion

Solution

(a) To start with, the object's momentum is $5 \times 3 = 15\,\mathrm{kg\,m\,s^{-1}}$.

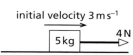

The momentum produced by a force of 4 N acting for 2 s = $4 \times 2 = 8\,\mathrm{kg\,m\,s^{-1}}$.

So the object's final momentum = $15 + 8 = 23\,\mathrm{kg\,m\,s^{-1}}$.

So its final velocity = momentum ÷ mass = $23 \div 5 = 4.6\,\mathrm{m\,s^{-1}}$.

(b) In this case the force is −4 N.

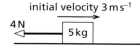

So the momentum produced = $-4 \times 2 = -8\,\mathrm{kg\,m\,s^{-1}}$.

So the final momentum = $15 - 8 = 7\,\mathrm{kg\,m\,s^{-1}}$.

So final velocity = $7 \div 5 = 1.4\,\mathrm{m\,s^{-1}}$.

Exercise A (answers p 154)

1 A force of 2 newtons acts for 6 seconds on an object that is initially at rest.

(a) Find the momentum, in $\mathrm{kg\,m\,s^{-1}}$, produced by the force.

(b) Given that the mass of the object is 3 kg, find its final velocity.

2 A force of 8 newtons acts for 3 seconds on an object of mass 2 kg that is initially at rest.

(a) Find the momentum produced by the force in this time.

(b) Find the final velocity of the object.

3 An object of mass 6 kg is moving with a velocity of $5\,\mathrm{m\,s^{-1}}$.

(a) What is the momentum of the object, in $\mathrm{kg\,m\,s^{-1}}$?

A force of 4 newtons acts on the object for 3 seconds, so as to increase its momentum.

(b) Find the momentum produced by the force in this time.

(c) What is the final momentum of the object?

(d) What is the final velocity of the object?

4 An object of mass 2.5 kg is moving with a velocity of $4\,\text{m}\,\text{s}^{-1}$.
The object is acted on by a force of 5.5 newtons in the direction of motion
for a period of 8 seconds. Find the final velocity of the object.

5 An object of mass 1.4 kg is moving with a velocity of $6.5\,\text{m}\,\text{s}^{-1}$.
A force of 3.5 newtons acts on the object for 2 seconds in the direction
opposite to the object's motion. Find the final velocity of the object.

B Force, mass and acceleration (answers p 154)

Suppose an object of mass m kg is initially moving with velocity $u\,\text{m}\,\text{s}^{-1}$.
A force of F newtons acts on the object for a time t seconds.
As a result, the object's final velocity is $v\,\text{m}\,\text{s}^{-1}$.

We can use the relationship 'force × time = change in momentum' to find
an equation linking F, t, m, u and v.

It is $\quad Ft = mv - mu$

From this it follows that $\quad Ft = m(v - u)$

$$\Rightarrow \quad F = m\left(\frac{v - u}{t}\right)$$

The expression $\dfrac{v - u}{t}$ represents $\dfrac{\text{change in velocity}}{\text{time}}$, which is the acceleration, a.

So $\quad F = ma$

This result is

Newton's second law of motion

K If a force of F newtons, acting on an object of mass m kg, causes an acceleration $a\,\text{m}\,\text{s}^{-2}$,
then $F = ma$. The acceleration continues for as long as the force is acting, and if the
force is constant, so is the acceleration.

This is one of the most frequently used equations in mechanics. When referring
to it, you can shorten 'Newton's second law' to 'N2L'.

In diagrams, a double-headed arrow is usually used to show an acceleration.

B1 A force acting on an object of mass 2.5 kg causes the object
to accelerate at $6\,\text{m}\,\text{s}^{-2}$.
Find the magnitude of the force.

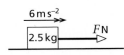

B2 A force of 24 N acts on an object of mass 3 kg.
Find the object's acceleration.

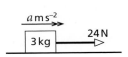

B3 A force of 4.5 N acts on an object and causes it to accelerate at $0.9\,\text{m}\,\text{s}^{-2}$.
Find the mass of the object.

A common situation to which Newton's second law can be applied is that of a vehicle moving on a horizontal road or track.

The force causing the vehicle's acceleration could be the tension in a cable or rope pulling the vehicle, or the thrust of a person pushing the vehicle.

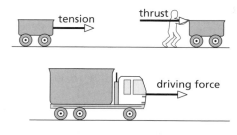

In a vehicle such as a car, lorry or train, the vehicle's engine exerts a **driving force** (or **propulsive force**). Although the engine is part of the vehicle, the driving force can be treated as if it were an external force. (The reason for this is given in chapter 6.)

There may also be forces acting in the opposite direction resisting the motion of the vehicle. Such forces of resistance include friction (dealt with in more detail in section F), air resistance, and the force of the vehicle's brakes.

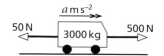

The force F that appears in the equation $F = ma$ is the resultant force on the vehicle, that is: driving force − resistance.

Forces of resistance stop acting as soon as the vehicle comes to rest. (For example, putting on a car's brakes will bring the car to rest, but keeping them on will not propel the car backwards!)

B4 A van of mass 3000 kg is being driven on a horizontal road. The van's engine exerts a driving force of 500 N. Resistances to motion amount to 50 N.

(a) What is the resultant horizontal force on the van?

(b) Use the equation $F = ma$ to calculate the acceleration of the van.

 If an object is moving with constant velocity, then its acceleration is zero. So the resultant force on the object is zero (propulsive force and resistance cancel out).

Example 2

A car of mass 1200 kg, travelling on a straight horizontal road, is accelerating at $0.4\,\mathrm{m\,s^{-2}}$. The driving force of the car's engine is 1520 N. Find the force of resistance.

Solution

Start by drawing a sketch. The sketch shows that $R\,\mathrm{N}$ stands for the unknown force of resistance. Vertical forces (which cancel out) are not shown here.

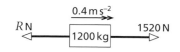

The resultant force acting on the car is $(1520 - R)\,\mathrm{N}$.

Use N2L ('Newton's second law'):

$$F = ma$$
$$1520 - R = 1200 \times 0.4 = 480$$
$$\Rightarrow \quad 1520 - 480 = R, \text{ so } R = 1040$$

The force of resistance is 1040 N.

Exercise B (answers p 154)

1 A lorry of mass 7500 kg is being driven along a straight horizontal road. The driving force of the lorry's engine is 8000 N. The force of resistance is 2000 N. Find the acceleration of the lorry.

2 A truck of mass 320 kg is pulled along a horizontal track by a horizontal cable. The truck is accelerating at $0.2\,\mathrm{m\,s^{-2}}$. Forces of resistance amount to 60 N. Find the tension in the cable.

3 The driving force of a railway locomotive is 24 000 N. The mass of the locomotive is 20 000 kg. Given that the locomotive is accelerating at $1.1\,\mathrm{m\,s^{-2}}$ along a straight horizontal track, find the force of resistance.

4 A car is travelling at a constant speed of $3\,\mathrm{m\,s^{-1}}$ along a straight horizontal road.

   (a) What is the acceleration of the car?

   (b) The driving force of the car's engine is 180 N. What is the force of resistance?

5 A van of mass 640 kg is being driven along a straight horizontal road. The engine is switched off and the brakes applied. The braking force is 200 N and other resistances to motion amount to 40 N.

   (a) The equation $F = ma$ is applied to this situation. If the direction of motion is taken as positive, explain why F is negative.

   (b) Find the value of the acceleration a, and explain what it means.

6 A motor boat is of mass 800 kg. The propulsive force of its engine can be varied. When the propulsive force is P N, the boat's acceleration is $1.5\,\mathrm{m\,s^{-2}}$. When the propulsive force is $2P$ N, the acceleration is $3.2\,\mathrm{m\,s^{-2}}$.

   Assuming that the force of resistance, R N, is the same in both cases, find the values of P and R.

C Solving problems in one dimension (answers p 154)

The equation $F = ma$ can be used together with the constant acceleration equations ($v = u + at$ and so on) to solve problems. The problems are generally of two types.

- Given F and m, use $F = ma$ to find a.
  Then use the constant acceleration equations to find other quantities.
- Given some of the values of u, v, s, t, use the constant acceleration equations to find a.
  Then use $F = ma$ to find F.

C1 A car of mass 1200 kg is travelling on a straight horizontal road. The driving force of the engine is 760 N. Resistance to motion is 40 N.

   (a) Find the acceleration of the car.

   (b) Find the time taken for the car to increase its velocity from $1.5\,\mathrm{m\,s^{-1}}$ to $4.5\,\mathrm{m\,s^{-1}}$.

   (c) Show that the distance travelled by the car during this time is 15 m.

C2 A van of mass 500 kg travelling on a straight horizontal road increases its velocity from $3\,\mathrm{m\,s^{-1}}$ to $6\,\mathrm{m\,s^{-1}}$ over a distance of 27 m.
Given that the resultant force on the van is of constant magnitude, find

(a) the acceleration of the van   **(b)** the resultant force on the van

Example 3

A boat of mass 400 kg has an outboard motor with a propulsive force of 350 N.
The boat is initially at rest. The motor is started and run for 6 seconds.
During this time a constant force of resistance acts on the boat.
At the end of the 6 seconds the velocity of the boat is $4.2\,\mathrm{m\,s^{-1}}$.

(a) Find the acceleration of the boat.

(b) Find the force of resistance on the boat.

The motor is switched off. The force of resistance remains the same.

(c) Find the deceleration of the boat.

(d) Find the time taken for the boat to come to rest.

(e) Find the distance travelled by the boat in this time.

Solution

(a) *Find a by using the constant acceleration equations.*
   $u = 0$, $v = 4.2$, $t = 6$, $a = ?$

   Use $v = u + at$: $4.2 = 0 + 6a$

   $\Rightarrow$ $a = 0.7$

   The acceleration is $0.7\,\mathrm{m\,s^{-2}}$.

(b) *Sketch a force diagram.*

   Apply N2L: $350 - R = 400 \times 0.7 = 280$

   $\Rightarrow$ $R = 70$

   The force of resistance is 70 N.

(c) *With the motor switched off, the only force on the boat is the resistance. As this acts in the opposite direction to the motion, its value is $-70\,\mathrm{N}$.*

   Apply N2L: $-70 = 400a$

   $\Rightarrow$ $a = -0.175$

   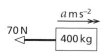

   The deceleration is $0.175\,\mathrm{m\,s^{-2}}$.

(d) For this part of the motion, $u = 4.2$, $v = 0$, $a = -0.175$, $t = ?$

   Use $v = u + at$: $0 = 4.2 - 0.175t$

   $\Rightarrow$ $t = \dfrac{4.2}{0.175} = 24$

   The time taken is 24 s.

(e) Use $s = \frac{1}{2}(u + v)t$: $s = \frac{1}{2}(4.2 + 0) \times 24 = 50.4$ (*Or you could use* $v^2 = u^2 + 2as$.)
   The distance travelled is 50.4 m.

Exercise C (answers p 154)

1 A lorry of mass 4500 kg has an engine with a driving force of 1800 N.
Given that there are no resistances to motion, find

(a) the acceleration of the lorry

(b) the time taken for the lorry to reach a speed of $5\,\mathrm{m\,s^{-1}}$ from rest on level ground

(c) the distance travelled by the lorry in this time

2 A boat of mass 250 kg has an engine with a propulsive force of 230 N.
As the boat moves through water it experiences a constant force of resistance R N.
The boat accelerates from rest and moves in a straight line.
After travelling for 10 seconds it is 40 m from its starting point.

(a) Find the acceleration of the boat.

(b) Find the value of R.

3 A car of mass 800 kg, whose engine has a driving force of 3600 N, is travelling
along a horizontal straight road with a constant velocity of $15\,\mathrm{m\,s^{-1}}$.

(a) Find the force of resistance.

The car's engine is disengaged. The force of resistance stays the same.

(b) Find the deceleration of the car.

(c) Find the distance the car travels before coming to rest.

4 A boat of mass 400 kg is at rest on a calm sea when a wind starts blowing with a
constant force on the boat. As a result the boat reaches a velocity of $1.5\,\mathrm{m\,s^{-1}}$
after travelling a distance of 50 m. Find the resultant force acting on the boat
during this motion.

5 A van of mass 7500 kg has an engine whose driving force is 4000 N.
When it travels on a straight horizontal road it is subject to a resistance R N,
which is always the same.
When the van carries no load it will accelerate from rest to $5\,\mathrm{m\,s^{-1}}$ in 10 s.

(a) Find the value of R.

(b) Find the time taken for the van to reach a speed of $5\,\mathrm{m\,s^{-1}}$ from rest
when it carries a load of mass 1500 kg.

6 A car accelerates uniformly along a straight horizontal road.
As it travels 200 metres, its speed increases from $12\,\mathrm{m\,s^{-1}}$ to $20\,\mathrm{m\,s^{-1}}$.

(a) Show that the acceleration of the car is $0.64\,\mathrm{m\,s^{-2}}$.

(b) Find the time it takes the car to travel this distance.

(c) The mass of the car is 1200 kg. Using the answer to part (a), find the magnitude
of the forward force that acts on the car during the above motion if:

(i) there is no resistance to its motion

(ii) a constant resistive force of magnitude 450 newtons acts on the car   AQA 2003

D Vertical motion (answers p 154)

From the time of the ancient Greeks, people believed that heavy objects fall to the ground faster than light objects. The Italian scientist Galileo Galilei (1564–1642) showed that not only was this untrue, but that all objects, whatever their mass, fall with the same constant acceleration (provided air resistance is ignored).

Galileo used an interesting argument to show that the earlier belief was incorrect.

Suppose a heavy object falls faster than a light object. What should happen if you connect a light object to a heavy one? Because the light object falls more slowly it should drag the heavy one back and cause it to fall more slowly.
On the other hand, the combined object is heavier than the heavy object alone and so should fall faster. The only way to resolve this dilemma is for the light and heavy objects to fall together.

Later measurements have shown the following to be true.

K In the absence of air resistance, all objects fall to the Earth with the same constant acceleration, whose value is approximately $9.8 \, \text{m s}^{-2}$.
This acceleration due to gravity is denoted by g. (In fact, there is a small variation in the value of g over the Earth's surface: it is larger at the equator than at the poles.)

From Newton's second law ($F = ma$) it follows that the force of gravity acting on an object of mass m kg is mg N. This downward force is, of course, the object's weight.

K An object of mass m kg has a weight of mg newtons.

Although g is an acceleration, in most problems it appears as a multiplier from mass m (kg) to weight mg (newtons).

D1 What is the weight, in newtons, of a ball of mass 1.5 kg?

D2 An object of mass 5 kg falls towards the ground.
Air resistance acting on the object is 2.5 N.

(a) Copy the sketch and complete it by adding the weight of the object in newtons.

(b) Use Newton's second law to find the object's acceleration.

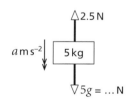

Example 4

A bucket of mass 2.5 kg is pulled upwards by a rope.
The bucket is accelerating at $2.2 \, \text{m s}^{-2}$. Find the tension in the rope.

Solution

The weight of the bucket $= mg = 2.5 \times 9.8 = 24.5 \, \text{N}$.

The sketch shows the two forces acting on the bucket.

Apply N2L: $T - 24.5 = 2.5 \times 2.2 = 5.5$
$\Rightarrow$ $T = 30$

The tension in the rope is 30 N.

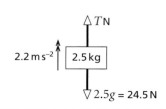

Exercise D (answers p 154)

1 A load of mass 4 kg is pulled upwards by a rope.
The tension in the rope is 45 N.

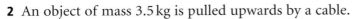

(a) Copy the sketch and label each force with its magnitude in newtons.

(b) What is the resultant upward force on the load?

(c) Find the acceleration of the load.

2 An object of mass 3.5 kg is pulled upwards by a cable.

(a) Suppose that the object is moving with constant speed.
Explain why the tension in the cable must be 3.5g newtons.

(b) Now suppose the object moves with an upward acceleration of 1.2 m s^{-2}.
Find the tension in the cable.

(c) The maximum tension that the cable can withstand is 50 newtons.
Find the maximum upward acceleration of the object, to 3 s.f.

3 A lift of mass 600 kg is attached to a cable which pulls it upwards.
The tension in the cable has a maximum possible value.

(a) When the lift is empty, its maximum possible upward acceleration is 2.5 m s^{-2}.
Find the maximum possible tension in the cable.

(b) Find the maximum possible upward acceleration of the lift when it carries a load of mass 100 kg.

4 A ball of mass 0.4 kg is dropped from the top of a cliff of height 35 m.
As it falls, the ball is subject to a constant force of air resistance of magnitude 1.5 N.

(a) Find the magnitude of the resultant downward force on the ball as it falls.

(b) Find the acceleration of the ball as it falls.

(c) Find the time it takes the ball to reach the foot of the cliff.

5 A stone of mass 0.5 kg is thrown upwards from the ground.
Air resistance on the stone has a constant magnitude of 0.7 N.

(a) Show that the deceleration of the stone as it travels upwards is 11.2 m s^{-2}.

(b) Find the acceleration of the stone as it travels downwards.

6 A lift of mass 600 kg is suspended from a single vertical cable.
The lift is initially at rest and then starts to accelerate upwards.
The tension in the cable remains constant at 6060 newtons while the lift is accelerating.
Assume that there is no resistance to the motion of the lift.

(a) Show that the acceleration of the lift is 0.3 m s^{-2}.

(b) Find the time that it would take the lift to travel 8 metres.

(c) Find the speed of the lift when it has travelled 8 metres. AQA 2003

E Resolving forces (answers p 155)

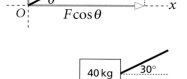

In chapter 3 (page 57) you saw that a force can be resolved into two components at right angles to one another.

The force F, acting at an angle θ to Ox, is resolved into components

      $F\cos\theta$ in direction Ox $F\sin\theta$ in direction Oy

Suppose a truck of mass 40 kg is pulled along a straight horizontal track by a light rope inclined at an angle of 30° to the horizontal, with no resistance. The tension in the rope is 10 newtons.

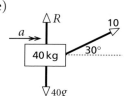

The forces acting on the truck are

- the weight, $40g$ newtons (there is no need to replace g by 9.8 at this stage)
- the normal reaction, R newtons, of the track on the truck
- the tension, 10 newtons, in the rope

These three forces are shown in the force diagram, in which the truck is treated as a particle.

The truck has an acceleration, $a\,\mathrm{m\,s^{-2}}$, which is shown by the double-headed arrow.

E1 The tension in the rope can be resolved into a horizontal component and a vertical component. Find the horizontal component.

E2 The acceleration of the truck is horizontal. The only force acting in this direction is the horizontal component of the tension. Use Newton's second law ($F = ma$) to find the acceleration of the truck.

E3 There is no vertical acceleration, so the resultant force in the vertical direction is zero. In other words, upward and downward forces balance each other.

The total upward force consists of R newtons and the vertical component of the tension. Use this fact, and the fact that $g = 9.8$, to find the value of R.

Example 5

A truck of mass 90 kg is pulled along a horizontal track by a rope inclined at 20° to the horizontal. The tension in the rope is 48 N. A horizontal force of resistance F N acts on the truck, which is moving with constant velocity. Find the value of F.

Solution

Sketch a force diagram.

The resultant horizontal force is $(48\cos 20° - F)\,\mathrm{N}$.

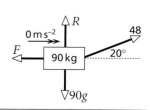

The velocity of the truck is constant, so its acceleration is 0.

Apply N2L: $48\cos 20° - F = 90 \times 0$. So $F = 48\cos 20° = 45.1$ (to 3 s.f.)

Example 6

A truck of mass 500 kg is pulled along a horizontal track by a rope inclined at 40° to the horizontal. A horizontal force of resistance, of magnitude 30 newtons, acts on the truck. The truck is accelerating at 0.2 m s⁻². Find

(a) the tension in the rope   **(b)** the normal reaction of the track on the truck

Solution

Sketch a force diagram and show the acceleration on it.

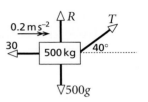

(a) The resultant horizontal force is $(T\cos 40° - 30)$ N.

Apply $F = ma$: $T\cos 40° - 30 = 500 \times 0.2$

$$\Rightarrow \qquad T = \frac{130}{\cos 40°} = 169.7$$

(b) Resolve vertically. (*There is no acceleration in this direction so upward and downward components balance.*)

$$T\sin 40° + R = 500g$$
$$\Rightarrow \qquad 169.7\sin 40° + R = 500 \times 9.8$$
$$\Rightarrow \qquad R = 4900 - 109.1 = 4790 \text{ (to 3 s.f.)}$$

The tension is 170 N and the normal reaction is 4790 N (to 3 s.f.).

Exercise E (answers p 155)

1 A boat of mass 400 kg is pulled by a light cable inclined at 20° to the horizontal. The tension in the cable is 220 N. A horizontal resisting force of 50 newtons acts on the boat.

   (a) Draw a force diagram.

   (b) Show that the horizontal force on the boat is 157 N.

   (c) Find the acceleration of the boat.

2 A truck of mass 90 kg is pulled along a straight horizontal track by a light rope inclined at 30° to the horizontal. The truck experiences a horizontal force of resistance of 25 newtons.

   (a) Given that the truck moves with a constant velocity, find

     (i) the tension in the rope

     (ii) the normal reaction of the track

   (b) Redo part (a) given that the truck accelerates at 0.5 m s⁻².

3 A truck of mass 800 kg is pulled along a straight horizontal track by a light cable inclined at 25° to the horizontal. A horizontal force of resistance, F newtons, acts on the truck. The tension in the cable is 320 newtons and the truck is accelerating at 0.3 m s⁻². Find

   (a) the value of F

   (b) the normal reaction of the track on the truck

4 A ship of mass 50 000 kg is being pulled by two horizontal cables each making an angle of 20° with the direction of motion of the ship. The tension in each cable is 4000 newtons. The ship experiences a horizontal force of resistance of 1500 newtons. Find the acceleration of the ship.

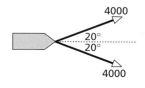

5 The diagram shows a design for a fairground ride. A trolley moves along a raised horizontal track. Hanging from the trolley is a light cable attached to a seat, in which a person sits. Trolley, cable and person move with an acceleration in the direction of the arrow, with the cable making a constant angle of 60° with the horizontal. Air resistance can be ignored.

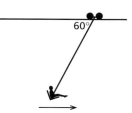

The mass of the seat plus person is 80 kg. The tension in the cable is T newtons.

(a) Explain why $T\sin 60° = 80g$ and hence find the value of T.

(b) Find the acceleration.

F Friction (answers p 155)

In chapter 3 (page 66), you saw that an object on a rough surface is able to resist a pulling force, but only up to a certain limit.

If the friction force is F, then $F \leq \mu R$, where R is the normal reaction of the surface on the object and μ is the coefficient of friction.

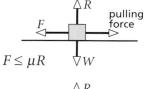

Once the object is moving, the magnitude of the friction force stays constant at μR.

(In reality the coefficient of friction is often smaller for a moving object than for a stationary one. This difference will be ignored.)

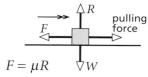

F1 A block of mass 60 kg is being pulled across a rough horizontal surface by a horizontal force P. The block is accelerating at $0.5\,\mathrm{m\,s^{-2}}$. The coefficient of friction between the block and the surface is 0.4.

(a) Sketch a diagram showing all the forces acting on the block.

(b) Explain why the normal reaction R of the surface on the block is $60g$ newtons.

(c) Find the friction force on the block.

(d) Find the value of P.

F2 The same block is pulled across the same surface, but this time the pulling force is 300 N inclined at 30° to the horizontal.

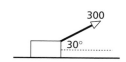

(a) Sketch a force diagram.

(b) By resolving vertically, find the normal reaction.

(c) Find the friction force on the block.

(d) By resolving horizontally and applying Newton's second law, find the acceleration of the block.

Example 7

A particle of mass $4\,\text{kg}$ is pulled across a rough horizontal surface by a light rope inclined at $40°$ to the horizontal. The coefficient of friction between the surface and the particle is 0.2. The tension in the rope is 16 newtons.
Find

(a) the normal reaction   **(b)** the friction force   **(c)** the acceleration of the particle

Solution

(a) Resolve vertically: $R + 16\sin 40° = 4g = 4 \times 9.8 = 39.2$
So $R = 39.2 - 16\sin 40° = 28.92\,\text{N}$

(b) $F = 0.2R = 5.784\,\text{N}$

(c) Resolve horizontally and apply N2L: $16\cos 40° - 5.784 = 4a$
So $a = \dfrac{6.473}{4} = 1.62$ (to 3 s.f.)

The acceleration is $1.62\,\text{m s}^{-2}$ (to 3 s.f.).

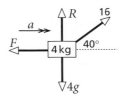

Exercise F (answers p 155)

1 A sledge of mass $15\,\text{kg}$ is pulled by a horizontal force of 78 newtons across a rough horizontal surface whose coefficient of friction is 0.5.
Find the acceleration of the sledge.

2 A box of mass $50\,\text{kg}$ is pushed across a rough horizontal floor by a horizontal force P newtons. The coefficient of friction between the floor and the box is 0.3. The box accelerates at $0.2\,\text{m s}^{-2}$. Find the value of P.

3 A particle of mass $3\,\text{kg}$ is sliding in a straight line across a smooth horizontal surface at a speed of $30\,\text{m s}^{-1}$. It encounters a rough patch of length $50\,\text{m}$, where the coefficient of friction between the surface and the particle is 0.4.

(a) Calculate the deceleration of the particle as it moves over the rough patch.

(b) Calculate the speed with which it leaves the rough patch.

4 A sledge of mass $10\,\text{kg}$ is pulled across a horizontal snow field by a light rope inclined at $30°$ to the horizontal.
The coefficient of friction between the sledge and the snow is 0.1.
The tension in the rope is 20 newtons.

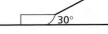

(a) Show that the normal reaction of the surface on the sledge is 88 newtons.

(b) Find the friction force on the sledge.

(c) Find the acceleration of the sledge.

5 A block of mass 20 kg is pushed across a rough floor by a force of 70 newtons inclined downwards at an angle of 35° to the horizontal. The coefficient of friction between the block and the floor is 0.2.

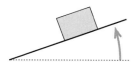

(a) Show that the normal reaction of the floor on the block is approximately 236 N.

(b) Find the magnitude of the friction force on the block.

(c) Find the acceleration of the block.

G Smooth inclined surfaces (answers p 155)

D **G1** Imagine an object resting on a perfectly smooth plane. The plane is horizontal to start with, but is gradually tilted so that its angle to the horizontal increases.

What will happen? Explain why.

We saw in chapter 3 that a perfectly smooth surface can provide a force at right angles to itself (normal reaction), but not a sideways force.

This is true whether the surface is horizontal or sloping.

G2 A plane is inclined at 35° to the horizontal.

Explain why the angle between the direction at right angles to the plane and the vertical is also 35°.

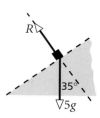

This diagram shows the forces acting on a particle of mass 5 kg placed on a smooth plane inclined at 35° to the horizontal. These forces are the weight (vertically downwards) and the normal reaction (at right angles to the plane).

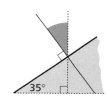

In all the situations looked at previously, we have resolved forces horizontally and vertically. However…

K In situations involving inclined planes it is usually best to resolve in these two directions:

  perpendicular to the plane

  parallel to (that is, up or down) the plane

These two directions are shown in the diagram above as dotted lines.

The next diagram shows how the weight, 5g, is resolved into

  a component $5g \cos 35°$ perpendicular to the plane

  a component $5g \sin 35°$ down the plane

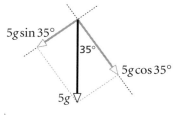

Bilborough College

brary and Information Cen'

D **G3** Here again is the force diagram for a particle of mass 5 kg on a smooth plane inclined at 35° to the horizontal.

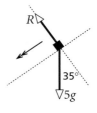

The particle accelerates down the plane.

(a) Explain why $R = 5g\cos 35°$, and hence find the value of R.

(b) By resolving forces down the plane and using Newton's second law, show that the acceleration of the particle is approximately 5.6 m s^{-2}.

G4 A particle of mass 1.5 kg slides down a smooth plane inclined at 25° to the horizontal.

(a) Sketch a diagram showing the forces acting on the particle.

(b) By resolving forces perpendicular to and parallel to the plane, find

   (i) the magnitude of the normal reaction of the plane on the particle

   (ii) the acceleration of the particle

Example 8

An object of mass 2.8 kg is pulled up a smooth plane inclined at 40° to the horizontal by a light string parallel to the plane. Given that the object is accelerating at 0.5 m s^{-2} up the plane, find

(a) the tension in the string

(b) the normal reaction between the plane and the object

Solution

Sketch the force diagram.

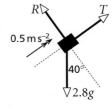

(a) Resolve up the plane.
The resultant component up the plane is $(T - 2.8g\sin 40°)$ N.

Apply N2L in this direction: $T - 2.8g\sin 40° = 2.8 \times 0.5$

$$\Rightarrow \qquad T = 2.8 \times 9.8 \times \sin 40° + 1.4$$
$$= 19.0 \text{ (to 3 s.f.)}$$

(b) Resolve perpendicular to the plane.
There is no acceleration perpendicular to the plane, so $R = 2.8g\cos 40°$
$$= 21.0 \text{ (to 3 s.f.)}$$

The tension is 19.0 N and the normal reaction 21.0 N.

Exercise G (answers p 156)

1 A particle of mass 4 kg slides down a smooth plane inclined at 30° to the horizontal.

(a) Sketch a diagram showing the forces acting on the particle.

(b) Find the acceleration of the particle.

(c) Find the magnitude of the normal reaction of the plane on the particle.

2 A sledge of mass 15 kg is pulled up a smooth slope inclined at 25° to the horizontal by a light rope parallel to the slope. The tension in the rope is 80 N. Find

(a) the acceleration of the sledge

(b) the normal reaction of the slope on the sledge

3 A child of mass 12 kg slides down a smooth slope inclined at 33° to the horizontal. The slope is 15 metres long and the child starts from rest at the top. Modelling the child as a particle, find

(a) the acceleration of the child

(b) the time taken to reach the foot of the slope

(c) the magnitude of the normal reaction on the child during the motion

H Rough inclined surfaces (answers p 156)

H1 Imagine an object resting on a rough plane. The plane is horizontal to start with, but is gradually tilted so that its angle to the horizontal increases.

What will happen? Explain why.

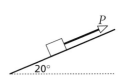

A rough plane is able to provide not only a normal reaction R but a friction force F on an object in contact with it. If the plane is inclined, the friction force may be either down or up the slope, depending on whether the object is moving (or is about to move) up or down the slope.

If the object is stationary, then $F \leq \mu R$. If it is moving, then $F = \mu R$.

H2 The diagram on the right shows the forces acting on a sledge of mass 3 kg (modelled as a particle) which is sliding down a rough plane inclined at 30° to the horizontal. The coefficient of friction is 0.2.

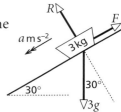

(a) Explain why the normal reaction of the plane on the sledge is $3g \cos 30°$ newtons.

(b) Find the value of F.

(c) Find the acceleration of the sledge down the plane.

H3 A load of mass 10 kg is hauled up a rough plane inclined at 20° to the horizontal, by a force P newtons parallel to the plane. The coefficient of friction between the load and the plane is 0.3.

(a) Sketch a diagram showing the forces acting on the load.

(b) Show that the normal reaction of the plane on the load is 92.1 N.

(c) Find the friction force on the load.

(d) Find the value of P

(i) when the load is moving with constant speed up the slope

(ii) when the load is accelerating at $2 \, \mathrm{m \, s^{-2}}$ up the slope

If an object is in equilibrium, the friction force F satisfies the inequality $F \le \mu R$.
This can be used to find an inequality involving μ.

H4 An object of mass 5 kg rests in equilibrium on a rough plane
inclined at 25° to the horizontal.
The diagram shows the forces acting on the particle.

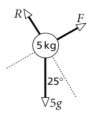

(a) Show that $R = 44.4$ (to 3 s.f.).

(b) Show that $F = 20.7$ (to 3 s.f.).

(c) Hence show that $\mu \ge 0.466$.

Example 9

A sledge of mass 15 kg is pulled up a slope inclined at 30° to the horizontal
by a rope parallel to the slope. The coefficient of friction between the sledge
and the slope is 0.3.

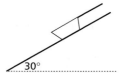

(a) Find the normal reaction of the slope on the sledge.

(b) Find the tension in the rope

   (i) when the sledge moves up the slope with a constant speed

   (ii) when the sledge accelerates up the slope at $2.5\,\mathrm{m\,s^{-2}}$

(c) State two modelling assumptions you have made in your solutions.

Solution

(a) Resolve perpendicular to the slope: $R = 15g\cos 30°$

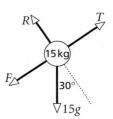

$$= 15 \times 9.8 \times \cos 30° = 127$$

   The normal reaction is 127 newtons (to 3 s.f.).

(b) (i) When the speed is constant, acceleration $= 0$.
     Friction force $F = 0.3R$
     Resolve up the slope and use N2L:

$$T - 0.3R - 15g\sin 30° = 15 \times 0$$
$$\Rightarrow \quad T = 0.3 \times 127 + 15 \times 9.8 \times \sin 30° = 112$$

   The tension in the rope is 112 newtons (to 3 s.f.).

  (ii) Resolve up the slope and use N2L:

$$T - 0.3R - 15g\sin 30° = 15 \times 2.5$$
$$\Rightarrow \quad T = 0.3 \times 127 + 15 \times 9.8 \times \sin 30° + 15 \times 2.5 = 149$$

   The tension in the rope is 149 newtons (to 3 s.f.).

(c) The sledge has been treated as a particle.
   The rope has been treated as light (of negligible mass or weight).

---

1 A particle of mass 10 kg slides down a rough plane inclined at 30°
to the horizontal. The coefficient of friction is 0.25.

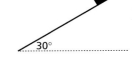

  (a) Draw a diagram showing the forces acting on the particle.

  (b) Show that the acceleration of the particle is 2.8 m s^{-2} (to 2 s.f.).

2 A box of mass 20 kg rests in limiting equilibrium on a rough plane
inclined at 30° to the horizontal.

  (a) Show that the normal reaction of the plane on the box is approximately 170 N.

  (b) Show that the coefficient of friction between the box and the plane is 0.58 (to 2 s.f.).

3 A sledge of mass 30 kg slides down a plane inclined at 20° to the horizontal.
The coefficient of friction between the sledge and the plane is 0.15.

  (a) Find the normal reaction of the plane on the sledge.

  (b) Show that the friction force on the sledge is 41.4 newtons (to 3 s.f.).

  (c) Find the acceleration of the sledge.

4 A box of mass 50 kg is pulled up a plane inclined at 15° to the horizontal
by a rope parallel to the plane. The coefficient of friction between the box
and the plane is 0.5. The box accelerates at 0.1 m s^{-2}.

  (a) Find the tension in the rope.

  (b) State any modelling assumptions you have made.

5 **(a)** A particle of mass 4 kg slides with constant speed down a plane inclined at 30°
to the horizontal. Find the coefficient of friction between the particle and the plane.

  (b) The same particle slides down a different plane, also inclined at 30° to the horizontal.
Given that the particle accelerates at 2 m s^{-2} down this plane, find the coefficient of
friction between the particle and the plane.

6 A small block of mass 2 kg is placed on a plane inclined at 40° to the horizontal.

  (a) Find the normal reaction of the plane on the block.

  (b) Show that if the coefficient of friction, μ, is greater than or equal to a certain value,
then the block will remain at rest on the plane. Find this value.

  (c) Given that $\mu = 0.4$, find the acceleration of the block down the plane.

7 A block, of mass 5 kg, is held at rest on a rough plane, which is inclined at
30° to the horizontal. The block is released and slides down the plane.
The coefficient of friction between the block and the plane is 0.2.

  (a) Draw a diagram to show the forces acting on the block as it slides.

  (b) Show that the magnitude of the friction force acting on the block is
approximately 8.5 N.

  (c) Find the acceleration of the block.

  (d) Find the speed of the block when it has travelled 1.2 metres down the slope.   AQA 2003

Motion in two dimensions

Force and acceleration are both vector quantities.
In vector form, Newton's second law is $\mathbf{F} = m\mathbf{a}$.

This equation can be used, along with the constant acceleration equations
($\mathbf{v} = \mathbf{u} + \mathbf{a}t$, $\mathbf{s} = \frac{1}{2}(\mathbf{u} + \mathbf{v})t$, $\mathbf{s} = \mathbf{u}t + \frac{1}{2}\mathbf{a}t^2$, $\mathbf{s} = \mathbf{v}t - \frac{1}{2}\mathbf{a}t^2$), to solve problems.

Example 10

A particle of mass 3 kg is moving with a velocity of $(2\mathbf{i} + 3\mathbf{j})\,\mathrm{m\,s^{-1}}$.
A constant force $\mathbf{F}$ newtons acts on the particle.
After 10 seconds the particle is moving with velocity $(5\mathbf{i} - 2\mathbf{j})\,\mathrm{m\,s^{-1}}$. Find

(a) the acceleration of the particle   (b) the magnitude of $\mathbf{F}$

Solution

(a) $\mathbf{u} = 2\mathbf{i} + 3\mathbf{j}$, $\mathbf{v} = 5\mathbf{i} - 2\mathbf{j}$, $t = 10$, $\mathbf{a} = ?$

Use $\mathbf{v} = \mathbf{u} + \mathbf{a}t$: $5\mathbf{i} - 2\mathbf{j} = 2\mathbf{i} + 3\mathbf{j} + 10\mathbf{a}$

$\Rightarrow 10\mathbf{a} = 3\mathbf{i} - 5\mathbf{j}$ so $\mathbf{a} = 0.3\mathbf{i} - 0.5\mathbf{j}$

The acceleration of the particle is $(0.3\mathbf{i} - 0.5\mathbf{j})\,\mathrm{m\,s^{-2}}$.

(b) Use N2L ($\mathbf{F} = m\mathbf{a}$): $\mathbf{F} = 3(0.3\mathbf{i} - 0.5\mathbf{j}) = 0.9\mathbf{i} - 1.5\mathbf{j}$

So $F = \sqrt{0.9^2 + 1.5^2} = 1.75$ (to 3 s.f.)

The magnitude of $\mathbf{F}$ is 1.75 N (to 3 s.f.).

Exercise I (answers p 157)

1 A particle of mass 5 kg is initially at the origin and moving with velocity $(\mathbf{i} + \mathbf{j})\,\mathrm{m\,s^{-1}}$.
It accelerates uniformly at $(4\mathbf{i} - 3\mathbf{j})\,\mathrm{m\,s^{-2}}$. Find

(a) the resultant force on the particle   (b) the velocity of the particle after 20 seconds

2 A particle of mass 4 kg is at rest at the origin at time $t = 0$.
A constant force $\mathbf{F}$ N acts on the particle.
At time $t = 10$ the position vector of the particle is $\begin{bmatrix} 150 \\ 80 \end{bmatrix}$ m. Find

(a) the acceleration of the particle   (b) the value of $\mathbf{F}$

3 A particle of mass 0.2 kg is moving with velocity $(5\mathbf{i} - 2\mathbf{j})\,\mathrm{m\,s^{-1}}$ when it is
acted on by a constant force of $(3\mathbf{i} + 4\mathbf{j})$ newtons. Find

(a) the acceleration of the particle   (b) the displacement of the particle after 4 s

4 A particle of mass 2.5 kg acted on by a constant force passes through a point A
with velocity $(2\mathbf{i} + 3\mathbf{j})\,\mathrm{m\,s^{-1}}$ and a point B with velocity $(10\mathbf{i} - \mathbf{j})\,\mathrm{m\,s^{-1}}$.
The time taken to travel from A to B is 5 seconds. Find

(a) the acceleration of the particle   (b) the displacement from A to B

(c) the magnitude of the force acting on the particle

Key points

- An object at rest or moving in a straight line with constant velocity will continue like that unless acted upon by a force. (Newton's first law)   (p 82)

- If a force of F newtons, acting on an object of mass m kg, causes an acceleration a m s^{-2}, then $F = ma$. (Newton's second law)   (p 85)

- If an object is moving with constant velocity, then its acceleration is zero. So the resultant force on the object is zero.   (p 86)

- An object of mass m kg has a weight of mg newtons ($g = 9.8$).   (p 90)

- In problems involving inclined planes, it is usually best to resolve forces in directions parallel to the plane and perpendicular to the plane.   (p 96)

- If an object is moving on a rough surface, the friction force F is equal to μR.   (pp 94, 98)

- In vector form, Newton's second law is $\mathbf{F} = m\mathbf{a}$.   (p 101)

Mixed questions (answers p 157)

1 A car moves along a straight road. When it passes a set of traffic lights, the car is travelling at a speed of $8 \, \text{m s}^{-1}$. The car then moves with constant acceleration for 10 seconds and travels 200 metres.

  (a) Show that the acceleration of the car is $2.4 \, \text{m s}^{-2}$.

  (b) Find the speed of the car at the end of the 10 seconds.

  (c) The road is horizontal and the car has mass 1200 kg. A constant resistance force of 1800 N acts on the car while it is moving.

    (i) Find the magnitude of the driving force that acts on the car while it is accelerating.

    (ii) At the end of the 10 second period the driving force is removed. The car then moves subject to the resistance force of 1800 N until it stops. Find the distance that the car travels while it is slowing down.   AQA 2002

2 A sledge, of mass 10 kg, is at rest on an icy, horizontal surface. A child, of mass 40 kg, is standing on the sledge. The child jumps off the sledge. Initially the child travels horizontally at $2 \, \text{m s}^{-1}$ and the sledge begins to slide in the opposite direction to the child.

  (a) Assuming that momentum is conserved, find the speed of the sledge, just after the child has jumped off it.

  (b) The coefficient of friction between the sledge and the ice is 0.2.

    (i) Find the magnitude of the friction force acting on the sledge while it is moving.

    (ii) Find the distance that the sledge slides before it comes to rest.   AQA 2002

3 The graph shows how the velocity, $v\,\text{m}\,\text{s}^{-1}$, of a cyclist varies with time, t seconds, as she moves along a straight horizontal road.

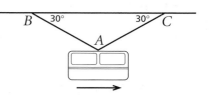

(a) Calculate the total distance travelled by the cyclist.

(b) Find the acceleration of the cyclist during the first 5 seconds of the motion.

(c) As the cyclist moves, a force of magnitude P newtons acts on the cyclist in the direction of motion. A constant horizontal resistance force of magnitude 50 newtons also acts. Model the cyclist and her bicycle as a particle of mass 65 kg.

   (i) Draw a diagram to show **all** the forces acting on the particle.

   (ii) Find the value of P during the first 5 seconds of the motion.　　AQA 2003

4 Two cables, AB and AC, are attached to a cable car, as shown in the diagram. The cable car has mass 450 kg.

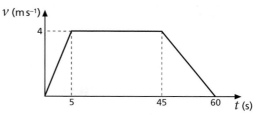

The cable car travels horizontally in the direction shown by the arrow. Model the cable car as a particle and assume that there is no air resistance present. As the cable car moves, the angles shown in the diagram do not change.

(a) The cable car travels at a constant speed. Show that the tension in each cable is 4410 N.

(b) The cable car now accelerates in the direction of the arrow at $0.5\,\text{m}\,\text{s}^{-2}$. Find the tension in each cable.

(c) Describe how your answers to part (b) would change if air resistance were taken into account.　　AQA 2002

5 A child slides down a steep, straight slide that is inclined at 60° to the horizontal. The child has mass 30 kg and the coefficient of friction between the slide and the child is 0.6. Assume that there is no air resistance.

(a) Draw a diagram to show the forces acting on the child, while sliding down the slide.

(b) Calculate the magnitude of the normal reaction force on the child.

(c) Show that the magnitude of the friction force that acts on the child is 88.2 N.

(d) Calculate the acceleration of the child.

(e) What modelling assumption have you made about the child in your solutions?　　AQA 2002

6 A ball is thrown vertically upwards from ground level. Throughout its motion it is acted on by gravity and a resistance force of constant magnitude. The ball reaches a maximum height of 1.5 metres after 0.5 seconds.

(a) Find **(i)** the initial speed of the ball

    (ii) its acceleration as it is moving upwards

The mass of the ball is 0.2 kg.

(b) Show that the magnitude of the resistance force is 0.44 N.

(c) Find the acceleration of the ball as it falls back to the ground.

(d) Find the total time that the ball is in the air.   AQA 2001

7 A box of mass 20 kg is pulled across a rough floor by a rope inclined at 25° to the horizontal. The coefficient of friction between the box and the ground is 0.3. The box is modelled as a particle. The diagram shows the forces acting on the box.

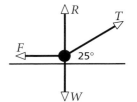

(a) Show that the weight of the box in newtons, W, is 196.

(b) Given that $T = 70$, show that $R = 166.4$, to 1 d.p.

(c) Find the value of F, the friction force acting on the box.

(d) Find the acceleration of the box.

(e) The box is initially at rest. Find the distance travelled by the box in 5 seconds.

8 A sledge, of mass 12 kg, is pulled up a rough slope which is inclined at an angle of 10° to the horizontal. The coefficient of friction between the slope and the sledge is 0.2.

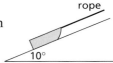

(a) The sledge is pulled by a rope that is parallel to the slope, as shown in the diagram.

    (i) Draw a diagram to show the forces acting on the sledge.

    (ii) Find the magnitude of the normal reaction force acting on the sledge.

    (iii) Given that the acceleration of the sledge is $0.5 \, \mathrm{m \, s^{-2}}$, show that the tension in the rope is approximately 50 N.

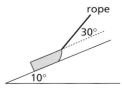

(b) The sledge is then pulled with the rope at an angle of 30° to the slope, as shown in the diagram. Find the acceleration of the sledge if the tension in the rope is 60 N.

(c) Write down **two** modelling assumptions you have made.   AQA 2002

9 Two constant forces $\mathbf{F_1} = (4\mathbf{i} + 16\mathbf{j})\,\mathrm{N}$ and $\mathbf{F_2} = (6\mathbf{i} - 11\mathbf{j})\,\mathrm{N}$ act on a particle. A force $\mathbf{F_3}$ also acts on the particle. The mass of the particle is 8 kg and the unit vectors $\mathbf{i}$ and $\mathbf{j}$ are perpendicular.

(a) In the case when the particle moves with constant velocity, find $\mathbf{F_3}$.

(b) In the case when the acceleration of the particle is $(2\mathbf{i} + 3\mathbf{j})\,\mathrm{m \, s^{-2}}$, find the magnitude of $\mathbf{F_3}$.   AQA 2001

Test yourself (answers p 157)

1 A go-kart of mass 500 kg is travelling in a horizontal straight line with constant acceleration. The go-kart's speed increases from $3.5\,\mathrm{m\,s^{-1}}$ to $11\,\mathrm{m\,s^{-1}}$ in 5 seconds.

  (a) Calculate the acceleration of the go-kart.

  (b) Calculate the distance the go-kart travels in the 5 seconds.

  (c) The resistance to the motion of the go-kart is 95 N.
     Find the driving force of the go-kart's engine.

2 After a collision, a car and a van, of combined mass 3000 kg, slide together along a straight horizontal road. The coefficient of friction between the road and the tyres of the vehicles as they slide is 0.7.

  (a) Model the car and the van as a single particle.

    (i) Show that the magnitude of the frictional force acting is 20 580 N.

    (ii) Find the acceleration of the car and van after the collision.

    (iii) The car and the van slide together for a distance of 5 metres before coming to rest. Using the result from part (a)(ii), show that just after the collision the car and van were moving at $8.28\,\mathrm{m\,s^{-1}}$ to three significant figures.

  (b) The mass of the car is 1200 kg and the mass of the van is 1800 kg. Before the collision, the van was stationary. Find the speed of the car just before the collision.   AQA 2003

3 A crate, of mass 50 kg, is at rest on a warehouse floor. The floor is rough and horizontal. The coefficient of friction between the crate and the floor is μ. A rope is attached to the crate at an angle of 30° to the horizontal. The tension in the rope is 100 N. The crate is shown in the diagram.

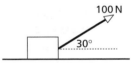

Model the crate as a particle.

  (a) Draw and label a diagram to show the forces acting on the crate.

  (b) Show that the magnitude of the normal reaction force acting on the crate is 440 N.

  (c) If the crate remains at rest, μ must satisfy the inequality $\mu \geq k$. Find k.

  (d) If $\mu = 0.1$, find the acceleration of the crate.   AQA 2004

4 A skier slides in a straight line directly down a slope inclined at 30° to the horizontal. The coefficient of friction between her skis and the slope is 0.3. The skier and her equipment are to be modelled as a particle of mass 80 kg. Assume that there is no air resistance present.

  (a) Draw a diagram to show the forces acting on the skier.

  (b) **(i)** Find the magnitude of the normal reaction force acting on the skier.

    (ii) Show that the magnitude of the friction force acting on the skier is 204 N to three significant figures.

  (c) Find the acceleration of the skier.   AQA 2003

6 Newton's laws of motion 2

In this chapter you will
- learn about the process of modelling
- use Newton's third law of motion to solve problems

A Modelling (answers p 158)

Many of the situations studied in mechanics are quite complicated. The first step is usually to simplify the situation. In this section we shall look at a particular mechanical system, the Lynton and Lynmouth Cliff Railway in Devon.

The railway is shown in this picture.
It connects Lynton, at the top of the cliff, with Lynmouth at the bottom.

There are two parallel tracks inclined at an angle of 35° to the horizontal.

A single car runs on each track. The two cars are connected by a cable that runs round a pulley wheel at the top.

(There is also a similar cable running round a pulley at the bottom, but the function of this cable is secondary.)

Each car is fitted with a water tank.
These tanks can be filled from a stream at the top and emptied into the sea at the bottom.

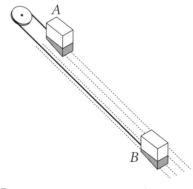

To understand how the railway works, suppose that one car (*A*) is at the top and the other (*B*) at the bottom and that both tanks are full.

People get into each car.

If *A* is heavier than *B*, it will start to descend and *B* will ascend.

If *A* is not heavier than *B*, water is let out of *B*'s tank until *A* is heavier than *B*.

When *B* gets to the top, its tank is filled and the whole process starts again.

D **A1** If the system consisted only of the things mentioned so far – cars, tracks, cable, water tanks – what do you think would happen to the cars once they had started to move?

What other things does the system need to be operated safely?

Imagine that the railway is being designed. The design of the track and the cars has been settled. Some of the questions that need to be considered are:

- How strong should the cable be?
- How fast will the cars travel?
- What will be the force on the cars' axles?

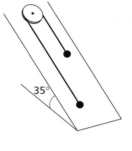

The first step in answering questions like these, or at least getting reasonable estimates, is to simplify the mechanism to its essentials, as shown in the diagram on the right.

The simplified version of the mechanism is called a **model**.

A model does not have to be a physical model. Most models in mechanics are descriptions in words, diagrams or symbols.

In the very simple model shown here, each car, including the people in it and the water in its tank, is modelled as a particle sliding on an inclined surface.

Having modelled the cars as particles, what about the cable? The cable (it is in fact about 370 m long) is itself quite heavy, but nowhere near as heavy as the cars. So in this simple model its mass could be ignored. In modelling language, the cable could be treated as 'light' (that is, of negligible mass).

Of course in practice such a 'light' cable could not do its job of pulling the heavy cars. But models often contain imaginary or 'ideal' elements, in this case a cable that is of negligible mass but strong.

It is also common to assume in a model like this that the cable is **inextensible**. This means that it will not stretch.

You may begin to wonder whether the simplified model is so unlike the real mechanism as to be useless. A model will be inadequate if an important factor is left out. For example, the model described so far would be inadequate if the mass of the cable is comparable with the mass of the cars, or if the cable is known to be highly elastic.

The process of modelling often starts with a highly simplified model. This model would include only the most important factors but would be good enough to answer some basic questions about the real mechanism or get good estimates of quantities. Then the model could be gradually improved to take account of other factors.

For example, in the model above the cars are modelled as particles. A particle is simple to deal with because all the forces on it act at the same point.

However, this is not true for the real car and a more detailed model would be needed in order to study the forces acting on the cars.

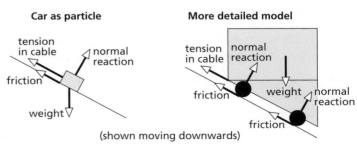

Car as particle — tension in cable, normal reaction, friction, weight

More detailed model — tension in cable, normal reaction, friction, weight, normal reaction, friction

(shown moving downwards)

The **modelling process** is shown in the diagram below.

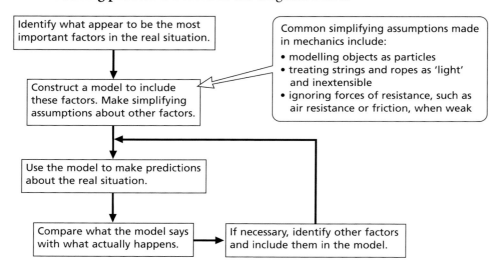

D **A2** Jack is studying the motion of an ice skater as she makes a complicated movement.
Would it be appropriate to model the skater as a particle?
Give reasons for your answer.

A3 There is an old joke about a mechanics exam question that starts
'An elephant of negligible mass …'.

Can you imagine circumstances in which an elephant could be said
to have negligible mass?

A4 A railway engineer is studying the motion of a tube train.
She is considering what might happen if both of these happen together:

• the brakes fail on a train as it is moving forward

• there is another train stopped ahead in the tunnel

Would it be realistic to ignore air resistance in this case?

What other factors do you think the model may need to include?

A5 A diver jumps from a diving board situated 5 metres above the surface
of the water in a swimming pool.
Why might it be inappropriate to model the diver as a particle?

In this book you have already met a number of examples where simplifying
assumptions have been made. More will occur in this chapter.

B Newton's third law of motion (answers p 158)

These diagrams show some situations where objects exert forces on one another.
(Other forces that may be acting on the objects are not shown.)

 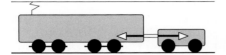 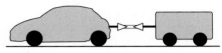

People leaning against each other   Engine pushing truck   Car towing trailer

Newton's third law of motion says

> If an object A exerts a force on an object B, then B exerts an equal and opposite
> force on A.

(Newton's own wording was 'Action and reaction are equal and opposite.')

For example, if you hit an object like a punch bag, you exert a force on the bag;
the bag exerts an equal force on your fist that you probably feel with some pain.

The three situations shown above frequently arise in mechanics.
Newton's third law applies whether the objects are stationary (as in the leaning people)
or moving with constant speed or acceleration (as in the pushing and towing).

In the case of the leaning people, the objects are in direct contact.
In the other cases, the forces are 'transmitted' between the objects by a bar
(where the force is a thrust) or a rope or bar (where the force is a tension).

B1 A car of mass 1200 kg is pulling a trailer
of mass 400 kg on a horizontal road.

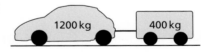

The car and trailer are connected by a
light horizontal rope.

The driving force of the car is 6000 N. The acceleration of the car and trailer is $a\,\mathrm{m\,s^{-2}}$.
Ignore friction and air resistance.

(a) Model the car as a particle.
Here is a diagram showing the forces acting on the car.
The tension in the rope is T N.
(The normal reaction R balances the weight.)

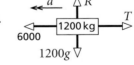

Use Newton's second law to write down an equation
involving T and a.

(b) Draw a diagram showing the forces acting on the trailer.
Why is the magnitude of the horizontal force equal to T N?

(c) By applying Newton's second law to the trailer, write down another equation
involving T and a.

(d) You now have two simultaneous equations. Solve them to find the values of T and a.

(e) The rope is described as 'light' so its mass can be ignored. What else has to be
true about the rope if the acceleration of the car and the trailer are to be equal?

In question B1 it is also possible to treat 'car + trailer' as a single particle of mass 1600 kg.

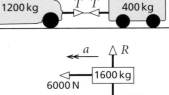

When this is done, the two forces of T and $-T$ cancel out. As far as the combined object is concerned, they are 'internal' forces. The only external force acting on the combined object is the driving force of the car.

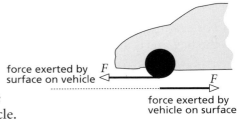

B2 (a) Write down the equation you get by applying Newton's second law to the combined particle 'car + trailer'.

(b) Solve the equation for a and check that the result is the same as before.

Note that if you use this 'combined object' method to find the acceleration, you still need to use Newton's second law on one of the separate objects to find the tension.

Driving force

Newton's third law explains how an engine inside a vehicle can provide an external driving force on the vehicle. The key to the explanation is the friction between the vehicle's wheels and the surface (road or rail).

The engine causes the wheels to push backwards on the surface with a force F. So, by Newton's third law, the surface provides an equal and opposite forward force F on the vehicle.

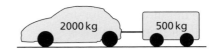

This works only if the surface is rough enough. For example, on an icy surface the wheels will spin and the vehicle will not move forwards.

Example 1

A car of mass 2000 kg tows a trailer of mass 500 kg on a straight horizontal road. The driving force of the car's engine is of magnitude 9000 N. Forces of resistance are 150 N on the car and 50 N on the trailer. Find

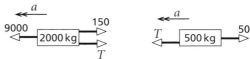

(a) the acceleration of the car and trailer

(b) the tension in the coupling between the car and the trailer

Solution

Draw separate force diagrams for car and trailer. (Vertical forces balance out and are not shown.)

Apply N2L to the car: $\qquad 9000 - 150 - T = 2000a \qquad (1)$

Apply N2L to the trailer: $\qquad T - 50 = 500a \qquad (2)$

Add (1) and (2): $\qquad 8800 = 2500a$ so $a = \frac{8800}{2500} = 3.52$

Substitute into (2): $\qquad T = 50 + 500 \times 3.52 = 1810$

(a) Acceleration $= 3.52 \, \text{m s}^{-2}$ **(b)** Tension $= 1810 \, \text{N}$

Exercise B (answers p 158)

1 A car of mass 3600 kg pulls a trailer of mass 400 kg on a straight horizontal road. The driving force of the car's engine is 3200 N. Resistance to motion may be ignored. Find

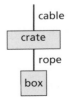

  (a) the acceleration of the car and trailer

  (b) the tension in the coupling between the car and the trailer

2 A van of mass 5200 kg pulls a trailer of mass 1200 kg on a straight horizontal road. The driving force of the van's engine is 4800 N. Horizontal resisting forces of 600 N and 200 N act on the van and the trailer respectively. Find

  (a) the acceleration of the van and trailer

  (b) the tension in the coupling between the van and the trailer

3 A railway engine pushes a carriage along a straight horizontal track. The mass of the engine is 10 500 kg. The mass of the carriage is 1500 kg. The engine and carriage are accelerating at $0.2 \, \text{m s}^{-2}$. Resistance to motion may be ignored. Find

  (a) the propulsive force of the engine

  (b) the magnitude of the force exerted by the engine on the carriage

4 A car pulls a trailer on a straight horizontal road. The mass of the car is 4200 kg; the mass of the trailer is 600 kg. There are no resistances to motion.

  The maximum tension in the coupling between the car and trailer is 480 N. Find

  (a) the maximum acceleration of the car and trailer

  (b) the driving force of the car's engine when the acceleration has its maximum value

5 A car of mass 1500 kg pulls a trailer of mass 500 kg on a straight horizontal road. Resistances to motion are constant at 200 N on the car and 100 N on the trailer.

  (a) Find the magnitude of the force in the towbar between the car and the trailer when the car and trailer travel with constant speed.

  (b) During the journey a braking force is applied to the car, with the result that the car and trailer decelerate at a constant rate of $0.2 \, \text{m s}^{-2}$.

   (i) By applying Newton's second law to the trailer, find the magnitude of the force in the towbar.

   (ii) Find the braking force applied to the car.

6 A crate of mass 120 kg is pulled vertically upwards by a cable attached to it. A box of mass 30 kg is attached to the underside of the crate by a light inextensible rope. The crate and box are accelerating upwards at $0.1 \, \text{m s}^{-2}$. Air resistance may be ignored.

  (a) Draw separate force diagrams for the crate and the box.

  (b) Find the tension in the cable.

  (c) Find the tension in the rope connecting the crate and the box.

C Pulleys and pegs (answers p 159)

This diagram shows two particles *A* and *B* connected by a light inextensible string that passes over a fixed pulley or peg.

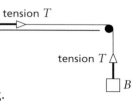

Particle *A* slides on a horizontal surface and particle *B* hangs vertically. Between the pulley and particle *A* the string is horizontal.

The force exerted by each particle on the other is transmitted by the string. Although the string changes direction as it goes round the pulley, the magnitude of the tension will be the same throughout, provided that the pulley (or peg) is frictionless, or 'smooth'. This will be assumed in all the work that follows.

D

C1 Imagine that particle *A* is held in position and then released. Describe what happens

    (a) if the horizontal surface is perfectly smooth

    (b) if the surface is rough

C2 In the diagram above, the mass of *A* is 3 kg and the mass of *B* is 2 kg. The horizontal surface is smooth.

    (a) Draw a diagram showing all the forces acting on *A*.

    (b) Let $a \, \mathrm{m\,s}^{-2}$ be the acceleration of particle *A*. Use Newton's second law to write down an equation connecting *T* and *a*.

    (c) Draw a diagram showing all the forces acting on *B*.

    (d) What fact about the string means that the magnitude of the acceleration of *B* is the same as that of *A*?

    (e) Use Newton's second law for *B* to write down another equation connecting *T* and *a*.

    (f) Solve the two equations to find the values of *a* and *T*.

C3 The masses of *A* and *B* are as before, but the surface is rough, with coefficient of friction 0.2.

    (a) Draw a diagram showing all the forces acting on *A*.

    (b) Explain why the normal reaction of the surface on *A* must be 3*g* newtons.

    (c) Assuming that *A* moves, explain why the friction force on *A* is 5.88 newtons.

    (d) Use Newton's second law for *A* to write down an equation connecting *T* and *a*.

    (e) Draw a force diagram for *B* and find a second equation connecting *T* and *a*.

    (f) Find the values of *a* and *T*.

C4 A particle of mass 4 kg situated on a horizontal surface is connected to a hanging particle of mass 3 kg by a string that passes over a smooth peg. Find the acceleration of the system and the tension in the string

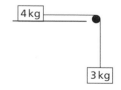

    (a) when the surface is smooth

    (b) when the surface is rough with $\mu = 0.5$

C5 The particles A and B both hang vertically, as shown in this diagram. The mass of A is greater than the mass of B.

Particle A is held and then released. Describe what happens.

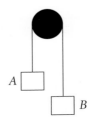

C6 The mass of A is 3 kg and the mass of B is 2 kg.
The tension in the string is T newtons.
The acceleration of A is a m s^{-2} downwards and that of B is a m s^{-2} upwards. Air resistance may be ignored.

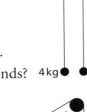

Particle A is released from rest.

(a) Draw a diagram showing all the forces on A.

(b) By applying Newton's second law to A, find an equation connecting T and a.

(c) Draw a diagram showing all the forces on B.

(d) By applying Newton's second law to B, find an equation connecting T and a.

(e) Find the values of a and T.

(f) Explain why the magnitude of the downward force exerted on the pulley is $2T$ and find its value.

C7 A particle of mass 3 kg is connected to a particle of mass 4 kg by a light inextensible string passing over a smooth pulley.

The particles are initially both at rest at the same level and are then released.

(a) Find the acceleration of each particle.

(b) Find the tension in the string.

(c) Find the distance travelled by each particle during the first 2 seconds.

(d) What is the difference in height between the particles after the 2 seconds?

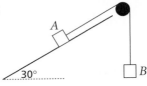

C8 Particles A, of mass 3 kg, and B, of mass 2 kg are arranged so that A slides on a smooth slope inclined at 30° to the horizontal. The string between A and the pulley is parallel to the slope.

(a) Before doing any calculation, say whether you think A will accelerate up or down the slope.

(b) This diagram shows the forces acting on particle A.

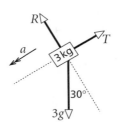

By resolving parallel to the slope, show that $14.7 - T = 3a$, where a is the acceleration down the slope.

(c) Draw a diagram of the forces acting on B. Find a second equation connecting T and a.

(d) Solve the two equations to find the values of a and T. What does the value of a tell you about the acceleration of the particles?

Example 2

Two particles, of mass 5 kg and 2 kg respectively, are connected by a light inextensible string passing over a smooth peg. Both particles hang vertically with one particle held at rest. The particle is released. Find

(a) the acceleration of the system   (b) the tension in the string

(c) the downward force on the peg

Solution

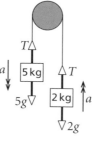

(a), (b) Apply N2L to the 5 kg particle: $5g - T = 5a$ (1)

Apply N2L to the 2 kg particle: $T - 2g = 2a$ (2)

Add (1) and (2): $3g = 7a$, so $a = 3 \times \dfrac{9.8}{7} = 4.2$

Substitute in (2): $T = 2g + 2a = 28$

Acceleration $= 4.2 \, \text{m s}^{-2}$; tension $= 28 \, \text{N}$

(c) The downward force on the peg is $2T$ N (see diagram) $= 56$ N.

Example 3

A particle A of mass 5 kg on a rough horizontal plane is connected by a light inextensible string passing over a smooth pulley to a second particle B of mass 2 kg that hangs freely.

The coefficient of friction between particle A and the plane is 0.1.

Particle A is held at rest and then released. Find

(a) the acceleration of the system

(b) the tension in the string

(c) the time taken, to the nearest 0.1 s, for B to fall 10 metres

Solution

(a) Resolve vertically the forces on A: $R = 5g = 49$

Friction force on particle A: $F = \mu R = 0.1 \times 49 = 4.9$

Apply N2L to A: $T - 4.9 = 5a$ (1)

Apply N2L to B: $2g - T = 2a$ (2)

Add (1) and (2): $2g - 4.9 = 7a$

      $\Rightarrow$ $7a = 19.6 - 4.9 = 14.7$, so $a = 2.1$

The acceleration is $2.1 \, \text{m s}^{-2}$.

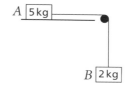

(b) From (1), $T = 5 \times 2.1 + 4.9 = 15.4$ The tension is 15.4 N.

(c) *Use the constant acceleration equations.* $u = 0, \ a = 2.1, \ s = 10, \ t = ?$

$s = ut + \frac{1}{2}at^2$ gives $10 = 1.05t^2 \Rightarrow t = \sqrt{\dfrac{10}{1.05}} = 3.1$ (to 1 d.p.)

The time taken is 3.1 s.

Example 4

A particle A of mass $5\,kg$ slides on a smooth plane inclined at $30°$ to the horizontal. The particle is connected to a particle B of mass $2\,kg$ by a light inextensible string passing over a smooth peg.

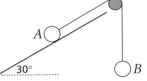

The system is released from rest. Find

(a) the acceleration of each particle

(b) the tension in the string

(c) the speed of particle A after it has travelled a distance of $8\,m$ (assuming that the string is long enough to allow this)

Solution

In this diagram the acceleration of A is shown as downwards. It may turn out to be upwards, in which case the value of a would turn out to be negative.

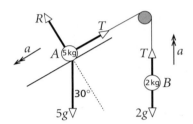

(a) The only motion of A is along the plane. So resolve forces in this direction and apply N2L:

$$5g \sin 30° - T = 5a \quad \text{so} \quad 24.5 - T = 5a \quad (1)$$

Apply N2L to B: $\quad T - 2g = 2a \quad \text{so} \quad T - 19.6 = 2a \quad (2)$

Add (1) and (2): $\quad 24.5 - 19.6 = 7a$

$$\Rightarrow \quad a = 0.7$$

The acceleration is $0.7\,m\,s^{-2}$.

(b) From (2), $T = 19.6 + 2a = 19.6 + 1.4 = 21$

The tension is $21\,N$.

(c) $u = 0$, $v = ?$, $a = 0.7$, $s = 8$

Use $v^2 = u^2 + 2as$. So $v^2 = 0 + 2 \times 0.7 \times 8 = 11.2$, from which $v = \sqrt{11.2} = 3.35$ (to 3 s.f)

The speed is $3.35\,m\,s^{-1}$ (to 3 s.f.).

Exercise C (answers p 159)

1 A particle of mass m_1 kg slides on a smooth horizontal surface. It is connected to a particle of mass m_2 kg by a light inextensible string passing over a smooth peg. The second particle hangs vertically as shown.

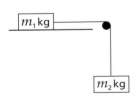

The system is released from rest. In each case below, find

(i) the acceleration of the system   (ii) the tension in the string

(a) $m_1 = 4$, $m_2 = 2$ (b) $m_1 = 2$, $m_2 = 4$ (c) $m_1 = 5$, $m_2 = 3$

2 Two particles of masses m_1 kg and mass m_2 kg are connected by a light inextensible string passing over a fixed smooth pulley. Both particles hang vertically. The system is released from rest. In each case below, find

    (i) the acceleration of the system   (ii) the tension in the string

    (iii) the downward force on the pulley

(a) $m_1 = 4$, $m_2 = 2$ **(b)** $m_1 = 5$, $m_2 = 3$ **(c)** $m_1 = 3.5$, $m_2 = 1.5$

3 A particle of mass m_1 kg slides on a rough horizontal surface with coefficient of friction μ. The particle is connected to a second particle of mass m_2 kg by a light inextensible string passing over a smooth peg. The second particle hangs vertically.

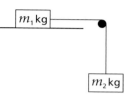

The system is released from rest. In each of the cases below, find

    (i) the acceleration of the system   (ii) the tension in the string

(a) $m_1 = 4$, $m_2 = 2$, $\mu = 0.1$ **(b)** $m_1 = 2$, $m_2 = 4$, $\mu = 0.2$

(c) $m_1 = 5$, $m_2 = 3$, $\mu = 0.5$ **(d)** $m_1 = 4$, $m_2 = 3$, $\mu = 0.5$

4 A particle of mass m_1 kg slides on a smooth plane inclined at angle α to the horizontal. It is connected to a particle of mass m_2 kg by a light inextensible string passing over a smooth peg. The second particle hangs vertically as shown.

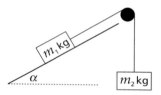

The system is released from rest. In each of the cases below, find

    (i) the acceleration and direction of motion of m_1 (ii) the tension in the string

(a) $m_1 = 4$, $m_2 = 3$, $\alpha = 30$ **(b)** $m_1 = 2$, $m_2 = 4$, $\alpha = 45$

(c) $m_1 = 5$, $m_2 = 3$, $\alpha = 45$ **(d)** $m_1 = 2$, $m_2 = 4$, $\alpha = 60$

5 Two small objects A and B, each of mass 0.3 kg, are connected by a light inextensible string passing over a smooth pulley and hang vertically. Initially the system is at rest.

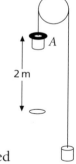

A 'collar' of mass 0.1 kg is placed on A. As a result the system accelerates. After A has fallen a distance of 2 metres, it passes through a ring which removes the collar. Find

(a) the acceleration of A while the collar is in place

(b) the time during which the collar is in place, to the nearest 0.1 s

(c) the distance travelled by A in the first 3 seconds after the collar is removed

6 A particle A of mass 5 kg is on a rough horizontal surface. The coefficient of friction between A and the surface is μ. A is connected to a particle B, of mass 2 kg, by a light inextensible string that passes over a fixed smooth peg.

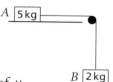

(a) Given that B hangs at rest, find the range of possible values of μ.

(b) When B is replaced by a particle C of mass 3 kg, the system accelerates at 0.49 m s^{-2}. Find the value of μ.

7 The Lynton and Lynmouth Cliff Railway is modelled as a pair of particles sliding on a smooth slope inclined at 35° to the horizontal. The particles are connected by a light inextensible cable passing round a smooth pulley at the top of the plane. Air resistance is ignored.

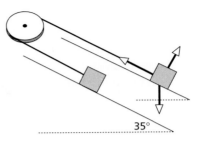

Diagram showing the forces acting on one of the particles

(a) Given that the masses of the particles are 8000 kg and 4000 kg, find the acceleration of the system and the tension in the cable.

(b) The railway is 360 m long. Imagine that the brakes fail when the heavier particle is at the top. Find the speed with which this particle reaches the bottom of the slope.

(c) State two features of the real railway that are left out of the model.

Key points

- Modelling assumptions are made in order to simplify a situation by including only the most important factors. If a model is inadequate it may be improved by including further factors. (p 108)

- If an object *A* exerts a force on an object *B*, then *B* exerts an equal and opposite force on *A*. (Newton's third law of motion) (p 109)

- If two objects are connected by a light string that passes round a frictionless peg or pulley, the magnitude of the tension in the string is the same throughout. (p 112)

Mixed questions (answers p 160)

1 The diagram shows a car pulling a trailer in a straight line along a horizontal road. The car has mass 1000 kg and the resistance forces acting on the car are of magnitude 1200 N. The trailer has mass 250 kg and the resistance forces acting on the trailer are of magnitude 300 N. The forward propulsive force of the engine of the car is 2000 N.

(a) (i) By considering the car and the trailer as a single body, show that the acceleration of the car and trailer is $0.4 \, \text{m s}^{-2}$.

(ii) By considering the forces acting only on the trailer, or otherwise, find the tension in the coupling between the car and the trailer.

When the car and the trailer are moving with velocity $12 \, \text{m s}^{-1}$, the coupling breaks and the trailer becomes separated from the car. During the subsequent motion the trailer moves under the resistance force alone.

(b) (i) Show that the deceleration of the trailer during the subsequent motion is $1.2 \, \text{m s}^{-2}$.

(ii) Find the distance moved by the trailer after the coupling breaks.

AQA 2002

2 Two particles are connected by a light inextensible string which passes over a smooth fixed peg, as shown in the diagram. The particle A, of mass 0.5 kg, is in contact with a rough horizontal surface, and the particle B, of mass 0.2 kg, hangs freely. The coefficient of friction between A and the surface is $\frac{2}{7}$.

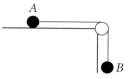

The system is released from rest with the string taut and A moves towards the peg.

(a) Show that the frictional force between A and the surface is of magnitude 1.4 N.

(b) Find the acceleration of the particles.

(c) Find the tension in the string.

(d) Find the time taken for the particles to travel 0.625 metres, given that A has not then reached the peg.

AQA 2002

3 Two particles, of masses 0.3 kg and m kg, are connected by a light, inextensible string which hangs over a smooth fixed peg, as shown in the diagram. The system is released from rest. During the subsequent motion, the 0.3 kg mass moves upwards and the tension in the string is 3.36 N.

(a) Show that the magnitude of the acceleration of the particles is 1.4 m s^{-2}.

(b) Find the value of m.

(c) Find the magnitude of the force the string exerts on the peg.

AQA 2002

4 Two particles, A and B, are connected by a light inextensible string which passes over a smooth light pulley. Particle A is on a smooth slope, at 45° to the horizontal, and particle B hangs with the string vertical, as shown in the diagram.

The mass of A is 14 kg and the mass of B is 6 kg.

(a) Using two equations of motion, show that the acceleration of the particles is 1.91 m s^{-2}, correct to three significant figures.

(b) Particle B is replaced by a particle C of mass m kg. After the particles have been set in motion, they move with a constant speed. Find m.

AQA 2004

5 The diagram shows two particles that are connected by a light inextensible string. The 5 kg particle, A, is on a rough horizontal surface and the 3 kg particle, B, hangs on the other end of the string as shown in the diagram. The string passes over a smooth light pulley.

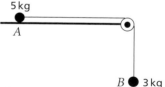

The coefficient of friction between A and the horizontal surface is 0.8.
The particles are set in motion with the string taut and A moving towards the pulley. The initial speed of both particles is 2 m s^{-1}. The particles slow down and stop before A reaches the pulley or B hits the floor.

(a) Show that, while the particles are moving, the magnitude of their acceleration is 1.225 m s^{-2}.

(b) Find the tension in the string while the particles are moving.

(c) Find the distance that the particles move before they come to rest.

AQA 2003

Test yourself (answers p 160)

1 The diagram shows a car pulling a trailer in a straight line on a horizontal stretch of road. The mass of the car is 1250 kg and the total resistance force acting on the car is 500 N.
The mass of the trailer is 250 kg and the total resistance force acting on the trailer is 100 N.

(a) During part of the journey, a constant braking force is applied to the car, causing the car and trailer to decelerate at a constant rate of $0.5 \, \text{m s}^{-2}$.

   (i) By considering the forces on the trailer, find the magnitude of the force in the towbar between the car and the trailer.

   (ii) Find the magnitude of the braking force applied to the car.

(b) Later in the journey, the car and trailer travel with constant speed. State the magnitude of the tension in the towbar.   AQA 2003

2 A block, of mass 6 kg, is held at rest on a rough horizontal table. The block is attached, by a light string that passes over a light smooth pulley, to a sphere of mass 4 kg that hangs freely, as shown in the diagram.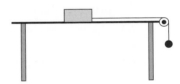

(a) The block is released and travels 60 cm in 2 seconds. Show that the acceleration of the block is $0.3 \, \text{m s}^{-2}$.

(b) Find the magnitude of the tension in the string.

(c) Find the magnitude of the friction force on the block.

(d) Find the coefficient of friction between the block and the table. Give your answer correct to two significant figures.   AQA 2001

3 A builder uses a rope that passes over a pulley to raise and lower concrete blocks while building a house. The diagram shows the initial position of two loads of the blocks.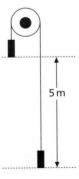

Each load consists of **8 blocks**, each of mass 5 kg. Initially the lower load is resting on the ground. When 2 blocks are accidentally removed from the lower load the system begins to move.

5 m

(a) Making any necessary modelling assumptions,

   (i) show that the acceleration of the loads is $1.4 \, \text{m s}^{-2}$

   (ii) find the tension in the rope

(b) State two assumptions made in part (a).

(c) Find the speed of the two loads when they are at the same level.   AQA 2001

7 Projectiles

In this chapter you will

- solve problems involving vertical motion under gravity
- learn about the motion of a projectile (a particle moving in two dimensions acted on by gravity)
- solve problems about projectiles including those involving release at height

A Vertical motion under gravity (answers p 161)

D **A1** Sarah is standing at a cliff edge. She drops a stone over the edge.

(a) Describe the motion of the stone from the time it leaves Sarah's hand until it hits the water.

(b) Sarah now drops a stone that is twice as heavy.
How do you think the motion of this stone will differ from that of the previous stone?

(c) She now throws a stone over the edge so that it leaves her hand with a velocity u m s^{-1} vertically downwards.
What effect will this have on the motion of the stone?

K If air resistance is ignored, the only force acting on a freely falling object is its weight. The object has acceleration vertically downwards of g m s^{-2}.
This acceleration is known as the **acceleration due to gravity** and is approximately equal to 9.8 m s^{-2}.

A2 Assuming that Sarah's stone started from rest, what would its velocity be after 2 seconds?

A3 Sarah throws the stone with an initial **upward** velocity of 15 m s^{-1}.
Calculate the velocity of the stone after

(a) 1 second   (b) 2 seconds   (c) 3 seconds   (d) 4 seconds

D **A4** Leroy throws a ball vertically upwards and catches it when it returns.

(a) Describe how the velocity of the ball changes during its motion.

(b) What is the velocity of the ball when it is at its maximum height?

(c) How does the velocity of the ball when Leroy catches it relate to its velocity when he threw it?

(d) Sketch a velocity–time graph for the motion of the ball after it leaves Leroy's hand.

(e) Sketch a displacement–time graph for the motion of the ball, where displacement is measured upwards from Leroy's hand.

K For vertical motion under gravity the acceleration is constant and equal to $9.8\,\mathrm{m\,s^{-2}}$ downwards and the motion is in a straight line, so the constant acceleration equations in one dimension can be applied.

$$v = u + at$$
$$s = \tfrac{1}{2}(u + v)t$$
$$s = ut + \tfrac{1}{2}at^2$$
$$s = vt - \tfrac{1}{2}at^2$$
$$v^2 = u^2 + 2as$$

Example 1

A stone is dropped off the edge of a cliff. It hits the water after 4 seconds. Calculate the height of the cliff above the water.

Solution

First list the known values and the unknown. Note that the stone is moving downwards so the downwards direction will be taken as positive and hence the acceleration due to gravity is positive.

$$u = 0, \ t = 4, \ a = 9.8, \ s = ?$$

Use $s = ut + \tfrac{1}{2}at^2$ to find the displacement.

$$s = 0 \times 4 + \tfrac{1}{2} \times 9.8 \times 4^2$$
$$\Rightarrow \ s = 78.4$$

The height of the cliff is $78.4\,\mathrm{m}$.

Example 2

A ball is thrown vertically upwards from ground level with initial speed $20\,\mathrm{m\,s^{-1}}$. Calculate the maximum height of the ball and the time it takes to reach this height.

Solution

At its maximum height the velocity of the ball is zero. It is moving upwards, so the upwards direction will be taken as positive and hence the acceleration due to gravity is negative.

$$u = 20, \ v = 0, \ a = -9.8, \ s = ?, \ t = ?$$

Use $v^2 = u^2 + 2as$ to find the displacement.

$$0 = 20^2 - 2 \times 9.8 \times s$$
$$\Rightarrow 0 = 400 - 19.6\,s$$
$$\Rightarrow s = \frac{400}{19.6} = 20.4 \text{ to 1 d.p.}$$

Use $v = u + at$ to find the time.

$$0 = 20 - 9.8 \times t$$
$$\Rightarrow t = \frac{20}{9.8} = 2.0 \text{ to 1 d.p.}$$

The ball reaches its maximum height of $20.4\,\mathrm{m}$ after $2.0\,\mathrm{s}$.

Example 3

A ball is thrown vertically upwards from ground level with an initial speed of $12\,\mathrm{m\,s^{-1}}$. Find the total time the ball is in the air.

Solution

During its motion the ball moves from ground level, where $s = 0$, to its maximum height and back to ground level. Substituting the known values into $s = ut + \frac{1}{2}at^2$ will give a quadratic equation which can be solved to find the times when the ball is at ground level.

$$u = 12, \ a = -9.8, \ s = 0, \ t = ?$$
$$s = ut + \tfrac{1}{2}at^2$$
$$\Rightarrow \quad 0 = 12t - \tfrac{1}{2}\times 9.8 \times t^2$$
$$\Rightarrow \quad 0 = 12t - 4.9t^2$$
$$\Rightarrow \quad 0 = t(12 - 4.9t)$$
$$\Rightarrow \quad t = 0 \text{ or } 2.448\ldots$$

The ball is thrown when $t = 0$, so $t = 2.448\ldots$ when the ball hits the ground.

The ball is in the air for 2.45 seconds (to 2 d.p.).

Exercise A (answers p 161)

1 A coin is dropped from the top of a high tower.

 (a) Find its velocity after 3 seconds.

 (b) How far has it fallen in this time?

 (c) It takes 5 seconds for the coin to hit the ground.
  How high is the top of the tower above the ground?

2 A stone is thrown off a cliff with an initial speed of $5\,\mathrm{m\,s^{-1}}$ downwards.
 The stone falls vertically downwards until it hits the water.
 If the top of the cliff is 30 metres above the water, find the speed of the stone when it hits the water.

3 A stone is thrown vertically upwards from ground level to dislodge a conker on a tree.
 The maximum speed the stone can be thrown with is $14.8\,\mathrm{m\,s^{-1}}$ and it must hit the conker with a speed of at least $5\,\mathrm{m\,s^{-1}}$ to dislodge it.
 What is the height of the highest conker the stone can dislodge?

4 A ball is thrown vertically upwards from ground level with an initial speed of $7\,\mathrm{m\,s^{-1}}$.
 Assume that no resistance forces act on the ball, so that it moves only under the influence of gravity.

 (a) Find the maximum height of the ball.

 (b) The ball hits the ground T seconds after it was thrown. Find T. 　　　AQA 2002

5 A toy rocket is catapulted vertically upwards from ground level and reaches a maximum height of 30 metres before returning to its starting position.

(a) Find the initial speed of the rocket.

(b) Find the total time the rocket is in the air.

6 A stone is thrown vertically upwards from ground level with initial speed $18\,\text{m}\,\text{s}^{-1}$.

(a) Find the times when it is $5\,\text{m}$ above ground level.

(b) For how long is the stone more than $5\,\text{m}$ above ground level?

7 A cricket ball is thrown vertically upwards from ground level with a speed of $25\,\text{m}\,\text{s}^{-1}$. For how long is the ball more than 20 metres above the ground?

8 A ball is thrown vertically upwards from ground level with an initial speed $u\,\text{m}\,\text{s}^{-1}$.

(a) Sketch a velocity–time graph for the motion of the ball.

(b) Find an expression, in terms of u, for the maximum height reached by the ball.

(c) Find an expression for the time when the ball is at its maximum height.

(d) State one modelling assumption you have made regarding the motion of the ball.

*9 A man throws a coin vertically upwards with a speed of $2\,\text{m}\,\text{s}^{-1}$. His hand is initially 1.2 metres above the ground.

(a) Find the time taken for the coin to hit the ground.

(b) Find the speed with which the coin hits the ground.

B Motion of a projectile (answers p 161)

An object that is thrown, dropped or launched into the air so that it moves under the influence of gravity alone is known as a **projectile**.
In the previous section we looked at projectiles that moved vertically in one dimension. In this section we will extend this into two dimensions.

The projectile will be modelled as a **particle**, an object that has mass but whose size can be ignored. The effects of air resistance and spin are considered negligible. If these effects are not negligible, then there will be forces other than weight acting on the particle, and it will not move as a projectile.

D   **B1** Suggest some examples of situations which can be modelled as projectiles. Suggest a situation which cannot be modelled as a projectile and explain why.

Consider the motion of a ball which is kicked off the edge of a cliff with an initial horizontal velocity $\mathbf{u} = 10\mathbf{i}\,\text{m}\,\text{s}^{-1}$ as shown. The only force acting on the ball is its weight, so the ball has constant vertical acceleration of $\mathbf{a} = -9.8\mathbf{j}\,\text{m}\,\text{s}^{-2}$.

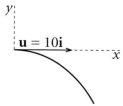

The constant acceleration equations in vector form can be applied.

B2 (a) By substituting the known values into $\mathbf{s} = \mathbf{u}t + \frac{1}{2}\mathbf{a}t^2$, show that the displacement, $\mathbf{s}$, of the ball at time t is given by $\mathbf{s} = 10t\mathbf{i} - 4.9t^2\mathbf{j}$.

(b) Show that $\mathbf{s} = 30\mathbf{i} - 44.1\mathbf{j}$ when $t = 3$.

(c) Complete this table of values for the displacement of the ball.

t	0	1	2	3	4
$\mathbf{s}$				$30\mathbf{i} - 44.1\mathbf{j}$	

(d) Plot these points on graph paper, using a scale of 1 cm to 10 m, and join them to show the path of the ball during the motion. Label the points where $t = 0$, $t = 1$, etc.

B3 (a) By substituting the known values into $\mathbf{v} = \mathbf{u} + \mathbf{a}t$, find an expression for the velocity, $\mathbf{v}$, of the ball at time t.

(b) Show that $\mathbf{v} = 10\mathbf{i} - 9.8\mathbf{j}$ when $t = 1$.

(c) Complete this table of values for the velocity of the ball.

t	0	1	2	3	4
$\mathbf{v}$	$10\mathbf{i}$	$10\mathbf{i} - 9.8\mathbf{j}$			

(d) Using a scale of 1 cm to $10\,\text{m}\,\text{s}^{-1}$, add the velocity vectors to the graph drawn in B2(d). Draw each vector from the point on the graph with the corresponding value of time.

It can be seen from the table of values and the graph that the horizontal component of velocity is constant throughout the motion as there is no force acting on the ball in that direction.

The vertical component of velocity is continuously increasing downwards because of the weight of the ball.

Hence the direction of the velocity of the ball is changing throughout its motion.

K Projectile motion takes place in a vertical plane and the path is in the shape of a parabola.

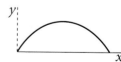

The horizontal component of a projectile's velocity is constant. The vertical component of a projectile's velocity changes throughout the motion due to its weight.

The magnitude and direction of the velocity of the projectile change throughout the motion.

D **B4** Another identical ball is dropped off the cliff (i.e. **u** = 0).

    (a) (i) Find an expression for the displacement, **s**, of the ball at time t.

      (ii) Find the displacement of the ball when $t = 0, 1, 2, 3$ and 4. Compare your answer with B2. Can you explain your answer?

    (b) (i) Find an expression for the velocity, **v**, of the ball at time t.

      (ii) Find the velocity of the ball when $t = 0, 1, 2, 3$ and 4. Compare your answer with B3. Can you explain your answer?

B5 A ball is thrown with an initial velocity $(10\mathbf{i} + 15\mathbf{j})\,\mathrm{m\,s^{-1}}$, where **i** and **j** are horizontal and vertical unit vectors respectively. The only force acting on the ball is its weight, so its acceleration is $-9.8\mathbf{j}\,\mathrm{m\,s^{-2}}$.

    (a) (i) Find an expression in terms of **i** and **j** for the displacement, **s**, of the ball from its starting point at time t.

      (ii) Find the displacement of the ball when $t = 0, 0.5, 1, 1.5, 2, 2.5$ and 3.

      (iii) Plot these points on graph paper and join them to show the path of the ball during the motion.

    (b) (i) Find an expression in terms of **i** and **j** for the velocity, **v**, of the ball at time t.

      (ii) Find the velocity of the ball when $t = 1, t = 2$ and $t = 3$.

      (iii) Draw the velocity vectors for these times on the graph drawn in (a)(iii) to show how the velocity of the ball changes during the motion.

Example 4

A ball is thrown with an initial velocity of $(4\mathbf{i} + 6\mathbf{j})\,\mathrm{m\,s^{-1}}$.
Find the magnitude and direction of the velocity after 1 second.

Solution

First list the known values and the unknowns. $\mathbf{u} = 4\mathbf{i} + 6\mathbf{j},\ \mathbf{a} = -9.8\mathbf{j},\ t = 1,\ \mathbf{v} = ?$

Use $\mathbf{v} = \mathbf{u} + \mathbf{a}t$ *to find* **v**. $\mathbf{v} = 4\mathbf{i} + 6\mathbf{j} + (-9.8\mathbf{j} \times 1) = 4\mathbf{i} - 3.8\mathbf{j}$

Sketch the vector.

Use Pythagoras to find the magnitude. $v = \sqrt{4^2 + 3.8^2} = \sqrt{30.44} = 5.5$ (to 1 d.p.)

Use trigonometry to find the direction. $\tan\theta = \dfrac{3.8}{4} = 0.95$ $\Rightarrow \theta = 43.5°$ (to 1 d.p.)

After 1 second the ball is travelling at $5.5\,\mathrm{m\,s^{-1}}$ at $43.5°$ below the horizontal.

Example 5

A stone is thrown over a cliff with initial velocity $\begin{bmatrix} 12 \\ 0 \end{bmatrix}$ m s^{-1}. The stone hits the water after 5 seconds.
Find the height of the cliff above the water and the speed of the stone as it hits the water.

Solution

First list the known values and the unknowns. $\mathbf{u} = \begin{bmatrix} 12 \\ 0 \end{bmatrix}$, $\mathbf{a} = \begin{bmatrix} 0 \\ -9.8 \end{bmatrix}$, $t = 5$, $\mathbf{s} = ?$, $\mathbf{v} = ?$

Use $\mathbf{s} = \mathbf{u}t + \frac{1}{2}\mathbf{a}t^2$ *to find* $\mathbf{s}$. $\mathbf{s} = \begin{bmatrix} 12 \\ 0 \end{bmatrix} \times 5 + \frac{1}{2}\begin{bmatrix} 0 \\ -9.8 \end{bmatrix} \times 5^2 = \begin{bmatrix} 60 \\ -122.5 \end{bmatrix}$

The height of the cliff is the vertical component of the displacement.   Height of cliff = 122.5 m

Use $\mathbf{v} = \mathbf{u} + \mathbf{a}t$ *to find* $\mathbf{v}$. $\mathbf{v} = \begin{bmatrix} 12 \\ 0 \end{bmatrix} + \begin{bmatrix} 0 \\ -9.8 \end{bmatrix} \times 5 = \begin{bmatrix} 12 \\ -49 \end{bmatrix}$

Find the magnitude of the velocity. $v = \sqrt{12^2 + 49^2} = 50.4$ m s^{-1} to 1 d.p.

Example 6

A ball is thrown with initial velocity $(8\mathbf{i} + 11\mathbf{j})$ m s^{-1}, where $\mathbf{i}$ and $\mathbf{j}$ are horizontal and vertical unit vectors.
Find the displacement and velocity of the ball after 2 seconds.

Solution

The only force acting on the ball is its weight, so it is moving as a projectile with acceleration of -9.8 m s^{-2}.

Use $\mathbf{s} = \mathbf{u}t + \frac{1}{2}\mathbf{a}t^2$ *to find* $\mathbf{s}$.

$\mathbf{u} = (8\mathbf{i} + 11\mathbf{j})$, $\mathbf{a} = -9.8\mathbf{j}$, $t = 2$, $\mathbf{s} = ?$, $\mathbf{v} = ?$
$\mathbf{s} = (8\mathbf{i} + 11\mathbf{j}) \times 2 - \frac{1}{2} \times 9.8\mathbf{j} \times 2^2$
$\Rightarrow \quad \mathbf{s} = (16\mathbf{i} + 22\mathbf{j}) - 19.6\mathbf{j}$
$\Rightarrow \quad \mathbf{s} = 16\mathbf{i} + 2.4\mathbf{j}$

Use $\mathbf{v} = \mathbf{u} + \mathbf{a}t$ *to find* $\mathbf{v}$.

$\mathbf{v} = (8\mathbf{i} + 11\mathbf{j}) - 9.8\mathbf{j} \times 2$
$\Rightarrow \quad \mathbf{v} = 8\mathbf{i} + 11\mathbf{j} - 19.6\mathbf{j}$
$\Rightarrow \quad \mathbf{v} = 8\mathbf{i} - 8.6\mathbf{j}$

After 2 seconds the displacement is $(16\mathbf{i} + 2.4\mathbf{j})$ m and the velocity is $(8\mathbf{i} - 8.6\mathbf{j})$ m s^{-1}.

Exercise B (answers p 163)

Take $\mathbf{i}$ and $\mathbf{j}$ as the horizontal and vertical unit vectors throughout this exercise.

1 An object is projected with initial velocity $12\mathbf{i}$ m s^{-1}.
  (a) Show that its velocity after 2 seconds is $(12\mathbf{i} - 19.6\mathbf{j})$ m s^{-1}.
  (b) Find its velocity after 5 seconds.

2 An object is projected with initial velocity $\begin{bmatrix} 2 \\ 3 \end{bmatrix}$ m s⁻¹.

    (a) Show that its displacement from the starting point after 1 second is $\begin{bmatrix} 2 \\ -1.9 \end{bmatrix}$ m.

    (b) Find its displacement after 4 seconds.

3 An object is projected with initial velocity $(10\mathbf{i} + 20\mathbf{j})$ m s⁻¹.

    (a) Find its displacement when $t = 0$, 1, 2, 3 and 4.

    (b) Plot these displacements on graph paper and join them to show the path of the object.

    (c) Find the velocity of the object when $t = 2$. Draw this vector on your graph.

    (d) Find the velocity of the object when $t = 4$. Draw this vector on your graph.

4 A ball is thrown with initial velocity $(4\mathbf{i} + 7\mathbf{j})$ m s⁻¹.

    (a) Find its velocity after 2 seconds.

    (b) Find its displacement after 2 seconds.

5 A football is kicked with an initial velocity of $(6\mathbf{i} + 12\mathbf{j})$ m s⁻¹.

    (a) What is the initial speed of the ball?

    (b) What angle does the initial velocity make with the horizontal?

    (c) What is the speed of the ball after 2 seconds?

    (d) What angle does the velocity make with the horizontal after 2 seconds?

6 Jack kicks a ball from ground level with initial velocity $\begin{bmatrix} 7 \\ 6 \end{bmatrix}$ m s⁻¹.
It hits a wall after 1 second.

    (a) Find the height at which the ball hits the wall.

    (b) At what speed does the ball hit the wall?

7 A stone is thrown off a cliff with initial velocity $(4\mathbf{i} + 3\mathbf{j})$ m s⁻¹.
The stone hits the water after 4 seconds.

    (a) Find the height of the cliff above the water.

    (b) How far from the base of the cliff does the stone hit the water?

8 An arrow is fired from a bow with an initial velocity of $(40\mathbf{i} + 7.5\mathbf{j})$ m s⁻¹.
It hits the target after 1.5 seconds.

    (a) What is the horizontal distance from the bow to the target?

    (b) Given that the arrow is fired from a height of 1 metre above ground level, at what height does the arrow hit the target?

*9 A ball is thrown with initial velocity $(5\mathbf{i} + 6\mathbf{j})$ m s⁻¹.

    (a) Write an expression for the velocity of the ball at time t.

    (b) When is the speed of the ball least?

    (c) What is the speed at this time?

C Projectile problems (answers p 163)

Consider a particle projected from the origin with velocity $10\,\text{m s}^{-1}$ at an angle of $40°$ to the horizontal.

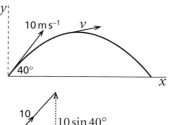

The initial velocity can be resolved into horizontal and vertical components; the horizontal and vertical components of the motion can be considered separately.

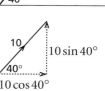

There is no force acting horizontally, so the horizontal component of the velocity remains constant.

Vertically, the weight of the particle causes an acceleration of $9.8\,\text{m s}^{-2}$ downwards.

At time t, the velocity of the particle can be found using $v = u + at$ in the horizontal and vertical directions.

Horizontally, $v_x = 10\cos 40°$

Vertically, $v_y = 10\sin 40° - 9.8t$

At time t, the displacement of the particle can be found using $s = ut + \frac{1}{2}at^2$ in the horizontal and vertical directions.

Horizontally, $x = 10t\cos 40°$

Vertically, $y = 10t\sin 40° - 4.9t^2$

Alternatively, if the initial velocity is given as a vector, the constant acceleration equations in vector form can be used to find the velocity and displacement of the particle at time t in vector form.

C1 A particle is projected from the origin with velocity $\begin{bmatrix} 5 \\ 8 \end{bmatrix}$.

    (a) Use $\mathbf{v} = \mathbf{u} + \mathbf{a}t$ to find an expression for the velocity of the particle, $\mathbf{v}$, at time t.

    (b) Use $\mathbf{s} = \mathbf{u}t + \frac{1}{2}\mathbf{a}t^2$ to find an expression for the displacement of the particle, $\mathbf{s}$, at time t.

K At time t, a particle projected from the origin with initial velocity U at an angle of θ to the horizontal will be at the point where

$$x = Ut\cos\theta \quad \text{and} \quad y = Ut\sin\theta - \frac{1}{2}gt^2$$

The velocity components are

$$v_x = U\cos\theta \quad \text{and} \quad v_y = U\sin\theta - gt$$

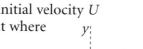
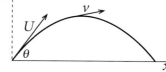

These equations can be used to solve problems involving projectiles.

Consider a particle projected from point O with initial velocity $15\,\text{m}\,\text{s}^{-1}$ at an angle of $30°$ to the horizontal.
The diagram shows the parabolic path of the projectile.

The **range** of the projectile is the horizontal distance travelled by the projectile from O to A.

The **time of flight** of the projectile is the time taken to travel from O to A, the time that the projectile is in the air.

At points O and A, $y = 0$.

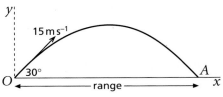

C2 (a) Write down the horizontal and vertical components of the initial velocity.

(b) Write an equation for the height of the particle, y, at time t.

(c) Use this equation to find the time of flight of the projectile.

(d) Write an equation for the horizontal distance, x, travelled by the particle at time t.

(e) By substituting the value of the time of flight into the equation found in part (d) find the range of the projectile.

The path of the projectile is symmetrical, so the projectile reaches its **maximum height** at the mid-point of the path.

When the projectile is at its maximum height the vertical component of its velocity is zero.

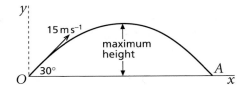

C3 (a) Write an equation for the y-component of the velocity of the particle at time t.

(b) Use this equation to find the time when the particle is at its maximum height.

(c) How does this time relate to the time of flight of the particle?

(d) By substituting the time found in part (b) into the equation for the height of the particle, find the maximum height of the projectile.

C4 (a) What horizontal distance has the particle travelled when it is at its maximum height?

(b) What is the direction of the velocity when the projectile is at its maximum height?

C5 A particle is projected from ground level with initial velocity $10\,\text{m}\,\text{s}^{-1}$ at an angle of $20°$ to the horizontal.

(a) Find the time of flight of the projectile.

(b) Find its range.

(c) Find its maximum height.

Example 7

A hockey ball is hit from ground level with an initial speed of $12\,\mathrm{m\,s^{-1}}$ at $40°$ to the horizontal.

For how long is the ball more than 2 metres above the ground?

Solution

Draw a sketch showing the known values.

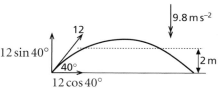

Use $s = ut + \frac{1}{2}at^2$ for vertical motion.

$$y = Ut\sin\theta - \tfrac{1}{2}gt^2$$
$$2 = 12\times t\times\sin 40° - \tfrac{1}{2}\times 9.8\times t^2$$
$$\Rightarrow 2 = 7.713t - 4.9t^2$$

Rearrange to give a quadratic equation.

$$4.9t^2 - 7.713t + 2 = 0$$

Solve using the quadratic formula.

$$t = \frac{7.713 \pm \sqrt{7.713^2 - 4\times 4.9\times 2}}{2\times 4.9}$$
$$\Rightarrow t = 0.33 \text{ or } 1.25 \text{ to 2 d.p.}$$

These are the two times when the ball is at a height of 2 metres.
The difference between these is the time above that height.

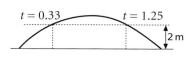

$$\text{Time above } 2\,\mathrm{m} = 1.25 - 0.33$$
$$= 0.92\,\mathrm{s} \text{ to 2 d.p.}$$

Example 8

A ball is kicked from ground level at a speed of $20\,\mathrm{m\,s^{-1}}$.

When it is at its maximum height it just passes over a fence $1.6\,\mathrm{m}$ high.
Find the angle of projection.

Solution

Draw a sketch showing the known values.

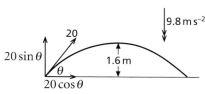

Use $v = u + at$ for vertical motion.

$$v_y = U\sin\theta - gt$$

At maximum height, $v_y = 0$

so $20\sin\theta - gt = 0$

Rearrange to find t in terms of θ. *Leave g in the expression.*	$t = \dfrac{20\sin\theta}{g}$
Use $s = ut + \frac{1}{2}at^2$ for vertical motion.	$y = Ut\sin\theta - \frac{1}{2}gt^2$

$$1.6 = 20 \times \frac{20\sin\theta}{g} \times \sin\theta - \frac{1}{2}g \times \frac{400\sin^2\theta}{g^2}$$

$$\Rightarrow 1.6 = \frac{200\sin^2\theta}{g}$$

$$\Rightarrow \sin^2\theta = \frac{1.6g}{200}$$

Substitute the value of g at this stage. $\sin\theta = \pm\sqrt{\dfrac{1.6g}{200}} = \pm 0.28$

We know that θ is less than 90°. $\theta = 16°$ to the nearest degree

Alternatively you could use $v^2 = u^2 + 2as$ for the vertical motion.

Exercise C (answers p 164)

1 A ball is thrown from ground level with initial speed $20\,\text{m s}^{-1}$ at an angle of $40°$ to the horizontal.

 (a) Find the time of flight of the ball (the length of time the ball is in the air).

 (b) Find the range of the ball.

2 A cricket ball is hit from ground level with initial velocity $\begin{bmatrix} 4 \\ 10 \end{bmatrix}\text{m s}^{-1}$.

 (a) Find the time of flight.

 (b) Find the range of the cricket ball.

3 A ball is kicked from ground level with initial speed $16\,\text{m s}^{-1}$ at an angle of $25°$ to the horizontal.
 Find the maximum height of the ball.

4 A hockey ball is hit with an initial velocity of $14\,\text{m s}^{-1}$ at an angle θ to the horizontal where $\sin\theta = 0.6$ as shown in the diagram.

 (a) Find the maximum height of the ball.

 (b) Find the range of the ball.

5 Ann throws a ball to Julian with initial velocity $\begin{bmatrix} 7 \\ 5 \end{bmatrix}\text{m s}^{-1}$ and Julian catches it at the same height.

 (a) For how long is the ball in the air?

 (b) How far apart are Ann and Julian?

6 A particle is projected from the origin with initial speed $V\,\mathrm{m\,s^{-1}}$ at an angle α to the horizontal.

   (a) Show that the time of flight of the particle is given by $t = \dfrac{2V\sin\alpha}{g}$.

   (b) Show that the range of the particle is given by $R = \dfrac{2V^2\sin\alpha\cos\alpha}{g}$.

7 A golf ball is hit so that it leaves the ground with an initial velocity of magnitude $15\,\mathrm{m\,s^{-1}}$, at an angle α to the horizontal, where $\tan\alpha = \frac{3}{4}$, as shown in the diagram.

   (a) How high does the ball go?

   (b) Given that the ground is horizontal, how far does the ball travel before its first bounce?

8 David takes a free kick in a football match. He kicks the ball with velocity $(10\mathbf{i} + 11\mathbf{j})\,\mathrm{m\,s^{-1}}$ from a point $20\,\mathrm{m}$ from the goal, where $\mathbf{i}$ and $\mathbf{j}$ are horizontal and vertical unit vectors. The height of the goal is $2.44\,\mathrm{m}$.

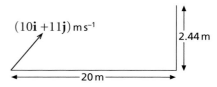

   (a) How long does the ball take to travel $20\,\mathrm{m}$ horizontally?

   (b) Assuming that the goalkeeper cannot reach the ball, does David score a goal?

   (c) Find the magnitude and direction of the velocity of the ball after it has travelled $20\,\mathrm{m}$ horizontally.

9 A ball is projected at an initial speed of $15\,\mathrm{m\,s^{-1}}$ and just passes over a wall $1.8\,\mathrm{m}$ high when it is at its maximum height.
Find the angle of projection of the ball.

10 Azmat throws a ball to Susan who is $80\,\mathrm{m}$ away and who catches it at the same height as it was thrown.
The ball is in the air for 5 seconds.
Find the initial speed of the ball and the angle at which it was thrown.

11 A ball is kicked from a point $5\,\mathrm{m}$ horizontally away from a wall $1\,\mathrm{m}$ high.
The ball just passes over the wall 1 second after it is kicked.

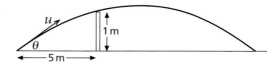

Find the initial speed of the ball and the angle at which it was kicked.

12 An arrow is fired at a target. It hits the target after 2.5 seconds at the same level as it was fired from.
Given that the arrow was fired at an initial speed of $50\,\mathrm{m\,s^{-1}}$, find the angle of projection and the range of the arrow.

13 Alison kicks a ball with a velocity of $10\,\mathrm{m\,s^{-1}}$ at an angle α to the horizontal where $\sin\alpha = 0.7$. The ball moves freely under gravity and passes over a wall 2 metres high when it is at its maximum height.

  (a) Find the time for the ball to reach its maximum height.

  (b) Find the vertical distance between the ball and the top of the wall at this time.

  (c) Find the length of time for which the ball is above the height of the wall.

14 A stone is catapulted from ground level at an angle of $35°$ to the horizontal. If the stone hits the ground $25\,\mathrm{m}$ from its point of projection, find its speed of release and the time it is in the air.

15 A particle is projected from point O with initial velocity $(a\mathbf{i} + b\mathbf{j})\,\mathrm{m\,s^{-1}}$. It hits the ground again $R\,\mathrm{m}$ from O after T seconds.

  Find a and b in terms of R, T and g.

D Release from a given height

Consider a particle projected with velocity $12\,\mathrm{m\,s^{-1}}$ at an angle of $50°$ to the horizontal from a height $4\,\mathrm{m}$ above ground level.

At time t, the particle is at the point (x, y).

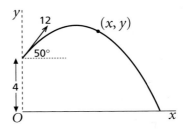

The horizontal component of the displacement of the particle is unaffected by the height of release.

$$x = 12t\cos 50°$$

The vertical component of the displacement is $4\,\mathrm{m}$ when the motion starts, causing the path of the projectile to be displaced vertically by $4\,\mathrm{m}$.

$$y = 12t\sin 50° - \tfrac{1}{2}gt^2 + 4$$

At time t, a projectile released at $U\,\mathrm{m\,s^{-1}}$ at θ to the horizontal from height $h\,\mathrm{m}$ above the ground is at the point where

$$x = Ut\cos\theta \quad \text{and} \quad y = Ut\sin\theta - \tfrac{1}{2}gt^2 + h$$

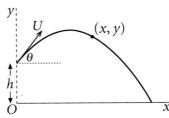

Example 9

A ball is thrown with an initial speed of $10\,\text{m}\,\text{s}^{-1}$ at an angle of $30°$ to the horizontal from a height of $1.5\,\text{m}$ above ground level.
Find its maximum height above the ground and the time when it hits the ground.

Solution

Draw a sketch showing the known values.

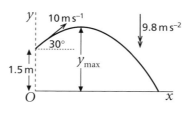

Use $v = u + at$ for vertical motion.

$$v_y = U\sin\theta - gt$$

At the maximum height $v_y = 0$,

so $10\sin 30° - gt = 0$

$$\Rightarrow t = \frac{10\sin 30°}{g}$$

Use $s = ut + \frac{1}{2}at^2$ for vertical motion.

Taking the height of release into account,

$$y = Ut\sin\theta - \frac{1}{2}gt^2 + h$$

$$y = 10\times\frac{10\sin 30°}{g}\times\sin 30° - \frac{1}{2}g\times\frac{100\sin^2 30°}{g^2} + 1.5$$

$$\Rightarrow y = \frac{50\sin^2 30°}{g} + 1.5 = 2.8 \text{ (to 1 d.p.)}$$

Alternatively you could use $v^2 = u^2 + 2as$ to find the maximum height.

Find the time when the ball hits the ground.   The ball hits the ground when $y = 0$,

so $10t\sin 30° - \frac{1}{2}\times 9.8t^2 + 1.5 = 0$

Rearrange to give a quadratic equation. $4.9t^2 - 5t - 1.5 = 0$

Solve using the quadratic formula.

$$t = \frac{5\pm\sqrt{5^2 + 4\times 4.9\times 1.5}}{2\times 4.9}$$

$$\Rightarrow t = -0.242 \text{ or } 1.263$$

The time is positive, so take the positive root. $t = 1.3$ (to 1 d.p.)

The maximum height of the ball is $2.8\,\text{m}$ and it hits the ground after $1.3\,\text{s}$.

Exercise D (answers p 164)

1 A javelin is thrown from a height of $1.75\,\text{m}$ at an angle of $45°$ to the horizontal with a speed of $25\,\text{m}\,\text{s}^{-1}$.

(a) Find the time when the javelin is at its greatest height.

(b) What is the greatest height of the javelin above the ground?

2 A discus is projected at an angle of 40° with a speed of 21 m s^{-1} and from a height above the ground of 2 m as shown in the diagram.

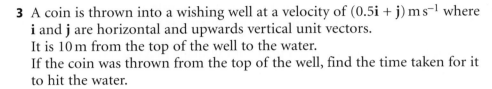

(a) Find an expression for the velocity of the discus at time t.

(b) Find an expression for the position vector with respect to O of the discus at time t.

(c) What is the length of the throw?

3 A coin is thrown into a wishing well at a velocity of $(0.5\mathbf{i} + \mathbf{j})$ m s^{-1} where $\mathbf{i}$ and $\mathbf{j}$ are horizontal and upwards vertical unit vectors.

It is 10 m from the top of the well to the water.

If the coin was thrown from the top of the well, find the time taken for it to hit the water.

4 Tim is standing 12 m away from the net on a tennis court. The net is 1 m high. He hits the tennis ball horizontally with speed U m s^{-1} from a height of 1.75 m.

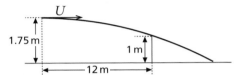

(a) Given that the ball just clears the top of the net, find the time taken for the ball to reach the net.

(b) Hence find the value of U.

(c) How far beyond the net does the ball land?

5 A small relief plane is flying horizontally at 30 m s^{-1}. Its height is 210 m. A package, released from the plane, just clears some trees which are 30 m high.

(a) At what horizontal distance from the trees is the package released?

(b) How far beyond the trees does the package land?

6 A particle is projected with initial velocity $\begin{bmatrix} 2U \\ U \end{bmatrix}$ m s^{-1} from a height h m above ground level. Find an expression, in terms of U, g and h, for the maximum height reached by the particle.

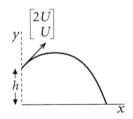

7 Two children throw stones into the sea.

Jill throws her stone at an angle of 60° to the horizontal and speed 10 m s^{-1}, while Jack throws his stone at a 40° angle and can only manage an initial speed of 5 m s^{-1}. Both stones are thrown simultaneously and both are released at a height 1.4 m above sea level.

(a) What is the maximum height of Jill's stone?

(b) Which stone lands in the water first?

(c) Whose stone lands further away, and how much further is it?

*8 A fairground game involves catapulting an object towards a target
on the ground 20 m away.
The object is released at a height of 1 m above ground level.
Assume that the ground is level and that the object moves as a projectile.
If the catapult is angled at 45° to the horizontal and the object hits the target,
find the speed at which the object leaves the catapult.

Key points

- When an object is falling freely under gravity it has downwards acceleration
  of g m s^{-2}. This acceleration due to gravity is approximately 9.8 m s^{-2}. (p 120)

- Projectile motion takes place in a vertical plane in the shape of a parabola.
  The only force acting is the weight of the particle. (p 124)

- At time t, the horizontal and vertical components of position of a particle
  projected at an initial velocity U m s^{-1} at an angle of θ to the horizontal
  are given by
  $$x = Ut\cos\theta \quad \text{and} \quad y = Ut\sin\theta - \tfrac{1}{2}gt^2$$ (p 128)

- At time t, the horizontal and vertical components of velocity of a particle
  projected at an initial velocity U m s^{-1} at an angle of θ to the horizontal
  are given by
  $$v_x = U\cos\theta \quad \text{and} \quad v_y = U\sin\theta - gt$$ (p 128)

- The range of a projectile is the horizontal
  distance from O to A.
  The time of flight is the time taken
  to travel from O to A.
  The maximum height of the projectile occurs
  at the mid-point of the path of the projectile
  when the vertical component of the velocity is zero. (p 129)

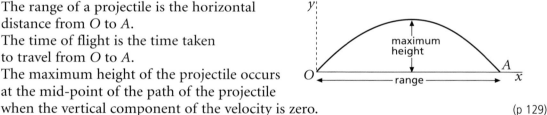

- At time t, a projectile released from height h above the ground is at
  the point where
  $$x = Ut\cos\theta \quad \text{and} \quad y = Ut\sin\theta - \tfrac{1}{2}gt^2 + h$$ (p 133)

Mixed questions (answers p 164)

1 An athlete puts a shot with initial velocity 8 m s^{-1} at an angle of 35°
to the horizontal.

(a) Find the range of the shot on horizontal ground, assuming that
it is thrown from ground level.

(b) The shot is actually released at a height of 1.5 metres. Find the range
of the shot taking into account the height of release.

(c) What modelling assumptions have been made in answering this question?

2 A particle is projected from a horizontal surface at a speed V and at an angle α above the horizontal.

    (a) Prove that the maximum height of the particle is $\dfrac{V^2 \sin^2 \alpha}{2g}$.

    (b) A ball is hit from ground level. The ball initially moves at an angle of 60° above the horizontal. The maximum height of the ball is 6 metres above the ground. Modelling the ball as a particle:

        (i) find the initial speed of the ball

        (ii) find the range of the ball   AQA 2003

3 Two particles, A and B, are connected by a light inextensible string which passes over a smooth fixed peg, as shown in the diagram.

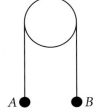

The particles A and B have masses 0.21 kg and 0.14 kg respectively. The system is released from rest. It may be assumed that, during the motion, neither particle reaches the peg.

    (a) Show that the magnitude of the acceleration of the particles during the subsequent motion is 1.96 m s^{-2}.

    (b) Find the speed of the particles after 2 seconds of the motion.

    (c) After 2 seconds of the motion, the string breaks and the particles move independently under the influence of gravity alone. Find the time between the string breaking and the particle B coming to instantaneous rest.

    (d) Sketch a velocity–time graph to show the motion of B between being released from rest and subsequently coming to instantaneous rest.   AQA 2003

4 A ball is thrown with initial velocity U m s^{-1} so that its range is equal to its maximum height.
What is its angle of projection?

Test yourself (answers p 165)

1 (a) A stone is released and falls vertically through a distance of 10 metres before hitting the ground.

        (i) Calculate the speed at which the stone hits the ground.

        (ii) Calculate the time between the stone being released and hitting the ground.

    (b) The same stone is released from a height of 10 metres above the surface of the Moon. On the Moon the acceleration due to gravity is much lower than on the Earth.

    If the calculations in parts (a)(i) and (a)(ii) were carried out for the motion of the stone on the Moon instead of the motion on the Earth, explain how your answers would be affected.   AQA 2001

2 A child throws a stone from the top of a vertical cliff and the stone subsequently lands in the sea. The stone is thrown from a height of 24.5 metres above the level of the sea. The initial velocity of the stone is horizontal and has magnitude $17\,\mathrm{m\,s^{-1}}$, as shown in the diagram.

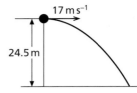

(a) Find the time between the stone being thrown and reaching the sea.

(b) Find the horizontal distance between the foot of the cliff and the point where the stone reaches the sea.

(c) Find the **speed** of the stone as it reaches the sea.

AQA 2002

3 George throws a ball from a point O, with velocity $\begin{bmatrix} 3U \\ 4U \end{bmatrix}$.

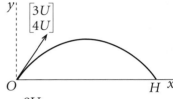

The ball subsequently lands at a point H, which is at the same horizontal level as O, as shown in the diagram.

(a) Show that the time taken by the ball to travel from O to H is $\dfrac{8U}{g}$.

(b) Find, in terms of g and U, the distance OH.

(c) Find, in terms of U, the initial speed of the ball.

(d) Find, in terms of g and U, the two times during the flight from O to H when the ball is moving with speed $\sqrt{18}U$.

AQA 2003

4 A ball is thrown so that it passes through the centre of a basket ball hoop, as shown in the diagram.

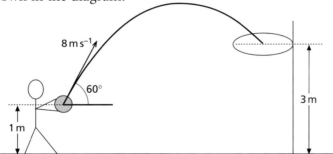

The ball is thrown from a height of 1 metre and the hoop is at a height of 3 metres above the ground. The initial velocity of the ball is $8\,\mathrm{m\,s^{-1}}$ at an angle of $60°$ above the horizontal.

(a) Find the maximum height of the ball above the ground.

(b) Find the time that it takes for the ball to reach the centre of the hoop.

(c) Find the horizontal distance from the initial position of the ball to the centre of the hoop.

AQA 2002

Answers

1 Kinematics in one dimension

A Velocity and displacement (p 6)

A1 (a) 60 m

(b) You need to know the direction he was walking and his starting point.

A2 (a) 120 m

(b) They walked in different directions.

A3 (a) 240 m   (b) −240 m   (c) 480 m

A4 (a) 4 km   (b) 2 km

A5 (a) 420 m   (b) 240 m

(c) 180 m in the positive direction

A6 (a) $7.5\,\mathrm{m\,s^{-1}}$

(b) The gradient of the graph

(c) The graph is a straight line.

A7 (a) March: gradient = 7.09 (to 2 d.p.)
June: gradient = 7.41 (to 2 d.p.)
The units for the gradients are metres per second.

(b) The velocity of each athlete.

(c) The graph is steeper, which means that the gradient and thus the velocity is greater.

(d) She ran with constant velocity on both occasions.

(e) Straight lines are unrealistic. The athlete starts from rest and increases her velocity, then runs at constant velocity for most of the race, possibly increasing it at the end of the race.

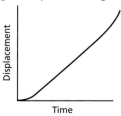

A8 (a) $5\,\mathrm{m\,s^{-1}}$ (b) $-3.3\,\mathrm{m\,s^{-1}}$ (to 1 d.p.)

(c) 150 m

A9 $1.875\,\mathrm{m\,s^{-1}}$

A10 350 m

A11 $4.375\,\mathrm{m\,s^{-1}}$

Exercise A (p 10)

1 (a) $10\,\mathrm{m\,s^{-1}}$ (b) $12.5\,\mathrm{m\,s^{-1}}$

(c) $15\,\mathrm{m\,s^{-1}}$ (d) $20.8\,\mathrm{m\,s^{-1}}$ (to 1 d.p.)

2 $\dfrac{150+150}{30+75} = 2.9\,\mathrm{m\,s^{-1}}$ (to 1 d.p.)

3 $\dfrac{150+60}{30+30} = 3.5\,\mathrm{m\,s^{-1}}$

4 $2.5\times60 + 1.7\times120 = 354\,\mathrm{m}$

5 (a) 810 m   (b) −90 m

(c) $10.8\,\mathrm{m\,s^{-1}}$ (d) $-1.2\,\mathrm{m\,s^{-1}}$

6 (a) $\dfrac{480+300}{180} = 4.3\,\mathrm{m\,s^{-1}}$ (to 1 d.p.)

(b) $\dfrac{480-300}{180} = 1\,\mathrm{m\,s^{-1}}$

7 Total time $= \dfrac{360}{80} = 4.5$ hours
Time for first half $= \dfrac{180}{75} = 2.4$ hours
Average speed for second half $= \dfrac{180}{4.5-2.5}$
$= 85.7\,\mathrm{km\,h^{-1}}$ (to 1 d.p.)

8 (a) He stopped for 20 s.   (b) $2\,\mathrm{m\,s^{-1}}$

(c) $1.5\,\mathrm{m\,s^{-1}}$ (d) $1.3\,\mathrm{m\,s^{-1}}$ (to 1 d.p.)

9 (a)
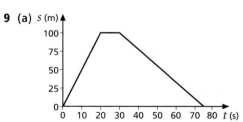

(b) $200 \div 75 = 2.7\,\mathrm{m\,s^{-1}}$ (to 1 d.p.)

(c) $0\,\mathrm{m\,s^{-1}}$

10 Tracy overtakes Simon after about 86 minutes, about 5 miles from Aycliffe.

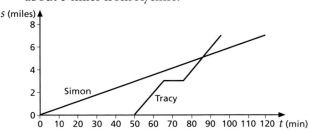

11 (a)

(b) They pass each other at about 12:33, 8.3 km from Blakesfield and about 13:07, 6.7 km from Blakesfield.

(c) At 12:40.

B Graphs of motion (p 11)

B1 (a) 0.25

(b) Metres per second per second

(c) The rate of increase of velocity, namely the acceleration, of the car.

B2 The rate of decrease of velocity, or deceleration, of the car.

B3 (a) $2\,\mathrm{m\,s^{-1}}$ **(b)** $4\,\mathrm{m\,s^{-1}}$

(c) $20\,\mathrm{m\,s^{-1}}$ **(d)** $40\,\mathrm{m\,s^{-1}}$

B4 $15\,\mathrm{m\,s^{-1}}$

B5 $0.1\,\mathrm{m\,s^{-2}}$

B6 (a) (i) Straight line   **(ii)** Line parallel to t-axis

(b) (i) Steeper line   **(ii)** Line higher above axis

(c) (i) Horizontal line   **(ii)** Line along t-axis

B7 No, because the acceleration is zero through each phase of the cyclist's motion. There is no way to represent the instantaneous changes at t_1 and t_2.

B8 (a) The velocity is increasing at a constant rate from zero to $V\,\mathrm{m\,s^{-1}}$ at $T\,\mathrm{s}$. The acceleration constant.

(b)

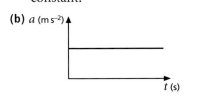

(c) The displacement is increasing at a faster and faster rate.

B9 *A:* constant velocity of $10\,\mathrm{m\,s^{-1}}$

B: velocity $10\,\mathrm{m\,s^{-1}}$, starts to decrease at constant rate

C: velocity $5\,\mathrm{m\,s^{-1}}$, constant deceleration of $0.25\,\mathrm{m\,s^{-2}}$

D: velocity $0\,\mathrm{m\,s^{-1}}$, constant deceleration of $0.25\,\mathrm{m\,s^{-2}}$

E: velocity $-5\,\mathrm{m\,s^{-1}}$, constant deceleration of $0.25\,\mathrm{m\,s^{-2}}$

F: velocity $-10\,\mathrm{m\,s^{-1}}$, now remains constant

G: constant velocity of $-10\,\mathrm{m\,s^{-1}}$

Exercise B (p 14)

1 (a) $0.2\,\mathrm{m\,s^{-1}}$ **(b)** $0.4\,\mathrm{m\,s^{-1}}$ **(c)** $2\,\mathrm{m\,s^{-1}}$

(d) $12\,\mathrm{m\,s^{-1}}$

2 Deceleration of $0.5\,\mathrm{m\,s^{-2}}$

3 (a) $0.2\,\mathrm{m\,s^{-2}}$ **(b)** $0\,\mathrm{m\,s^{-2}}$ **(c)** $-0.4\,\mathrm{m}$

4 (a) The displacement increases at a steady rate until t_1, it is constant until t_2 and then it decreases at a faster steady rate until it reaches zero.

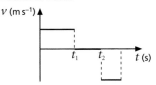

(b) The displacement is decreasing at a steady rate throughout the motion, the object passes through the origin at time t_1.

5 (a) The velocity is decreasing at a constant rate throughout the motion.

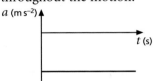

(b) The velocity is constant and negative until time t_1, then it increases at a steady rate until time t_2, when it is positive. After t_2 the velocity remains constant.

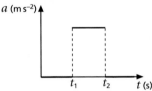

6 (a) v (m s^{-1})

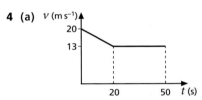

(b) $0.3 \, \text{m s}^{-2}$ **(c)** $-0.45 \, \text{m s}^{-2}$

(d) a (m s^{-2})

C Area under a velocity–time graph (p 15)

C1 (a) 180   **(b)** 180   **(c)** Metres

(d) Aisha's displacement

C2 (a) 120   **(b)** −120   **(c)** 0 m

C3 195 m

C4 (a) The velocity increases at a steady rate from zero until it reaches its maximum of $15 \, \text{m s}^{-1}$ after 45 s. It then continues at this constant value for a further 75 s.

(b) 337.5 m   **(c)** 1462.5 m

Exercise C (p 17)

1 2250 m

2 (a) 60 m   **(b)** 300 m

3 (a) v (m s^{-1})

(b) 1602 m

4 (a) v (m s^{-1})

(b) 720 m

5 1170 m

6 Displacement of car at time Ts
$$= \tfrac{1}{2} \times T \times (0.25T)$$
Displacement of van at time Ts $(T > 30)$
$$= \tfrac{1}{2} \times 30 \times 10 + (T - 30) \times 10$$
The car overtakes the van when the displacement of the car is equal to the displacement of the van.
$$\Rightarrow \frac{T^2}{8} = 10T - 150$$
$$\Rightarrow T^2 - 80T + 1200 = 0$$
$$\Rightarrow T = 20, 60$$
As $T > 30$, the car overtakes the van after 60 s.

7 (a) The area under the velocity graph for $0 < t < T$ is equal to the area under the graph for $T < t < 9$.
So $4T = 2(9 - T) \Rightarrow T = 3$

(b) 24 m

D Motion with constant acceleration (p 18)

D1 $a = \dfrac{v - u}{t} \Rightarrow at = v - u \Rightarrow v = u + at$

D2 $15\,\text{m s}^{-1}$

D3 $14\,\text{m s}^{-1}$

D4 $277.5\,\text{m}$

D5 $20\,\text{s}$

Exercise D (p 20)

1 $10\,\text{m s}^{-1}$

2 $12\,\text{m s}^{-1}$

3 $210\,\text{m}$

4 $0.2\,\text{m s}^{-2}$

5 $20\,\text{m s}^{-1}$

6 $4\,\text{m s}^{-1}$

7 (a) $11\,\text{m s}^{-1}$ (b) $375\,\text{m}$

8 (a) $120\,\text{m}$ (b) $0.07\,\text{m s}^{-2}$ (to 2 d.p.)

9 (a) $40\,\text{s}$ (b) $320\,\text{m}$

E Constant acceleration equations (p 21)

E1 $s = \frac{1}{2}(u + v)t \Rightarrow s = \frac{1}{2}(u + u + at)t$
$\Rightarrow s = \frac{1}{2}(2u + at)t \Rightarrow s = ut + \frac{1}{2}at^2$

E2 $120\,\text{m}$

E3 (a) $u = v - at$

(b) $s = \frac{1}{2}(u + v)t \Rightarrow s = \frac{1}{2}(v - at + v)t$
$\Rightarrow s = \frac{1}{2}(2v - at)t \Rightarrow s = vt - \frac{1}{2}at^2$

E4 (a) $t = \dfrac{v - u}{a}$

(b) $s = \frac{1}{2}(u + v)t \Rightarrow s = \frac{1}{2}(u + v)\left(\dfrac{v - u}{a}\right)$
$\Rightarrow s = \dfrac{v^2 - u^2}{2a}$
$\Rightarrow v^2 = u^2 + 2as$

E5 $20.6\,\text{m s}^{-1}$ (to 1 d.p.)

E6 $15.8\,\text{m s}^{-1}$ (to 1 d.p.)

Exercise E (p 22)

1 $7.5\,\text{m s}^{-1}$

2 $26.0\,\text{m s}^{-1}$ (to 1 d.p.)

3 Acceleration $= 2.4\,\text{m s}^{-2}$ (to 1 d.p.),
distance $= 189\,\text{m}$

4 Distance $= 440\,\text{m}$, final speed $= 30\,\text{m s}^{-1}$

5 Deceleration $= 1.722\,\text{m s}^{-2}$, time $= 12.2\,\text{s}$ (to 1 ⊔

6 (a) Area of rectangle $= ut$
Area of triangle $= \frac{1}{2}at \times t = \frac{1}{2}at^2$
$\Rightarrow s = ut + \frac{1}{2}at^2$

(b) Area of large rectangle $= vt$
Area of triangle $= \frac{1}{2}at^2$
$\Rightarrow s = vt - \frac{1}{2}at^2$

7 (a) $0.4\,\text{m s}^{-2}$ (b) $36\,\text{m s}^{-1}$

8 (a) Substituting into $v = u + at$ gives $18 = 5 + $ ⊔
$\Rightarrow 13 = 25a \Rightarrow a = 0.52$

(b) $287.5\,\text{m}$ (c) $13.2\,\text{m s}^{-1}$

9 $61.2\,\text{s}$ (to 1 d.p.)

10 (a) $1.27\,\text{m s}^{-1}$ (to 2 d.p.)   (b) $v = \dfrac{u}{\sqrt{2}}$

Mixed questions (p 24)

1 (a) The gradient of the velocity–time graph is
negative and constant for $0 \leq t \leq 5$ indicati⊔
that the car has constant deceleration.

(b) $1.2\,\text{m s}^{-2}$ (c) $345\,\text{m}$ (d) $23\,\text{m s}^{-}$

2 (a) $0.8\,\text{m s}^{-2}$ (b) $150\,\text{m}$

3 (a) $0.16\,\text{m s}^{-2}$ (b) $0.13\,\text{m s}^{-2}$

(c) Distance travelled while accelerating $= 8\,\text{m}$
Distance travelled while decelerating $= 9.6$
So distance at constant speed $= 22.4\,\text{m}$
Time at constant speed $= 22.4 \div 1.6 = 14\,\text{s}$
So total time $= 36\,\text{s}$

4 (a) $4.5\,\text{s}$ (b) $-10\,\text{m s}^{-2}$ (c) $202.5\,\text{⊔}$

5 (a) $10\,\text{s}$

(b)
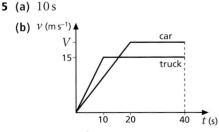

(c) $17.5\,\text{m s}^{-1}$

6 (a) (i) $\frac{2U}{3}\,\mathrm{m\,s^{-2}}$ **(ii)** $12U\,\mathrm{m}$

  (b) $U = 2$

7 The car travels at constant velocity for time T s.
When overtaking the car has to travel
$(50 + 16 + 50 + 4) = 120\,\mathrm{m}$ further than the lorry.
The velocity–time graphs for the car and the lorry
are as shown.

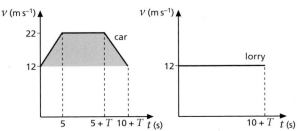

The shaded area represents the extra distance
travelled by the car.
So $120 = \frac{1}{2}(10 + T + T)\times 10$
$\Rightarrow 24 = 2T + 10 \Rightarrow T = 7$
The car takes 17 s to get from its initial to its final
position.
In this time the lorry has travelled $12 \times 17 = 204\,\mathrm{m}$.
The car has travelled a total of $324\,\mathrm{m}$.

Test yourself (p 26)

1 (a) $467.5\,\mathrm{m}$

  (b) (i) $0.73\,\mathrm{m\,s^{-2}}$ (to 2 d.p.) **(ii)** $0\,\mathrm{m\,s^{-2}}$

    (iii) $-0.55\,\mathrm{m\,s^{-2}}$

2 (a) $16\,\mathrm{m}$ **(b)** $8\,\mathrm{m\,s^{-1}}$ **(c)** $14.5\,\mathrm{s}$

3 (a)

v (m s⁻¹) graph: shape rising from 5, plateau at V, descending to 70 on t (s) axis, with 60 marked.

  (b) $V = 4.8$

4 (a) $82.5\,\mathrm{m}$ **(b)** $35\,\mathrm{s}$

  (c) $2.36\,\mathrm{m\,s^{-1}}$ (to 2 d.p.)

5 (a) (i) The graph is a straight line.

    (ii) $0.67\,\mathrm{m\,s^{-2}}$ (to 2 d.p.)

  (b) $T = 21$

2 Kinematics in two dimensions

Answers are given to three significant figures
where appropriate.

A Displacement (p 28)

A1 Alexia's possible finishing points lie on a circle of
radius $50\,\mathrm{m}$, centred on her starting point.

A2 (a) x-component $= 36 \sin 30° = 18.0\,\mathrm{m}$
      y-component $= 36 \cos 30° = 31.2\,\mathrm{m}$

  (b) $\begin{bmatrix} 18.0 \\ 31.2 \end{bmatrix}\mathrm{m}$

A3 (a)

$60\mathbf{i} + 80\mathbf{j}$ (vector diagram with θ, 60 and 80 marked)

  (b) $\sqrt{80^2 + 60^2} = 100\,\mathrm{m}$

  (c) $\tan^{-1}\left(\frac{80}{60}\right) = 53.1°$ to the x-direction

A4 (a) $20°$

  (b) x-component $= 30 \cos 20° = 28.2\,\mathrm{m}$
      y-component $= -30 \sin 20° = -10.3\,\mathrm{m}$

  (c) $(28.2\mathbf{i} - 10.3\mathbf{j})\,\mathrm{m}$

Exercise A (p 31)

1 (a) (i) $\begin{bmatrix} 20 \\ 15 \end{bmatrix}\mathrm{km}$ **(ii)** $(20\mathbf{i} + 15\mathbf{j})\,\mathrm{km}$

  (b) (i) $\begin{bmatrix} -20 \\ 0 \end{bmatrix}\mathrm{km}$ **(ii)** $(-20\mathbf{i})\,\mathrm{km}$

  (c) (i) $\begin{bmatrix} 18 \\ -6 \end{bmatrix}\mathrm{km}$ **(ii)** $(18\mathbf{i} - 6\mathbf{j})\,\mathrm{km}$

  (d) (i) $\begin{bmatrix} -5 \\ 10 \end{bmatrix}\mathrm{km}$ **(ii)** $(-5\mathbf{i} + 10\mathbf{j})\,\mathrm{km}$

2 (a)

$\begin{bmatrix} 8 \\ 3 \end{bmatrix}$ (vector diagram with θ, 8 and 3 marked)

  (b) Magnitude $= \sqrt{8^2 + 3^2} = 8.54$
    Direction $= \tan^{-1}\left(\frac{3}{8}\right) = 20.6°$ to the x-direction

3 (a) $\sqrt{15^2 + 12^2} = 19.2\,\mathrm{m}$

  (b) $\tan^{-1}\left(\frac{12}{15}\right) = 38.7°$ clockwise from the vector $\mathbf{i}$

4 $(100 \sin 70°\,\mathbf{i} + 100 \cos 70°\,\mathbf{j})\,\mathrm{m} = (94.0\mathbf{i} + 34.2\mathbf{j})\,\mathrm{m}$

5 $\begin{bmatrix} 35.4 \\ -35.4 \end{bmatrix}$ m

6 Distance $= \sqrt{15^2 + 20^2} = 25\,\text{m}$

$\tan^{-1}\left(\frac{20}{15}\right) = 53.1°$, so bearing is $323.1°$

B Resultant displacement (p 31)

B1

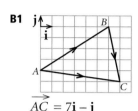

$\overrightarrow{AC} = 7\mathbf{i} - \mathbf{j}$

B2 (a) $(6\mathbf{i} + 4\mathbf{j}) + (\mathbf{i} - 5\mathbf{j}) = (6 + 1)\mathbf{i} + (4 - 5)\mathbf{j}$
$= 7\mathbf{i} - \mathbf{j}$

(b)

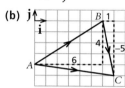

Total displacement in x-direction $= 6 + 1 = 7$
Total displacement in y-direction $= 4 - 5 = -1$

B3 (a) $\sqrt{7^2 + 1^2} = 7.07\,\text{m}$

(b) $\sqrt{6^2 + 4^2} + \sqrt{1^2 + 5^2} = 12.3\,\text{m}$

Exercise B (p 33)

1 $\begin{bmatrix} 150 \\ -30 \end{bmatrix}$

2 (a) $2\mathbf{i} + 2\mathbf{j}$

(b) 2.83 units at an angle of $45°$ to the vector $\mathbf{i}$

3 Let fourth vector be $a\mathbf{i} + b\mathbf{j}$.
$(-2 + 5 + 16 + a)\mathbf{i} + (-3 - 7 + 4 + b)\mathbf{j} = 10\mathbf{i} - 2\mathbf{j}$
$\Rightarrow (19 + a)\mathbf{i} + (b - 6)\mathbf{j} = 10\mathbf{i} - 2\mathbf{j}$
Hence the fourth vector is $-9\mathbf{i} + 4\mathbf{j}$.

4 (a) $(5\mathbf{i} + 8\mathbf{j})\,\text{m}$ (b) $\sqrt{5^2 + 8^2} = 9.43\,\text{m}$

(c) $\sqrt{8^2 + 2^2} + \sqrt{3^2 + 10^2} = 18.7\,\text{m}$

5 The resultant displacement is $(80\mathbf{i} + 10\mathbf{j})\,\text{m}$.
The displacement is $80.6\,\text{m}$ at an angle of $7.1°$
with the vector $\mathbf{i}$.

C Position vector (p 33)

C1 $\mathbf{r}_B = 5\mathbf{i} - \mathbf{j}$

C2 $\mathbf{s} = \mathbf{i} - 3\mathbf{j}$

C3 $(6\mathbf{i} - 2\mathbf{j}) + (-3\mathbf{i} + \mathbf{j}) = 3\mathbf{i} - \mathbf{j}$

C4 (a) $\mathbf{r}_C = 3\mathbf{i} + 2\mathbf{j}$, $\mathbf{r}_D = \mathbf{i} + 3\mathbf{j}$ (b) $-2\mathbf{i} + \mathbf{j}$

C5 $(\mathbf{i} + 3\mathbf{j}) - (3\mathbf{i} + 2\mathbf{j}) = -2\mathbf{i} + \mathbf{j}$

C6 $(4\mathbf{i} + 3\mathbf{j}) - (-2\mathbf{i} + 5\mathbf{j}) = (4 + 2)\mathbf{i} + (3 - 5)\mathbf{j}$
$= 6\mathbf{i} - 2\mathbf{j}$

C7 (a) When $t = 0$, $\mathbf{r} = 20\mathbf{j}$
When $t = 10$, $\mathbf{r} = 300\mathbf{i} - 20\mathbf{j}$

(b) $300\mathbf{i} - 40\mathbf{j}$

(c) $303\,\text{m}$

(d) The speedboat is due east when the
$\mathbf{j}$-component of the position vector is zero.
$20 - 4t = 0 \Rightarrow t = 5$

Exercise C (p 35)

1 $\begin{bmatrix} 12 \\ -1 \end{bmatrix}$

2 (a) $(4\mathbf{i} + 2\mathbf{j})\,\text{km}$ (b) $4.47\,\text{km}$

3 $\begin{bmatrix} 4 \\ -2 \end{bmatrix} - \begin{bmatrix} -3 \\ 6 \end{bmatrix} = \begin{bmatrix} 7 \\ -8 \end{bmatrix}$

4 $(25\mathbf{i} - 40\mathbf{j}) - (40\mathbf{i} - 30\mathbf{j}) = (-15\mathbf{i} - 10\mathbf{j})\,\text{m}$

5 (a) $-2\mathbf{j}$ (b) $300\mathbf{i} + 38\mathbf{j}$

(c)

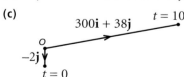

(d) $(300\mathbf{i} + 38\mathbf{j}) - (-2\mathbf{j}) = (300\mathbf{i} + 40\mathbf{j})\,\text{m}$

6 (a) $18\mathbf{i} + 3.1\mathbf{j}$

(b) The ball hits the ground when the
$\mathbf{j}$-component of the position vector is zero.
$8t - 4.9t^2 = 0 \Rightarrow t(8 - 4.9t) = 0$
$\Rightarrow t = 0, t = 1.63$
$t = 0$ when the ball is kicked, so the ball hits
the ground when $t = 1.63$.

(c) The horizontal distance covered is the
$\mathbf{i}$-component of the position vector.
The ball has covered $18 \times 1.63 = 29.3$ m.

7 (a) When $2t - 10 = 0$, hence when $t = 5$

(b) $\mathbf{r} = 31\mathbf{j}$, so the particle is 31 m from its starting
point at this time.

8 (a) The object is south-east of the origin when
$8t - 12 = -(t^2 - 8) \Rightarrow t^2 + 8t - 20 = 0$
$\Rightarrow (t + 10)(t - 2) = 0 \Rightarrow t = -10, t = 2$
When $t = 2$, $\mathbf{r} = 4\mathbf{i} - 4\mathbf{j}$
When $t = -10$, $\mathbf{r} = -92\mathbf{i} + 92\mathbf{j}$
The object is south-east of the origin when
$t = 2$.

(b) 5.66 km

Velocity (p 36)

1 (a) $4\mathbf{i} + 2\mathbf{j}$ **(b)** $20\mathbf{i} + 10\mathbf{j}$ **(c)** $10\mathbf{i} + 5\mathbf{j}$

2 (a) $4.47 \,\mathrm{m\,s}^{-1}$ **(b)** $\theta = 26.6°$

3 (a)

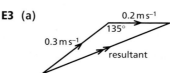

(b) $45°$

(c) $\mathbf{i}$-component $= 55 \cos 45° = 38.9$
$\mathbf{j}$-component $= -55 \sin 45° = -38.9$

(d) $(38.9\mathbf{i} - 38.9\mathbf{j}) \,\mathrm{m\,s}^{-1}$

4 (a) $(15\mathbf{i} + 25\mathbf{j}) \,\mathrm{m}$ **(b)** $\dfrac{15\mathbf{i} + 25\mathbf{j}}{5} = (3\mathbf{i} + 5\mathbf{j}) \,\mathrm{m\,s}^{-1}$

5 (a) $\mathbf{r} = 3\mathbf{i}$ **(b)** $\mathbf{r} = 63\mathbf{i} + 240\mathbf{j}$

(c) $(60\mathbf{i} + 240\mathbf{j}) \,\mathrm{m}$ **(d)** $\dfrac{60\mathbf{i} + 240\mathbf{j}}{30} = (2\mathbf{i} + 8\mathbf{j}) \,\mathrm{m\,s}^{-1}$

Exercise D (p 37)

1 (a) $20\mathbf{j} \,\mathrm{m\,s}^{-1}$ **(b)** $-5\mathbf{i} \,\mathrm{m\,s}^{-1}$

2 (a) $\begin{bmatrix} 3 \\ 1 \end{bmatrix} \mathrm{m}$ **(b)** $\begin{bmatrix} 30 \\ 10 \end{bmatrix} \mathrm{m}$

3 (a) $14.4 \,\mathrm{m\,s}^{-1}$

(b) $33.7°$ below the vector $\mathbf{i}$

4 $\begin{bmatrix} 20 \sin 65° \\ 20 \cos 65° \end{bmatrix} = \begin{bmatrix} 18.1 \\ 8.5 \end{bmatrix} \mathrm{m\,s}^{-1}$

5 $15 \cos 30° \mathbf{i} + 15 \sin 30° \mathbf{j} = (13.0\mathbf{i} + 7.5\mathbf{j}) \,\mathrm{m\,s}^{-1}$

6 (a) $(-30\mathbf{i} + 240\mathbf{j}) \,\mathrm{m}$

(b) $\dfrac{-30\mathbf{i} + 240\mathbf{j}}{60} = (-0.5\mathbf{i} + 4\mathbf{j}) \,\mathrm{m\,s}^{-1}$

7 When $t = 0$, $\mathbf{r} = 10\mathbf{i} + \mathbf{j}$
When $t = 30$, $\mathbf{r} = -80\mathbf{i} + 151\mathbf{j}$
Displacement $= -90\mathbf{i} + 150\mathbf{j}$
Average velocity $= \dfrac{-90\mathbf{i} + 150\mathbf{j}}{30} = (-3\mathbf{i} + 5\mathbf{j}) \,\mathrm{m\,s}^{-1}$

8 (a) $200\mathbf{i} - 22\mathbf{j}$ **(b)** $800\mathbf{i} - 52\mathbf{j}$

(c) $\dfrac{600\mathbf{i} - 30\mathbf{j}}{10} = (60\mathbf{i} - 3\mathbf{j}) \,\mathrm{m\,s}^{-1}$

9 (a) $4t\mathbf{i} - 3t\mathbf{j}$

(b) $(20 + 4t)\mathbf{i} + (30 - 3t)\mathbf{j}$

(c) $260\mathbf{i} - 150\mathbf{j}$

10 $\mathbf{r} = (10t - 30)\mathbf{i} + (12 - 3t)\mathbf{j}$
When $t = 20$, $\mathbf{r} = 170\mathbf{i} - 48\mathbf{j}$

E Resultant velocity (p 39)

E1 $0.1 \,\mathrm{m\,s}^{-1}$

E2 (a) $0.361 \,\mathrm{m\,s}^{-1}$ **(b)** $33.7°$

E3 (a)

(b) Scale drawing leading to resultant of
$0.46 \,\mathrm{m\,s}^{-1}$ at $27°$ to the direction of motion of
the tray.

E4 $3 \,\mathrm{m\,s}^{-1}$

E5 (a)

(b) $-1 \,\mathrm{m\,s}^{-1}$, taking the direction of the current as
positive

E6 (a) $2.24 \,\mathrm{m\,s}^{-1}$ **(b)** $63.4°$ to the bank

E7 (a)

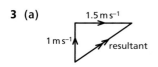

(b) 1.41 m s^{-1} at 45° to the river bank.

E8 1.80 m s^{-1} at 56.3° to the river bank.

Exercise E (p 41)

1 $(50\mathbf{i} + 5\mathbf{j})$ m s^{-1}

2 $\begin{bmatrix} -3 \\ 2 \end{bmatrix} + \begin{bmatrix} 2 \\ -1 \end{bmatrix} = \begin{bmatrix} -1 \\ 1 \end{bmatrix}$ km h^{-1}

3 (a)

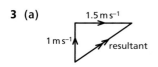

(b) 1.80 m s^{-1} (c) 33.7°

4 (a) $(\mathbf{i} + 6\mathbf{j})$ m s^{-1} (b) 6.08 m s^{-1}
  (c) 80.5° with the vector $\mathbf{i}$

5 (a) 3.20 m s^{-1} at 51.3° to the bank
  (b) 3.91 m s^{-1} at 39.8° to the bank

F Resultant velocity problems (p 42)

F1 (a) 1.73 m s^{-1} (b) 60° to the bank

F2 (a)

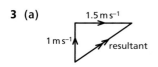

(b) 1.50 m s^{-1}

(c) 56.3° to the bank

F3 $-4\sin 40°\,\mathbf{i} - 4\cos 40°\,\mathbf{j}$

F4 (a) Resultant velocity
$= (10\sin\theta\,\mathbf{i} - 10\cos\theta\,\mathbf{j}) + (-4\sin 40°\,\mathbf{i} - 4\cos 40°\,\mathbf{j})$
$= (10\sin\theta - 4\sin 40°)\mathbf{i} - (10\cos\theta + 4\cos 40°)\mathbf{j}$
The $\mathbf{i}$-component of the resultant is zero.
$\Rightarrow (10\sin\theta - 4\sin 40°) = 0$
$\Rightarrow 10\sin\theta = 4\sin 40°$

(b) $\theta = 14.9°$ (c) $-12.7\mathbf{j}$ m s^{-1}

F5 (a) $\dfrac{4}{\sin\theta} = \dfrac{10}{\sin 40°}$

$\Rightarrow \sin\theta = \dfrac{4\sin 40°}{10} \Rightarrow \theta = 14.9°$

(b) $180° - 40° - 14.9° = 125.1°$

$\dfrac{v}{\sin 125.1°} = \dfrac{10}{\sin 40°} \Rightarrow v = 12.7$ m s^{-1}

Exercise F (p 44)

1 (a)

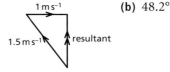

(b) 48.2°

(c) 1.12 m s^{-1} (d) 44.7 seconds

(e) The current is constant across the width of river.
The girl can maintain the speed and directio[n] throughout the motion.
She can paddle immediately at 1.5 m s^{-1}.

2 (a)

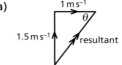

Resultant velocity = 1.80 m s^{-1}, $\theta = 56.3°$

Distance $= \dfrac{50}{\sin 56.3°} = 60.1$ m

Time taken $= \dfrac{60.1}{1.80} = 33$ s (to 2 s.f.)

(b) Distance downstream $= \dfrac{50}{1.5} = 33$ m (to 2 s.f[.])

3 (a) Resultant velocity = velocity of plane + velocity of wind
$\Rightarrow$ velocity of wind $= (\mathbf{i} + 3\mathbf{j}) - (3\mathbf{i} + 2\mathbf{j})$
$= -2\mathbf{i} + \mathbf{j}$
Magnitude = 2.24 m s^{-1}

(b)

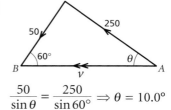

$\theta = 26.6°$ to the negative $\mathbf{i}$-direction

4 (a)

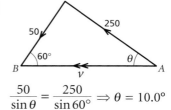

$\dfrac{50}{\sin\theta} = \dfrac{250}{\sin 60°} \Rightarrow \theta = 10.0°$
The plane flies on a bearing of 280°.

(b) $\dfrac{v}{\sin 110°} = \dfrac{250}{\sin 60°} \Rightarrow v = 271\,\text{km h}^{-1}$

Time taken $= \frac{100}{271} = 0.369$ hours $= 22.1$ min

5 (a)

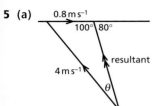

(b) $\dfrac{0.8}{\sin \theta} = \dfrac{4}{\sin 100°} \Rightarrow \theta = 11.4°$

The boat is directed at 68.6° to the bank.

(c) $\dfrac{v}{\sin 68.6°} = \dfrac{4}{\sin 100°} \Rightarrow v = 3.78$

The magnitude of the resultant velocity of the boat is $3.78\,\text{m s}^{-1}$.

6 Velocity of water $= v\,\text{m s}^{-1}$

Resultant velocity downstream $= 2.4 + v$

Time taken to row downstream $= \dfrac{50}{2.4 + v}$

Resultant velocity upstream $= 2.4 - v$

Time taken to row upstream $= \dfrac{50}{2.4 - v}$

$\dfrac{50}{2.4 + v} + \dfrac{50}{2.4 - v} = 75$

$50(2.4 - v) + 50(2.4 + v) = 75(2.4 + v)(2.4 - v)$

$240 = 432 - 75v^2$

$v = 1.6$

G Acceleration (p 45)

1 (a) $(2\mathbf{i} + \mathbf{j})\,\text{m s}^{-1}$ **(b)** $(4\mathbf{i} + 2\mathbf{j})\,\text{m s}^{-1}$

  (c) $(10\mathbf{i} + 5\mathbf{j})\,\text{m s}^{-1}$

2 (a)

                  (b) $5.39\,\text{m s}^{-2}$

    5 $(-2\mathbf{i} + 5\mathbf{j})\,\text{m s}^{-2}$

        2

  (c) 68.2° to the negative $\mathbf{i}$-direction

3 $-2\mathbf{i} - \mathbf{j}$

4 (a) $(-20\mathbf{i} + 30\mathbf{j})\,\text{m s}^{-1}$

  (b) $(-\mathbf{i} + 1.5\mathbf{j})\,\text{m s}^{-2}$

      1.5 $(-\mathbf{i} + 1.5\mathbf{j})\,\text{m s}^{-2}$

          1

Exercise G (p 47)

1 (a) $\begin{bmatrix} 1 \\ -1 \end{bmatrix}\text{m s}^{-1}$ **(b)** $\begin{bmatrix} 5 \\ -5 \end{bmatrix}\text{m s}^{-1}$

2 $(-\mathbf{i} + \mathbf{j}) + 3(2\mathbf{i} - \mathbf{j}) = (5\mathbf{i} - 2\mathbf{j})\,\text{m s}^{-1}$

3 (a) $(2\mathbf{i} + 6\mathbf{j})\,\text{m s}^{-1}$ **(b)** $(0.2\mathbf{i} + 0.6\mathbf{j})\,\text{m s}^{-2}$

4 $\dfrac{(-10\mathbf{i} - 5\mathbf{j})}{5} = (-2\mathbf{i} - \mathbf{j})\,\text{m s}^{-2}$

5 The acceleration is $2.24\,\text{m s}^{-2}$ at 63.4° clockwise from the vector $\mathbf{i}$.

6 $\begin{bmatrix} 4 \div 4 \\ 2 \div 4 \end{bmatrix} = \begin{bmatrix} 1 \\ 0.5 \end{bmatrix}\text{m s}^{-2}$

H Constant acceleration equations in two dimensions

Exercise H (p 49)

1 $(38\mathbf{i} - 19\mathbf{j})\,\text{m s}^{-1}$

2 $\begin{bmatrix} 70 \\ 10 \end{bmatrix}\text{m}$

3 $(2.5\mathbf{i} + 1.25\mathbf{j})\,\text{m}$

4 $(570\mathbf{i} - 990\mathbf{j})\,\text{m}$

5 $(-5\mathbf{i} + \mathbf{j})\,\text{m s}^{-1}$

6 (a) $\begin{bmatrix} 20 \\ 10 \end{bmatrix}\text{m}$ **(b)** $\begin{bmatrix} 0.2 \\ -0.05 \end{bmatrix}\text{m s}^{-2}$

7 $(-3\mathbf{i} + 9.5\mathbf{j})\,\text{m s}^{-1}$

8 $5\mathbf{j}\,\text{m s}^{-1}$

9 $\begin{bmatrix} -1.5 \\ 3 \end{bmatrix}\text{m s}^{-1}$

10 (a) $\mathbf{v} = (3 - 2t)\mathbf{i} + (1 + t)\mathbf{j}$

   (b) $9.22\,\text{m s}^{-1}$

11 (a) $(-0.8\mathbf{i} + 1.1\mathbf{j})\,\text{m s}^{-2}$

   (b) $\mathbf{r} = (6t - 0.4t^2)\mathbf{i} + (0.55t^2 - 2t)\mathbf{j}$

12 (a) $(11\mathbf{i} - 11\mathbf{j})\,\text{m s}^{-1}$ **(b)** $242\,\text{m}$

   (c) Velocity $= (25\mathbf{i} - 39\mathbf{j})\,\text{m s}^{-1}$,
      so speed $= 46.3\,\text{m s}^{-1}$

13 (a) $(\mathbf{i} - 3\mathbf{j})\,\text{m s}^{-2}$ **(b)** $(54\mathbf{i} - 28\mathbf{j})\,\text{m}$

Mixed questions (p 51)

1 (a) $a = 2$

 (b) (i) $4\mathbf{i} + 12\mathbf{j}$ **(ii)** $-2\mathbf{i} - 4\mathbf{j}$

 (c) 16.5 units

2 (a) $6.5\,\mathrm{m\,s^{-1}}$ **(b)** $22.6°$

3 (a) $\mathbf{r}_A = 6t\mathbf{i}$
 $\mathbf{r}_B = 4t\mathbf{i} + (5 - t)\mathbf{j}$

 (b) $t = 5$

 (c) The displacement of B from A is $\mathbf{r}_B - \mathbf{r}_A$
 $= (4t - 6t)\mathbf{i} + (5 - t)\mathbf{j} = -2t\mathbf{i} + (5 - t)\mathbf{j}$.
 The distance is the magnitude of the
 displacement.
 $d^2 = (-2t)^2 + (5 - t)^2$
 $\Rightarrow d^2 = 4t^2 + 25 - 10t + t^2$
 $\Rightarrow d^2 = 5t^2 - 10t + 25$

 (d) The ships are 5 km apart when
 $25 = 5t^2 - 10t + 25 \Rightarrow 5t^2 - 10t = 0$
 $\Rightarrow 5t(t - 2) = 0 \Rightarrow t = 0, t = 2$
 Initially $t = 0$, so they are again 5 km apart
 after 2 hours.

4 (a) $40\mathbf{i} - 5\mathbf{j}$ **(b)** $(3\mathbf{i} - \mathbf{j})\,\mathrm{m\,s^{-1}}$
 (c) $(\mathbf{i} - 2\mathbf{j})\,\mathrm{m\,s^{-1}}$ **(d)** $(10\mathbf{i} - 20\mathbf{j})\,\mathrm{m}$

5 (a) $\dfrac{x}{\sin 10°} = \dfrac{50}{\sin 50°} \Rightarrow x = \dfrac{50\sin 10°}{\sin 50°} = 11.3$

 Alternatively, resolve the velocities into
 components. The resultant is directed due
 north, so the sum of the components in the
 east direction is zero.
 $\Rightarrow x\sin 50° = 50\sin 10°$
 $\Rightarrow x = \dfrac{50\sin 10°}{\sin 50°} = 11.3$

 (b) (i) $49.2\,\mathrm{km\,h^{-1}}$ **(ii)** $56.5\,\mathrm{km\,h^{-1}}$

Test yourself (p 53)

1 (a) $68.8\,\mathrm{m}$

 (b) (i) $200\,\mathrm{s}$ **(ii)** $66.7\,\mathrm{s}$

2 (a) 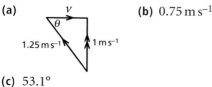 **(b)** $0.75\,\mathrm{m\,s^{-1}}$

 (c) $53.1°$

3 (a) $4\mathbf{j}\,\mathrm{m\,s^{-1}}$

 (b) Using $\mathbf{v} = \mathbf{u} + \mathbf{a}t$, $6\mathbf{i} = 4\mathbf{j} + 10\mathbf{a}$
 $\Rightarrow 10\mathbf{a} = 6\mathbf{i} - 4\mathbf{j} \Rightarrow \mathbf{a} = 0.6\mathbf{i} - 0.4\mathbf{j}$
 Hence the acceleration is $(0.6\mathbf{i} - 0.4\mathbf{j})\,\mathrm{m\,s^{-2}}$.
 The magnitude of the acceleration is
 $0.721\,\mathrm{m\,s^{-2}}$.

 (c) $(30\mathbf{i} + 20\mathbf{j})\,\mathrm{m}$

4 (a) $(2\mathbf{i} - 1.5\mathbf{j})\,\mathrm{m\,s^{-2}}$ **(b)** $10\,\mathrm{m\,s^{-1}}$

 (c) The particle starts at the origin, so its position
 vector is its displacement at time t.
 $\mathbf{s} = (\mathbf{i} - 0.75\mathbf{j})t^2 = t^2\mathbf{i} - 0.75\,t^2\mathbf{j}$
 If the particle passes through $60\mathbf{i} - 45\mathbf{j}$, then
 $60\mathbf{i} - 45\mathbf{j} = t^2\mathbf{i} - 0.75\,t^2\mathbf{j}$.
 Equating coefficients of $\mathbf{i}$ and $\mathbf{j}$
 $\Rightarrow 60 = t^2$ and $45 = 0.75\,t^2$
 $\Rightarrow t = \sqrt{60}$ and $t = \sqrt{60}$
 Both values of t are the same, hence the
 particle passes through $(60\mathbf{i} - 45\mathbf{j})\,\mathrm{m}$.

3 Forces

A Forces as vectors (p 54)

A1 D

A2 (a)

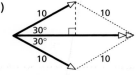

(b) Resultant $= 2 \times 10 \cos 30° = 17.3\,\text{N}$ (to 3 s.f.)

A3 (a)

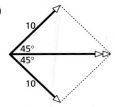

(b) $14.1\,\text{N}$ (to 3 s.f.)

Exercise A (p 56)

1

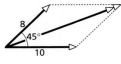

(a) Magnitude $16.6\,\text{N}$

(b) Angle between resultant and $10\,\text{N}$ force $20°$

2 (a)

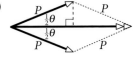

(b) $10\,\text{N}$ (c) $36.9°$

3 (a) $5.83\,\text{N}$ (b) $31.0°$ (c) $5.83\,\text{N}, 31.0°$

4 (a) $7520\,\text{N}$ (to 3 s.f.)

(b) Along the line bisecting the angle between the forces

5 (a)

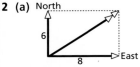

(b) Magnitude of resultant
$$= \text{length of diagonal}$$
$$= P \cos(\tfrac{1}{2}\theta) + P \cos(\tfrac{1}{2}\theta)$$
$$= 2P \cos(\tfrac{1}{2}\theta)$$

B Resolving a force (p 57)

B1 $5.14\,\text{N}$ in direction p
$6.13\,\text{N}$ in direction q

B2 (a) $19.0\,\text{N}$ (b) $6.18\,\text{N}$

B3 (a) $9.85\,\text{N}$ (b) $24.0°$

B4 (a) $8.66\ldots\,\text{N}$ (b) $4.69\ldots\,\text{N}$

(c) $8.66\ldots + 4.69\ldots = 13.359$ (to 3 d.p.)

(d) $5\,\text{N}$ (e) $-1.71\ldots\,\text{N}$

(f) $5 - 1.71\ldots = 3.290$ (to 3 d.p.)

(g) (i) $13.8\,\text{N}$ (ii) $13.8°$

Exercise B (p 59)

1 (a) $10\,\text{N}$ (b) $17.3\,\text{N}$

2 (a) $9.64\,\text{N}$ (b) $11.49\,\text{N}$

3 (a) $4.915\,\text{N}$ (b) $3.441\,\text{N}$ (c) $8.915\,\text{N}$

(d) $9.556\,\text{N}$ (e) $21.1°$

4 (a) $4\mathbf{i} + \mathbf{j}$ or $\begin{bmatrix} 4 \\ 1 \end{bmatrix}$ (b) $4.12\,\text{N}, 14.0°$

5 $10.2\,\text{N}, 68.3°$

6 $7.08\,\text{N}, 72.3°$

C Resolving coplanar forces in equilibrium (p 60)

C1 (a) (i) $P \cos 35°$ (ii) $P \sin 35°$

(b) The total component in direction Ox is zero, so $P \cos 35° - 10 \cos 75° = 0$.

(c) The total component in direction Oy is zero, so $P \sin 35° + 10 \sin 75° - Q = 0$.

(d) 3.16 (e) 11.47

C2 (a) The total component in direction Ox is zero, so $U \cos 40° - V \cos 70° = 0$.

(b) $U \sin 40°, V \sin 70°$

(c) The overall component in direction Oy is zero, so the total y-components of U and V must be $5\,\text{N}$.

(d) $U = 1.82, V = 4.08$

Exercise C (p 61)

1 (a) $P\cos 25° = Q\cos 25°$, so $P = Q$

(b) Resolve in direction Oy:
$$P\sin 25° + Q\sin 25° = 5$$
$$\Rightarrow \quad P\sin 25° + P\sin 25° = 5$$
$$\Rightarrow \quad 2P\sin 25° = 5$$
$$\Rightarrow \quad P = \frac{5}{2\sin 25°} = 5.92$$

2 (a) $10\sin 60° = P\sin 45°$
$$\Rightarrow \quad P = \frac{10\sin 60°}{\sin 45°} = 12.2 \text{ (to 3 s.f)}$$

(b) 13.7

3 (a) $5\cos 30° = 8\cos\theta$
$$\Rightarrow \cos\theta = \frac{5\cos 30°}{8} = 0.541\ldots$$
$$\Rightarrow \quad \theta = 57.2°$$

(b) 9.22

4 (a) 36.9° **(b)** 9

(c) 12 N in direction opposite to removed force

5 (a) Resolve in direction Ox:
$$P\cos\theta + 6\cos 60° = 10$$
$$\Rightarrow \quad P\cos\theta + 3 = 10$$
$$\Rightarrow \quad P\cos\theta = 7$$

(b) Resolve in direction Oy:
$$P\sin\theta = 6\sin 60°$$

(c) $\dfrac{P\sin\theta}{P\cos\theta} = \dfrac{6\sin 60°}{7}$
$$\Rightarrow \tan\theta = \frac{6\sin 60°}{7}$$
$$= 0.742\ldots$$
$$\Rightarrow \quad \theta = 36.6°$$

(d) 8.72

6 $p = 5, q = 1$

7 $P = 4.48, Q = 3.66$

D Weight, tension and thrust (p 63)

D1 (a) **(b)**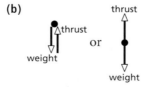

D2 (a) tension / A / tension / weight **(b)** tension / tension / B / weight

Exercise D (p 65)

1 (a) 15 / 25° / T / W

(b) (i) 6.34 N **(ii)** 13.6 N

2 (a) 6.39 N **(b)** 2.18 N

3 (a) 22.4 N **(b)** 27.5 N

4 (a) 59.0° **(b)** 23.3 N

5 (a) Resolve vertically: $T\cos\alpha + T\cos\alpha = W$
$$\Rightarrow \quad 2T\cos\alpha = W$$
$$\Rightarrow \quad T = \frac{W}{2\cos\alpha}$$

(b) As α increases, $\cos\alpha$ decreases, so T increases

(c) As α approaches 90°, T gets larger and larger without limit.

6 18.1 N (upper), 11.5 N (lower)

E Friction (p 66)

E1 The object remains stationary at first, but eventually it moves.

E2 (a) R / F / 8 / 20

(b) (i) 8 N **(ii)** 20 N

(c) 0.4

E3 4.2 N

E4 (a) Resolve vertically

(b) 7.5 N

(c) $F \le \mu R$
$$\Rightarrow \quad 7.5 \le 0.3W$$
$$\Rightarrow \quad W \ge \frac{7.5}{0.3} = 25$$

E5

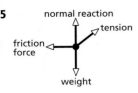

E6

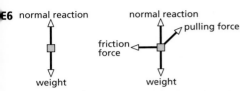

The vertical component of the pulling force plus the normal reaction equals the weight, so the normal reaction is less than the weight.

E7 (a)

R, 20, $25°$, F, 40

(b) Resolve vertically: $R + 20\sin 25° = 40$
So $R = 40 - 20\sin 25° = 31.5$

(c) Resolve horizontally: $F = 20\cos 25° = 18.1$

(d) $18.1 \leq 31.5\mu$, so $\mu \geq \dfrac{18.1}{31.5} = 0.57$

Exercise E (p 69)

1 (a)

R, μR, 12, 15

(b) 0.8

2 3.6

3 (a) 8 N

(b) F (friction) $= 4\cos 30° = 3.464$
$F \leq \mu R$, so $3.464 \leq 8\mu$
so $\mu \geq \dfrac{3.464}{8} = 0.433$

4 (a) Resolve horizontally: $F = 1.5\cos 40°$
$= 1.15$

(b) 2.87 N

(c) 3.84 N

5 (a) Resolve vertically: $R + P\sin 45° = 7$
so $R = 7 - P\sin 45°$
$= 7 - 0.707P$

(b) F (friction) $= P\cos 45° = 0.707P$
$F \leq \mu R \quad \Rightarrow \quad 0.707P \leq 0.25 \times (7 - 0.707P)$
$\Rightarrow \quad 0.707P \leq 1.75 - 0.177P$
$\Rightarrow \quad 0.884P \leq 1.75$
$\Rightarrow \quad P \leq \dfrac{1.75}{0.884} = 1.98$

6 (a) 3.40 N

(b) $F = 3\cos 60° = 1.5$
$F \leq \mu R \quad \Rightarrow \quad 1.5 \leq 3.40\mu$
$\Rightarrow \quad \mu \geq \dfrac{1.5}{3.40} = 0.44$

7 Friction force to left:

Resolve horizontally: $F + P = 6\cos 45°$
$\Rightarrow \quad F = 6\cos 45° - P = 4.243 - P$
Resolve vertically: $R + 6\sin 45° = 10$
$\Rightarrow \quad R = 10 - 6\sin 45° = 5.757$
$F \leq \mu R \Rightarrow 4.243 - P \leq 0.2 \times 5.757$
$\Rightarrow P \geq 4.243 - 0.2 \times 5.757 = 3.09$ (to 2 d.p.)

Friction force to right

Resolve horizontally: $F + 6\cos 45° = P$
$\Rightarrow \quad F = P - 6\cos 45° = P - 4.243$
Resolve vertically: $R + 6\sin 45° = 10$
$\Rightarrow \quad R = 10 - 6\sin 45° = 5.757$
$F \leq \mu R \Rightarrow P - 4.243 \leq 0.2 \times 5.757$
$\Rightarrow P \leq 4.243 + 0.2 \times 5.757 = 5.39$ (to 2 d.p.)

Mixed questions (p 71)

1 (a) $(8\mathbf{i} + 2\mathbf{j})\,\text{N}$ or $\begin{bmatrix} 8 \\ 2 \end{bmatrix}\text{N}$

(b) 8.25 N, 14.0°

2 (a) 5.20 N　　　**(b)** 30°

3 (a) $\begin{bmatrix} 21.7 \\ 12.5 \end{bmatrix}$　　　**(b)** $\begin{bmatrix} -7.5 \\ -26.6 \end{bmatrix}$

4 (a) 38.8° **(b)** 9.07

5 6.22 N (left), 4.06 N (right)

6 (a) Resolve vertically: $R + T\sin 30° = 5$
$$\Rightarrow \quad R = 5 - T\sin 30°$$
$$= 5 - 0.5T$$

(b) $F = T\cos 30° = 0.866T$
$$F \le \mu R \quad \Rightarrow \quad 0.866T \le 0.5\times(5 - 0.5T)$$
$$\Rightarrow \quad 0.866T \le 2.5 - 0.25T$$
$$\Rightarrow \quad 1.116T \le 2.5$$
$$\Rightarrow \quad T \le \frac{2.5}{1.116} = 2.24$$

Test yourself (p 72)

1 (a) $(9\mathbf{i} - 4\mathbf{j})\,\text{N}$ **(b)** 9.85 N **(c)** 24.0°

2 (a) Resolve horizontally:
$$6 = 8\cos 60° + a\cos 60°$$
$$\Rightarrow \ 6 = 4 + \tfrac{1}{2}a$$
$$\Rightarrow \ a = 4$$

(b) 3.46 N

3 $P = 17.3$, $Q = 10$

4 (a)

(b) $F = 12 + 15\cos 30° = 25.0$ (to 3 s.f.)

(c) $R = 75.0$ **(d)** $W = 82.5$

5

(a) 13 N

(b) Resolve horizontally:
$$F = P + 4\cos 30°$$
$$= P + 3.464$$
$$F \le \mu R \quad \Rightarrow \quad P + 3.464 \le 0.3\times 13$$
$$\Rightarrow \quad P \le 3.9 - 3.464 = 0.436$$

4 Momentum

A Mass and momentum (p 73)

A1 The lighter ball will move faster.

A2 $2\,\text{m s}^{-1}$

A3 $4\,\text{kg}$

Exercise A (p 74)

1 $14\,\text{kg m s}^{-1}$ in the same straight line

2 (a) $17.5\,\text{kg m s}^{-1}$

(b) B is moving in the opposite direction to A. The momentum of B is $-7.5\,\text{kg m s}^{-1}$.

3 (a) $(8\mathbf{i} + 6\mathbf{j})\,\text{kg m s}^{-1}$ **(b)** $(4\mathbf{i} - 8\mathbf{j})\,\text{kg m s}^{-1}$
(c) $(-10\mathbf{i} - 4\mathbf{j})\,\text{kg m s}^{-1}$ **(d)** $(-6\mathbf{i} + 30\mathbf{j})\,\text{kg m s}^{-1}$

4 (a) $\begin{bmatrix} 15 \\ 25 \end{bmatrix}\,\text{kg m s}^{-1}$ **(b)** $\begin{bmatrix} 21 \\ -14 \end{bmatrix}\,\text{kg m s}^{-1}$

(c) $\begin{bmatrix} -3.2 \\ -4 \end{bmatrix}\,\text{kg m s}^{-1}$

B Conservation of momentum

Exercise B (p 77)

1 $4\,\text{m s}^{-1}$ forwards

2 $5\,\text{m s}^{-1}$ forwards

3 $0.2\,\text{m s}^{-1}$

4 $0.4\,\text{m s}^{-1}$
(There is no need to bother with the first collision. The total momentum after the second collision is equal to the original momentum.)

5 Total momentum before collision
$$= mU + 4m\left(\tfrac{1}{2}U\right)$$
$$= 3mU$$
So if $V\,\text{m s}^{-1}$ is the final velocity,
$$3mU = 5mV$$
$$\Rightarrow \qquad V = \tfrac{3}{5}U$$

6 1.2

7 0.75

C Conservation of momentum in two dimensions (p 78)

C1 $3(4\mathbf{i} + 4\mathbf{j}) + 2(2\mathbf{i} - 3\mathbf{j}) = 3(2\mathbf{i} - \mathbf{j}) + 2\mathbf{v}_2$

$\Rightarrow 12\mathbf{i} + 12\mathbf{j} + 4\mathbf{i} - 6\mathbf{j} = 6\mathbf{i} - 3\mathbf{j} + 2\mathbf{v}_2$

$\Rightarrow \qquad\qquad 10\mathbf{i} + 9\mathbf{j} = 2\mathbf{v}_2$

$\Rightarrow \qquad\qquad\qquad \mathbf{v}_2 = 5\mathbf{i} + 4.5\mathbf{j}$

C2 $3(4\mathbf{i} + 4\mathbf{j}) + 2(2\mathbf{i} - 3\mathbf{j}) = 5\mathbf{v}$

$\Rightarrow 12\mathbf{i} + 12\mathbf{j} + 4\mathbf{i} - 6\mathbf{j} = 5\mathbf{v}$

$\Rightarrow \qquad\qquad 16\mathbf{i} + 6\mathbf{j} = 5\mathbf{v}$

$\Rightarrow \qquad\qquad\qquad \mathbf{v} = 3.2\mathbf{i} + 1.2\mathbf{j}$

Exercise C (p 79)

1 $(3.5\mathbf{i} + 2.5\mathbf{j})\,\mathrm{m\,s^{-1}}$

2 $\begin{bmatrix} -2 \\ 3 \end{bmatrix}\mathrm{m\,s^{-1}}$

3 $(2.4\mathbf{i} - 4.1\mathbf{j})\,\mathrm{m\,s^{-1}}$

4 $\begin{bmatrix} 5 \\ 0 \end{bmatrix}$

5 (a) (i) $(3\mathbf{i} + 4.5\mathbf{j})\,\mathrm{kg\,m\,s^{-1}}$ **(ii)** $(3\mathbf{i} + 4.5\mathbf{j})\,\mathrm{kg\,m\,s^{-1}}$

(b) $(-5\mathbf{i} - 8\mathbf{j})\,\mathrm{m\,s^{-1}}$

Mixed questions (p 80)

1 (a) $5\,\mathrm{m\,s^{-1}}$ **(b)** $1\,\mathrm{m\,s^{-1}}$

(c) $1.33\,\mathrm{m\,s^{-1}}$ (to 2 d.p.)

2 Let $v\,\mathrm{m\,s^{-1}}$ be the velocity of B after collision.

$mu - 4mu = -\tfrac{1}{2}um + 4mv$

$\Rightarrow \qquad -3u = -\tfrac{1}{2}u + 4v$

$\Rightarrow \qquad 4v = -2\tfrac{1}{2}u$

$\Rightarrow \qquad v = -\tfrac{5}{8}u$

So the speed of B is $\tfrac{5}{8}u\,\mathrm{m\,s^{-1}}$.

3 $0.451\,\mathrm{m\,s^{-1}}$

4 (a) $5 \times 4 = 5 \times 1.2 + m \times 1.4$

$\Rightarrow 20 = 6 + 1.4m$

$\Rightarrow 14 = 1.4m \Rightarrow m = 10$

(b) 18.6

Test yourself (p 81)

1 (a) Momentum of pellet $= 0.5 \times 20 = 10\,\mathrm{kg\,m\,s^{-1}}$

Let $v\,\mathrm{m\,s^{-1}}$ be the trolley's velocity after the first impact.

Then $10 = 10.5v$

$\Rightarrow \qquad v = \dfrac{10}{10.5} = \dfrac{20}{21}$

(b) $\dfrac{20}{11} = 1.82\,\mathrm{m\,s^{-1}}$ (to 2 d.p.)

2 $\begin{bmatrix} 0 \\ -1 \end{bmatrix}\mathrm{m\,s^{-1}}$

3 (a) (i) $\begin{bmatrix} 1 \\ 0.5 \end{bmatrix}\mathrm{kg\,m\,s^{-1}}$ **(ii)** $\begin{bmatrix} 1 \\ 0.5 \end{bmatrix}\mathrm{kg\,m\,s^{-1}}$

(b) $\begin{bmatrix} -5 \\ -3 \end{bmatrix}\mathrm{m\,s^{-1}}$

5 Newton's laws of motion 1

A Force and momentum (p 82)

A1 (a) (i) The object accelerates.

(ii) The object moves at a constant velocity.

(b) (i) The object accelerates for twice as long and so reaches twice the velocity.

(ii) The object accelerates at twice the rate and so reaches twice the velocity.

A2 The heavier object accelerates at a smaller rate than the lighter object, and reaches a lower velocity.

A3 (a) $40\,\mathrm{kg\,m\,s^{-1}}$ (b) $8\,\mathrm{m\,s^{-1}}$

A4 (a) $20\,\mathrm{kg\,m\,s^{-1}}$ (b) $6\,\mathrm{kg\,m\,s^{-1}}$

(c) $26\,\mathrm{kg\,m\,s^{-1}}$ (d) $6.5\,\mathrm{m\,s^{-1}}$

A5 (a) The object decelerates.

(b) The object comes to rest and then accelerates away from you.

Exercise A (p 84)

1 (a) $12\,\mathrm{kg\,m\,s^{-1}}$ (b) $4\,\mathrm{m\,s^{-1}}$

2 (a) $24\,\mathrm{kg\,m\,s^{-1}}$ (b) $12\,\mathrm{m\,s^{-1}}$

3 (a) $30\,\mathrm{kg\,m\,s^{-1}}$ (b) $12\,\mathrm{kg\,m\,s^{-1}}$

(c) $42\,\mathrm{kg\,m\,s^{-1}}$ (d) $7\,\mathrm{m\,s^{-1}}$

4 $21.6\,\mathrm{m\,s^{-1}}$

5 $1.5\,\mathrm{m\,s^{-1}}$

B Force, mass and acceleration (p 85)

B1 $15\,\mathrm{N}$

B2 $8\,\mathrm{m\,s^{-2}}$

B3 $5\,\mathrm{kg}$

B4 (a) $450\,\mathrm{N}$ (b) $0.15\,\mathrm{m\,s^{-2}}$

Exercise B (p 87)

1 $0.8\,\mathrm{m\,s^{-2}}$

2 $124\,\mathrm{N}$

3 $2000\,\mathrm{N}$

4 (a) $0\,\mathrm{m\,s^{-2}}$ (b) $180\,\mathrm{N}$

5 (a) The direction of F is opposite to the directio of motion.

(b) $a = -0.375$ (deceleration)

6 $P = 1360$, $R = 160$

C Solving problems in one dimension (p 87)

C1 (a) $0.6\,\mathrm{m\,s^{-2}}$ (b) $5\,\mathrm{s}$

(c) $s = \frac{1}{2}(u + v)t = \frac{1}{2}(1.5 + 4.5)\times 5 = 15$

C2 (a) $0.5\,\mathrm{m\,s^{-2}}$ (b) $250\,\mathrm{N}$

Exercise C (p 89)

1 (a) $0.4\,\mathrm{m\,s^{-2}}$ (b) $12.5\,\mathrm{s}$ (c) $31.25\,\mathrm{m}$

2 (a) $0.8\,\mathrm{m\,s^{-1}}$ (b) 30

3 (a) $3600\,\mathrm{N}$ (b) $4.5\,\mathrm{m\,s^{-2}}$ (c) $25\,\mathrm{m}$

4 $9\,\mathrm{N}$

5 (a) 250 (b) $12\,\mathrm{s}$

6 (a) $v^2 = u^2 + 2as$

$$20^2 = 12^2 + 400a$$
$$a = \frac{400 - 144}{400}$$
$$= 0.64$$

(b) $12.5\,\mathrm{s}$

(c) (i) $768\,\mathrm{N}$ (ii) $1220\,\mathrm{N}$ (to 3 s.f.)

D Vertical motion (p 90)

D1 $14.7\,\mathrm{N}$

D2 (a) $49\,\mathrm{N}$ (b) $9.3\,\mathrm{m\,s^{-2}}$

Exercise D (p 91)

1 (a) (b) $5.8\,\mathrm{N}$ (c) $1.45\,\mathrm{m\,s^-}$

2 (a) In the equation $F = ma$, $a = 0$ so the resultan force on the object is zero. The tension must be equal to the weight.

(b) $38.5\,\mathrm{N}$ (c) $4.49\,\mathrm{m\,s^{-2}}$

3 (a) $7380\,\mathrm{N}$ (b) $0.743\,\mathrm{m\,s^{-2}}$ (to 3 s.f.)

4 (a) 2.42 N   **(b)** 6.05 m s^{-2} **(c)** 3.40 s

5 (a) Resultant force $= -0.5g - 0.7 = -5.6$ N
   Apply N2L: $-5.6 = 0.5a$
   $\Rightarrow$ $a = -11.2$

(b) 8.4 m s^{-2}

6 (a) $F = ma$
   $6060 - 600 \times 9.8 = 600a$
   $a = \dfrac{6060 - 5880}{600}$
   $\qquad = 0.3$

(b) 7.30 s   **(c)** 2.19 m s^{-1}

E Resolving forces (p 92)

E1 8.66 N

E2 0.217 m s^{-2} (to 3 s.f.)

E3 387

Exercise E (p 93)

All answers are to 3 s.f.

1 (a)

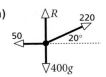

(b) Horizontal force $= 220 \cos 20° - 50 = 157$ N

(c) 0.392 m s^{-2}

2 (a) (i) 28.9 N   **(ii)** 868 N

(b) (i) 80.8 N   **(ii)** 842 N

3 (a) 50.0   **(b)** 7700 N

4 0.120 m s^{-2}

5 (a) Resolve vertically (vertical acceleration $= 0$)
   $T = 905$

(b) 5.66 m s^{-2}

F Friction (p 94)

All answers are to 3 s.f.

F1 (a)

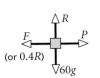

(b) Resolve vertically; no vertical acceleration

(c) 235 N   **(d)** 265 N

F2 (a)

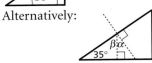

(b) 438 N

(c) 175 N   **(d)** 1.41 m s^{-2}

Exercise F (p 95)

1 0.3 m s^{-2}

2 157

3 (a) 3.92 m s^{-2} **(b)** 22.5 m s^{-1}

4 (a) Resolve vertically:
   $R + 20 \sin 30° = 10g$,
   so $R = 98 - 10 = 88$

(b) 8.8 N   **(c)** 0.852 m s^{-2}

5 (a) Resolve vertically:
   $R = 20g + 70 \sin 35° = 236$

(b) 47.2 N   **(c)** 0.507 m s^{-2}

G Smooth inclined surfaces (p 96)

G1 The block will accelerate down the plane.
The acceleration increases as the angle increases.
This is because the component of the weight
acting down the plane increases as the angle
increases.

G2 As the plane is tilted, the normal to
the plane rotates from a vertical
position to 35° from the vertical.

Alternatively: $\beta = 90° - 35° = 65°$
so $\alpha = 90° - \beta = 35°$

G3 (a) Resolve perpendicular to the plane:
   $R = 40.1$ (to 3 s.f.)

(b) $5g \sin 35° = 5a$, so $a = 9.8 \sin 35° = 5.6$

G4 (a)

(b) (i) 13.3 N

(ii) 4.14 m s⁻²

Exercise G (p 97)

1 (a)

(b) 4.9 m s⁻²   **(c)** 33.9 N

2 (a) 1.19 m s⁻²   **(b)** 133 N

3 (a) 5.34 m s⁻²   **(b)** 2.4 s (to 1 d.p.) **(c)** 98.6 N

H Rough inclined surfaces (p 98)

H1 The block does not move down the plane until the component of the weight down the plane is greater than the friction force up the plane. Then the block accelerates and the acceleration increases as the angle increases.

H2 (a) Resolve perpendicular to the plane:
There is no acceleration in this direction, so $R = 3g\cos 30°$.

(b) 5.09   **(c)** 3.20 m s⁻²

H3 (a)

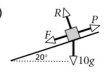

(b)

Resolve perpendicular to the plane:
$R = 10g\cos 20° = 92.1$ (to 3 s.f.)

(c) 27.6 N

(d) (i) 61.1   **(ii)** 81.1

H4 (a) Resolve perpendicular to the plane:
$R = 5g\cos 25° = 44.4$ (to 3 s.f.)

(b) Resolve parallel to the plane:
$F = 5g\sin 25° = 20.7$ (to 3 s.f.)

(c) $F \le \mu R$, so $20.7 \le 44.4\mu$
so $\mu \ge \dfrac{20.7}{44.4} = 0.466$

Exercise H (p 100)

1 (a)

(b) Resolve perpendicular to the plane:
$R = 10g\cos 30° = 84.9$
So $F = 0.25R = 21.2$

Resolve down the plane, and use N2L:
$10g\sin 30° - 21.2 = 10a$
$\Rightarrow a = 2.8$ (to 2 s.f.)

2 (a)

Resolve perpendicular to the plane:
$R = 20g\cos 30° = 170$ (to 3 s.f.)

(b) Resolve parallel to the plane:
$\mu R = 20g\sin 30°$
So $170\mu = 98$
$\Rightarrow \mu = \dfrac{98}{170} = 0.58$ (to 2 s.f.)

3 (a) 276 N   **(b)** $0.15 \times 276 = 41.4$ (to 3 s.f.)
(c) 1.97 m s⁻²

4 (a) $T = 0.1 \times 50 + 25g\cos 15° + 50g\sin 15$
$= 368$

(b) The box is treated as a particle; the rope is light.

5 (a) 0.577 (to 3 s.f.)   **(b)** 0.342 (to 3 s.f.)

6 (a) 15.0 N (to 3 s.f.)

(b)

Resolve parallel to the plane:
If the block is at rest, $F = 2g\sin 40° = 12.6$
$F \le \mu R$, so $12.6 \le 15.0\mu$
so $\mu \ge \dfrac{12.6}{15.0} = 0.84$

(c) 3.30 m s⁻² (to 3 s.f.)

7 (a)

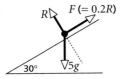

(b) $R = 5g\cos 30° = 42.4\ldots$
$F = \mu R = 0.2 \times 42.4\ldots = 8.5$ (to 2 s.f.)

(c) $3.20\,\text{m s}^{-2}$

(d) $2.77\,\text{m s}^{-1}$

I Motion in two dimensions

Exercise I (p 101)

1 (a) $(20\mathbf{i} - 15\mathbf{j})\,\text{N}$ **(b)** $(81\mathbf{i} - 59\mathbf{j})\,\text{m s}^{-1}$

2 (a) $\begin{bmatrix} 3 \\ 1.6 \end{bmatrix}\text{m s}^{-2}$ **(b)** $\begin{bmatrix} 12 \\ 6.4 \end{bmatrix}$

3 (a) $(15\mathbf{i} + 20\mathbf{j})\,\text{m s}^{-2}$ **(b)** $(140\mathbf{i} + 152\mathbf{j})\,\text{m}$

4 (a) $(1.6\mathbf{i} - 0.8\mathbf{j})\,\text{m s}^{-2}$ **(b)** $(30\mathbf{i} + 5\mathbf{j})\,\text{m}$

(c) $4.47\,\text{N}$ (to 3 s.f.)

Mixed questions (p 102)

1 (a) $s = ut + \frac{1}{2}at^2$
$200 = 8 \times 10 + 50a$
$a = \dfrac{200 - 80}{50} = 2.4$

(b) $32\,\text{m s}^{-1}$

(c) (i) $4680\,\text{N}$ **(ii)** $341\,\text{m}$

2 (a) $8\,\text{m s}^{-1}$

(b) (i) $19.6\,\text{N}$ **(ii)** $16.3\,\text{m}$

3 (a) $200\,\text{m}$ **(b)** $0.8\,\text{m s}^{-2}$

(c) (i) 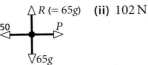   **(ii)** $102\,\text{N}$

4 (a) Let T_1 be the tension in AC.
Let T_2 be the tension in AB.
Resolve horizontally:
$T_1 \cos 30° = T_2 \cos 30°$
So $T_1 = T_2$
Resolve vertically:
$T_1 \sin 30° + T_2 \sin 30° = 450g$
So $T_1 = T_2 = \dfrac{450g}{2\sin 30°} = 4410$

(b) $T_1 = 4540\,\text{N}$, $T_2 = 4280\,\text{N}$

(c) Tension in AB decreases; tension in AC increases.

5 (a)   **(b)** $147\,\text{N}$

(c) $F = 0.6 \times 147 = 88.2$ **(d)** $5.55\,\text{m s}^{-2}$

(e) The child has been treated as a particle.

6 (a) (i) $6\,\text{m s}^{-1}$ **(ii)** $-12\,\text{m s}^{-2}$

(b) Use N2L vertically:
$-0.2 \times 9.8 - R = -12 \times 0.2$
So $R = 2.4 - 1.96 = 0.44$

(c) $7.6\,\text{m s}^{-2}$

(d) $1.13\,\text{s}$

7 (a) $W = 20g = 20 \times 9.8 = 196\,\text{N}$

(b) Resolve vertically:
$R + 70\sin 25° = 196$
$\Rightarrow R = 196 - 70\sin 25° = 166.4$ (to 1 d.p.)

(c) 49.9

(d) $0.677\,\text{m s}^{-2}$

(e) $8.46\,\text{m}$

8 (a) (i)

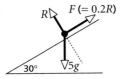   **(ii)** $116\,\text{N}$

(iii) Resolve up the slope and use N2L:
$T - 12g\sin 10° - 0.12 \times 116 = 12 \times 0.5$
So $T = 12 \times 9.8\sin 10° + 23.2 + 6$
$= 50$ approximately

(b) $1.20\,\text{m s}^{-2}$

(c) The sledge is treated as a particle; there is no air resistance.

9 (a) $-10\mathbf{i} - 5\mathbf{j}$ **(b)** $19.9\,\text{N}$

Test yourself (p 105)

1 (a) $1.5\,\text{m s}^{-2}$ **(b)** $36.25\,\text{m}$ **(c)** $845\,\text{N}$

2 (a) (i) Normal reaction $= 3000g = 29\,400\,\text{N}$
Friction force $= 0.7 \times 29\,400 = 20\,580\,\text{N}$

(ii) $-6.86\,\mathrm{m\,s^{-2}}$

(iii) Use $v^2 = u^2 + 2as$:
$$0^2 = u^2 - 2 \times 6.86 \times 5$$
So $u = \sqrt{68.6} = 8.28$

(b) $20.7\,\mathrm{m\,s^{-1}}$ (to 3 s.f.)

3 (a)

R, 100, F, 30°, 50g diagram

(b) Resolve vertically:
$R + 100\sin 30° = 50 \times 9.8$
So $R = 490 - 50 = 440$

(c) 0.197

(d) $0.852\,\mathrm{m\,s^{-2}}$

4 (a) R, $F = 0.3R$, 30°, 80g diagram

(b) (i) 679 N   **(ii)** $F = 0.3 \times 679 = 204$

(c) $2.35\,\mathrm{m\,s^{-2}}$

6 Newton's laws of motion 2

A Modelling (p 106)

A1 The cars would accelerate. Brakes are needed!

A2 It would not be appropriate.
The relative positions of different parts of the skater's body are important.

A3 For example, an elephant stepping on to an ocean-going oil tanker would not have a detectable effect.

A4 Air resistance in a tunnel cannot be ignored. Mass and speed of train, gradient and curvature of track, friction of rails, etc. need to be included

A5 The dimensions of the diver are comparable with the distance fallen. As with the skater, the different positions of arms, legs and trunk are important.

B Newton's third law of motion (p 109)

B1 (a) $6000 - T = 1200a$

(b)

T ← 400 kg, normal reaction, 400g diagram

Reason: Newton's third law

(c) $T = 400a$ **(d)** $a = 3.75$, $T = 1500$

(e) It must be inextensible.

B2 (a) $6000 = 1600a$ **(b)** $a = 3.75$

Exercise B (p 111)

1 (a) $0.8\,\mathrm{m\,s^{-2}}$ **(b)** 320 N

2 (a) $0.625\,\mathrm{m\,s^{-2}}$ **(b)** 950 N

3 (a) 2400 N   **(b)** 300 N

4 (a) $0.8\,\mathrm{m\,s^{-2}}$ **(b)** 3840 N

5 (a) 100 N

(b) (i) 0 N   **(ii)** 100 N

6 (a) Crate, T, S, 120g; Box, S, 30g diagram

(b) 1485 N   **(c)** 297 N

C Pulleys and pegs (p 112)

C1 (a) Both particles accelerate.

(b) What happens depends on
- the relative masses of the particles
- the roughness of the surface

The particles either remain stationary or accelerate.

C2 (a)
(b) $T = 3a$
(c)

(d) The string is inextensible.

(e) $2g - T = 2a$ (f) $a = 3.92$, $T = 11.76$

C3 (a)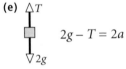

(b) There is no vertical acceleration, so the normal reaction must be equal to the weight.

(c) $0.2 \times R = 0.2 \times 3 \times 9.8 = 5.88$

(d) $T - 5.88 = 3a$

(e)
$2g - T = 2a$

(f) $a = 2.74$, $T = 14.1$ (to 3 s.f.)

C4 (a) Acceleration $4.2\,\text{m s}^{-2}$, tension $16.8\,\text{N}$

(b) Acceleration $1.4\,\text{m s}^{-2}$, tension $25.2\,\text{N}$

C5 Both particles accelerate, A down and B up.

C6 (a) $\triangle T$ (with a arrow, $3g$)

(b) $3g - T = 3a$

(c) $\triangle T$ (with a arrow, $2g$)

(d) $T - 2g = 2a$

(e) $a = 1.96$, $T = 23.5$ (to 3 s.f.)

(f) The tension in the string is the same throughout its length. The downward force on the pulley is $T + T$ (see diagram). The downward force is 47 N.

C7 (a) $1.4\,\text{m s}^{-2}$ (b) $33.6\,\text{N}$ (c) $2.8\,\text{m}$ (d) $5.6\,\text{m}$

C8 (a) This is difficult to guess! The correct answer comes out of the following working.

(b) $3g \sin 30° - T = 3a$
So $14.7 - T = 3a$

(c) $\triangle T$
$T - 2g = 2a$
$2g$

(d) $a = -0.98$ (deceleration)
$T = 17.64$
A moves up the slope.

Exercise C (p 115)

1 (a) (i) $3.27\,\text{m s}^{-2}$ (ii) $13.1\,\text{N}$
(b) (i) $6.53\,\text{m s}^{-2}$ (ii) $13.1\,\text{N}$
(c) (i) $3.68\,\text{m s}^{-2}$ (ii) $18.4\,\text{N}$

2 (a) (i) $3.27\,\text{m s}^{-2}$ (ii) $26.1\,\text{N}$ (iii) $52.3\,\text{N}$
(b) (i) $2.45\,\text{m s}^{-2}$ (ii) $36.8\,\text{N}$ (iii) $73.5\,\text{N}$
(c) (i) $3.92\,\text{m s}^{-2}$ (ii) $20.6\,\text{N}$ (iii) $41.2\,\text{N}$

3 (a) (i) $2.61\,\text{m s}^{-2}$ (ii) $14.4\,\text{N}$
(b) (i) $5.88\,\text{m s}^{-2}$ (ii) $15.7\,\text{N}$
(c) (i) $0.638\,\text{m s}^{-2}$ (ii) $27.7\,\text{N}$
(d) (i) $1.4\,\text{m s}^{-2}$ (ii) $25.2\,\text{N}$

4 (a) (i) $1.4\,\text{m s}^{-2}$ (up slope) (ii) $25.2\,\text{N}$
(b) (i) $4.22\,\text{m s}^{-2}$ (up slope) (ii) $22.3\,\text{N}$
(c) (i) $0.656\,\text{m s}^{-2}$ (down slope) (ii) $31.4\,\text{N}$
(d) (i) $3.70\,\text{m s}^{-2}$ (up slope) (ii) $24.4\,\text{N}$

5 (a) $1.4\,\text{m s}^{-2}$ (b) $1.7\,\text{s}$ (c) $7.1\,\text{m}$

6 (a) $\mu \geq 0.4$ (b) 0.52

7 (a) Acceleration $= 1.87\,\text{m s}^{-2}$, tension $= 30\,000\,\text{N}$

(b) $36.7\,\text{m s}^{-1}$

(c) The braking system, the mass and elasticity of the cable, friction at the pulley, friction on the rails, etc. are all left out.

Mixed questions (p 117)

1 (a) (i) Resultant horizontal force

$= 2000 - 1500 = 500\,\text{N}$

Total mass $= 1250\,\text{kg}$

So $500 = 1250a \Rightarrow a = 0.4$

(ii) $400\,\text{N}$

(b) (i) Horizontal force $= -300\,\text{N}$

Mass $= 250\,\text{kg}$

So $-300 = 250a \Rightarrow a = -1.2$

(ii) $60\,\text{m}$

2 (a) R (normal reaction) $= 0.5g$

F (friction force) $= \mu R = \frac{2}{7} \times 0.5g = 1.4$

(b) $0.8\,\text{m s}^{-2}$ **(c)** $1.8\,\text{N}$ **(d)** $1.25\,\text{s}$

3 (a) N2L ($3g$ particle): $T - 0.3g = 0.3a$

$3.36 - 0.3 \times 9.8 = 0.3a$

$\Rightarrow \quad a = 1.4\,\text{m s}^{-2}$

(b) $m = 0.4$ **(c)** $6.72\,\text{N}$

4 (a) N2L (A): $T - 14g\sin 45° = 14a$

N2L (B): $6g - T = 6a$

Add: $6g - 14g\sin 45° = 20a$

$\Rightarrow \qquad\qquad a = -1.91$

(A accelerates down the slope.)

(b) $9.90\,\text{kg}$

5 (a) Normal reaction on $A = 5g$

Friction force on $A = 0.8 \times 5g = 4g$

N2L (particle A): $T - 4g = 5a$

N2L (particle B): $3g - T = 3a$

Add: $-g = 8a$

So $a = \dfrac{-9.8}{8} = -1.225$

Magnitude of acceleration $= 1.225\,\text{m s}^{-2}$

(b) $33.1\,\text{N}$ **(c)** $1.63\,\text{m}$

Test yourself (p 119)

1 (a) (i)

If $T\,\text{N}$ is tension in towbar

$T - 100 = 250 \times (-0.5) = -125$

So $T = -25$ (i.e. $25\,\text{N}$ thrust)

(ii)

$B + 500 - 25 = 1250 \times 0.5$

$\Rightarrow \qquad B = 150$

Braking force is $150\,\text{N}$

(b) $100\,\text{N}$

2 (a) $s = ut + \frac{1}{2}at^2$

$0.6 = 0 + \frac{1}{2} \times a \times 4$

$\Rightarrow \quad a = 0.3$

(b) $38\,\text{N}$ **(c)** $36.2\,\text{N}$ **(d)** 0.62

3 (a) (i) N2L (heavier load): $40g - T = 40a$

N2L (lighter load): $T - 30g = 30a$

Add: $10g = 70a$

$\Rightarrow \quad a = \dfrac{98}{70} = 1.4$

(ii) $336\,\text{N}$

(b) Smooth pulley

Light string

Inextensible string

No air resistance

(c) $2.65\,\text{m s}^{-1}$

7 Projectiles

Answers are given to three significant figures where appropriate.

A Vertical motion under gravity (p 120)

A1 (a) The stone starts from rest and moves vertically downwards with constant acceleration until it hits the water.

(b) The motion is not affected by the weight of the stone: it will move with the same constant acceleration.

(c) The stone starts moving with velocity $u\,\mathrm{m\,s^{-1}}$ and moves vertically downwards with the same constant acceleration as before.
It hits the water with a greater velocity than in the previous cases.

A2 $19.6\,\mathrm{m\,s^{-1}}$ downwards.

A3 (a) $5.2\,\mathrm{m\,s^{-1}}$ upwards

(b) $4.6\,\mathrm{m\,s^{-1}}$ downwards

(c) $14.4\,\mathrm{m\,s^{-1}}$ downwards

(d) $24.2\,\mathrm{m\,s^{-1}}$ downwards

A4 (a) The velocity decreases at a constant rate from its original value to zero and continues to decrease finishing with a negative value.

(b) Zero

(c) The velocity has the same magnitude but it is acting downwards rather than upwards.

(d) 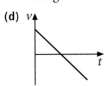 (e)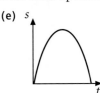

Exercise A (p 122)

1 (a) $29.4\,\mathrm{m\,s^{-1}}$ downwards

(b) $44.1\,\mathrm{m}$ (c) $122.5\,\mathrm{m}$

2 $24.8\,\mathrm{m\,s^{-1}}$

3 $9.9\,\mathrm{m}$

4 (a) $2.5\,\mathrm{m}$ (b) $1.43\,\mathrm{s}$

5 (a) $24.2\,\mathrm{m\,s^{-1}}$ (b) $4.95\,\mathrm{s}$

6 (a) $0.30\,\mathrm{s}$, $3.37\,\mathrm{s}$ (b) $3.07\,\mathrm{s}$

7 $3.12\,\mathrm{s}$

8 (a)

(b) $v^2 = u^2 - 2gs$, and $v = 0$ at maximum height
$$\Rightarrow s = \frac{u^2}{2g}$$

(c) $v = u - gt$, and $v = 0$ at maximum height
$$\Rightarrow t = \frac{u}{g}$$

(d) The only force acting on the ball is its weight; air resistance is negligible.

9 (a) The coin hits the ground when $s = -1.2$, so $-1.2 = 2t - 4.9t^2$. The time is positive when the coin hits the ground, so take the positive root of this equation.
The coin hits the ground after 0.74 seconds.

(b) $5.25\,\mathrm{m\,s^{-1}}$

B Motion of a projectile (p 123)

B1 Stones, snowballs, hockey balls, cricket balls thrown from the outfield and basketballs are all situations that can reasonably be modelled as projectiles.
If the motion of the object is affected by wind or spin it cannot be modelled as a projectile.
Polishing half of a cricket ball can accentuate swing when it is bowled, and so it cannot be modelled as a projectile.

B2 (a) $\mathbf{u} = 10\mathbf{i}$, $\mathbf{a} = -9.8\mathbf{j}$
$$\Rightarrow \mathbf{s} = (10\mathbf{i}) \times t + \tfrac{1}{2} \times (-9.8\mathbf{j}) \times t^2$$
$$\Rightarrow \mathbf{s} = 10t\mathbf{i} - 4.9t^2\mathbf{j}$$

(b) $\mathbf{s} = (10 \times 3)\mathbf{i} - (4.9 \times 3^2)\mathbf{j} \Rightarrow \mathbf{s} = 30\mathbf{i} - 44.1\mathbf{j}$

(c)

t	0	1	2	3	4
s	0	$10\mathbf{i} - 4.9\mathbf{j}$	$20\mathbf{i} - 19.6\mathbf{j}$	$30\mathbf{i} - 44.1\mathbf{j}$	$40\mathbf{i} - 78.4\mathbf{j}$

(d) (and B3(d))

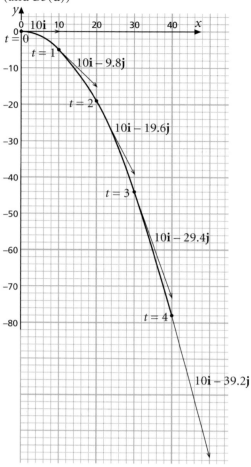

B3 (a) $\mathbf{u} = 10\mathbf{i}$, $\mathbf{a} = -9.8\mathbf{j}$
$\Rightarrow \mathbf{v} = 10\mathbf{i} + (-9.8\mathbf{j}) \times t \Rightarrow \mathbf{v} = 10\mathbf{i} - 9.8t\mathbf{j}$

(b) $\mathbf{v} = 10\mathbf{i} + (-9.8 \times 1)\mathbf{j} \Rightarrow \mathbf{v} = 10\mathbf{i} - 9.8\mathbf{j}$

(c)

t	0	1	2	3	4
v	$10\mathbf{i}$	$10\mathbf{i} - 9.8\mathbf{j}$	$10\mathbf{i} - 19.6\mathbf{j}$	$10\mathbf{i} - 29.4\mathbf{j}$	$10\mathbf{i} - 39.2\mathbf{j}$

(d) See B2(d).

B4 (a) (i) $\mathbf{s} = -4.9t^2\mathbf{j}$

(ii)

t	0	1	2	3	4
s	0	$-4.9\mathbf{j}$	$-19.6\mathbf{j}$	$-44.1\mathbf{j}$	$-78.4\mathbf{j}$

The **j**-components of the displacement a the same as those in B2, but the **i**-components of displacement are zero i this case. In both cases the ball had no initial vertical component of velocity, so the displacements are the same in this direction. The initial horizontal velocity B2 caused the horizontal displacement.

(b) (i) $\mathbf{v} = -9.8t\mathbf{j}$

(ii)

t	0	1	2	3	4
v	0	$-9.8\mathbf{j}$	$-19.6\mathbf{j}$	$-29.4\mathbf{j}$	$-39..$

The **j**-components of the velocity are the same as those in B2, but the **i**-componen are zero in this case. In both cases the ba had no initial vertical component of velocity, so the vertical velocities are caused by the acceleration due to gravity The initial horizontal velocity in B2 caused the constant horizontal velocity.

B5 (a) (i) $\mathbf{u} = 10\mathbf{i} + 15\mathbf{j}$, $\mathbf{a} = -9.8\mathbf{j}$, $\mathbf{s} = \mathbf{u}t + \frac{1}{2}\mathbf{a}t^2$
$\Rightarrow \mathbf{s} = (10\mathbf{i} + 15\mathbf{j}) \times t + \frac{1}{2} \times (-9.8\mathbf{j}) \times t^2$
$\Rightarrow \mathbf{s} = 10t\mathbf{i} + (15t - 4.9t^2)\mathbf{j}$

(ii)

t	0	0.5	1	1.5
s	0	$5\mathbf{i} + 6.275\mathbf{j}$	$10\mathbf{i} + 10.1\mathbf{j}$	$15\mathbf{i} + 11.4$

	2	2.5	3
	$20\mathbf{i} + 10.4\mathbf{j}$	$25\mathbf{i} + 6.875\mathbf{j}$	$30\mathbf{i} + 0.9$

(iii) (and (b)(iii))

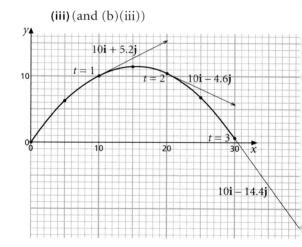

(b) (i) $\mathbf{u} = 10\mathbf{i} + 15\mathbf{j}$, $\mathbf{a} = -9.8\mathbf{j}$, $\mathbf{v} = \mathbf{u} + \mathbf{a}t$

$\Rightarrow \mathbf{v} = (10\mathbf{i} + 15\mathbf{j}) + (-9.8\mathbf{j}) \times t$

$\Rightarrow \mathbf{v} = 10\mathbf{i} + (15 - 9.8t)\mathbf{j}$

(ii)

t	1	2	3
$\mathbf{v}$	$10\mathbf{i} + 5.2\mathbf{j}$	$10\mathbf{i} - 4.6\mathbf{j}$	$10\mathbf{i} - 14.4\mathbf{j}$

(iii) See (a)(iii).

Exercise B (p 126)

1 (a) $\mathbf{v} = \mathbf{u} + \mathbf{a}t \Rightarrow \mathbf{v} = 12\mathbf{i} + (-9.8) \times 2\mathbf{j}$
$\Rightarrow \mathbf{v} = 12\mathbf{i} - 19.6\mathbf{j}$

(b) $(12\mathbf{i} - 49\mathbf{j})\,\mathrm{m\,s^{-1}}$

2 (a) $\mathbf{s} = \mathbf{u}t + \frac{1}{2}\mathbf{a}t^2$

$\Rightarrow \mathbf{s} = \begin{bmatrix} 2 \\ 3 \end{bmatrix} \times 1 + \frac{1}{2}\begin{bmatrix} 0 \\ -9.8 \end{bmatrix} \times 1^2$

$\Rightarrow \mathbf{s} = \begin{bmatrix} 2 \\ 3 - 4.9 \end{bmatrix} \Rightarrow \mathbf{s} = \begin{bmatrix} 2 \\ -1.9 \end{bmatrix}$

(b) $\begin{bmatrix} 8 \\ -66.4 \end{bmatrix}\mathrm{m}$

3 (a)

t	0	1	2	3	4
$\mathbf{s}$	0	$10\mathbf{i} + 15.1\mathbf{j}$	$20\mathbf{i} + 20.4\mathbf{j}$	$30\mathbf{i} + 15.9\mathbf{j}$	$40\mathbf{i} + 1.6\mathbf{j}$

(b) (and (c) and (d))

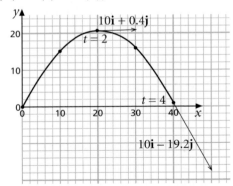

(c) $(10\mathbf{i} + 0.4\mathbf{j})\,\mathrm{m\,s^{-1}}$ **(d)** $(10\mathbf{i} - 19.2\mathbf{j})\,\mathrm{m\,s^{-1}}$

4 (a) $(4\mathbf{i} - 12.6\mathbf{j})\,\mathrm{m\,s^{-1}}$ **(b)** $(8\mathbf{i} - 5.6\mathbf{j})\,\mathrm{m}$

5 (a) $13.4\,\mathrm{m\,s^{-1}}$ **(b)** $63.4°$ **(c)** $9.68\,\mathrm{m\,s^{-1}}$

(d) $51.7°$ below the horizontal

6 (a) $1.1\,\mathrm{m}$ **(b)** $7.96\,\mathrm{m\,s^{-1}}$

7 (a) $66.4\,\mathrm{m}$ **(b)** $16\,\mathrm{m}$

8 (a) $60\,\mathrm{m}$ **(b)** $1.225\,\mathrm{m}$

9 (a) $\mathbf{v} = 5\mathbf{i} + (6 - 9.8t)\mathbf{j}$

(b) The speed is least when $6 - 9.8t = 0$
$\Rightarrow t = 0.612$
The speed is least $0.612\,\mathrm{s}$ after the ball is thrown.

(c) $5\,\mathrm{m\,s^{-1}}$

C Projectile problems (p 128)

C1 (a) $\mathbf{v} = \begin{bmatrix} 5 \\ 8 - 9.8t \end{bmatrix}$ **(b)** $\mathbf{s} = \begin{bmatrix} 5t \\ 8t - 4.9t^2 \end{bmatrix}$

C2 (a) Horizontal component $= 15\cos 30°$
Vertical component $= 15\sin 30°$

(b) $y = 15t\sin 30° - \frac{1}{2}gt^2 \Rightarrow y = 7.5t - 4.9t^2$

(c) At A, $y = 0 \Rightarrow 7.5t - 4.9t^2 = 0$
$\Rightarrow t(7.5 - 4.9t) = 0 \Rightarrow t = 0$ or 1.53
$t = 0$ at O, so at A $t = 1.53$
The time of flight is $1.53\,\mathrm{s}$.

(d) $x = 15t\cos 30°$

(e) The range is $19.9\,\mathrm{m}$.

C3 (a) $v_y = 15\sin 30° - gt \Rightarrow v_y = 7.5 - 9.8t$

(b) At maximum height $v_y = 0 \Rightarrow 7.5 - 9.8t = 0$
$\Rightarrow t = 0.765\,\mathrm{s}$

(c) The time when the particle is at its maximum height is half of the time of flight because of the symmetry of the path of the projectile.

(d) $2.87\,\mathrm{m}$.

C4 (a) When the particle is at its maximum height, the horizontal distance travelled is half of the range, i.e. $9.9\,\mathrm{m}$.

(b) When the projectile is at its maximum height, the vertical component of the velocity is zero, so the direction of the velocity is horizontal.

C5 (a) The particle hits the ground when $y = 0$.
$\Rightarrow 10t\sin 20° - \frac{1}{2}gt^2 = 0$
$\Rightarrow t(10\sin 20° - 4.9t) = 0 \Rightarrow t = 0$ or 0.698
Initially $t = 0$, so the time of flight is $0.698\,\mathrm{s}$.

(b) $x = 10t\cos 20° \Rightarrow x = 6.559$
The range is $6.56\,\mathrm{m}$.

(c) The particle is at its maximum height when
$t = 0.35 \Rightarrow y = 0.5968$
The maximum height is $0.597\,\mathrm{m}$.

Exercise C (p 131)

1 (a) 2.62 s   (b) 40.2 m

2 (a) 2.04 s   (b) 8.16 m

3 2.33 m

4 (a) 3.6 m   (b) 19.2 m

5 (a) 1.02 s   (b) 7.14 m

6 (a) The time of flight is the time when $y = 0$, and
$$y = Vt\sin\alpha - \tfrac{1}{2}gt^2 \Rightarrow Vt\sin\alpha - \tfrac{1}{2}gt^2 = 0$$
$$\Rightarrow t(V\sin\alpha - \tfrac{1}{2}gt) = 0$$
$$\Rightarrow t = 0 \text{ or } t = \frac{2V\sin\alpha}{g}$$

  Initially $t = 0$, so time of flight $t = \dfrac{2V\sin\alpha}{g}$.

(b) $x = R$ when $t = \dfrac{2V\sin\alpha}{g}$.

$$x = Vt\cos\alpha \Rightarrow R = V \times \frac{2V\sin\alpha}{g} \times \cos\alpha$$
$$\Rightarrow R = \frac{2V^2\sin\alpha\cos\alpha}{g}$$

7 (a) 4.13 m   (b) 22.0 m

8 (a) 2 s

(b) When $t = 2$, $y = 2.4$ m so he does score a goal.

(c) 13.2 m s^{-1} at 40.7° below the horizontal

9 23.3°

10 29.3 m s^{-1} at 56.9° to the horizontal

11 7.73 m s^{-1} at 49.7° to the horizontal

12 The angle of projection is 14.2°. The range is 121 m.

13 (a) 0.714 s   (b) 0.5 m   (c) 0.639 s

14 The speed of release is 16.1 m s^{-1}. It is in the air for 1.89 s.

15 $a = \dfrac{R}{T}$, $b = \dfrac{gT}{2}$

D Release from a given height

Exercise D (p 134)

1 (a) 1.80 s   (b) 17.7 m

2 (a) $\mathbf{v} = (21\cos 40°)\mathbf{i} + (21\sin 40° - 9.8t)\mathbf{j}$

  or $\mathbf{v} = \begin{bmatrix} 21\cos 40° \\ 21\sin 40° - 9.8t \end{bmatrix}$

(b) $\mathbf{s} = (21t\cos 40°)\mathbf{i} + (21t\sin 40° - 4.9t^2 + 2)\mathbf{j}$

  or $\mathbf{s} = \begin{bmatrix} 21t\cos 40° \\ 21t\sin 40° - 4.9t^2 + 2 \end{bmatrix}$

(c) 46.6 m

3 1.53 s

4 (a) 0.391 s   (b) 30.7   (c) 6.33 m

5 (a) 182 m   (b) 14.4 m

6 $\dfrac{U^2}{2g} + h$

7 (a) 5.23 m

(b) Jill's stone lands in the water after 1.92 s. Jack's stone lands in the water after 0.96 s. Jack's stone lands in the water first.

(c) Jill's stone lands 9.58 m away. Jack's stone lands 3.66 m away. Jill's stone lands 5.92 m further.

8 The object hits the target when $Ut\cos 45° = 20$ and $Ut\sin 45° - 4.9t^2 + 1 = 0$.
$$\Rightarrow t = \frac{20}{U\cos 45°}$$
$$\Rightarrow 20\tan 45° - \frac{4.9 \times 400}{U^2\cos^2 45°} + 1 = 0$$
$$\Rightarrow 21 = \frac{3920}{U^2} \Rightarrow U = 13.7$$

The object leaves the catapult at 13.7 m s^{-1}.

Mixed questions (p 136)

1 (a) 6.14 m   (b) 7.82 m

(c) The shot can be modelled as a particle. Air resistance is negligible. The shot travels in a vertical plane.

2 (a) At maximum height $v_y = 0 \Rightarrow V\sin\alpha - gt = 0$

$$\Rightarrow t = \frac{V\sin\alpha}{g}$$

At maximum height,

$$y = V \times \frac{V\sin\alpha}{g} \times \sin\alpha - \tfrac{1}{2} \times g \times \left(\frac{V\sin\alpha}{g}\right)^2$$

$$\Rightarrow y = \frac{V^2\sin^2\alpha}{2g}$$

(b) (i) $12.5\,\mathrm{m\,s^{-1}}$ **(ii)** $13.9\,\mathrm{m}$

3 (a) Apply N2L to A: $0.21g - T = 0.21a$
Apply N2L to B: $T - 0.14g = 0.14a$
Adding gives $0.07g = 0.35a$, so $a = 1.96$

(b) $3.92\,\mathrm{m\,s^{-1}}$ **(c)** $0.4\,\mathrm{s}$

(d)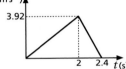

4 $76.0°$

Test yourself (p 137)

1 (a) (i) $14\,\mathrm{m\,s^{-1}}$ **(ii)** $1.43\,\mathrm{s}$

(b) The speed would be lower, as the acceleration is lower.
The time taken would be greater, as the acceleration and speed are lower.

2 (a) $2.24\,\mathrm{s}$ **(b)** $38.0\,\mathrm{m}$ **(c)** $27.7\,\mathrm{m\,s^{-1}}$

3 (a) At H, $y = 0 \Rightarrow 4Ut - \tfrac{1}{2}gt^2 = 0$

$$\Rightarrow t(4U - \tfrac{1}{2}gt) = 0 \Rightarrow t = 0 \text{ or } \frac{8U}{g}$$

But $t = 0$ at O, so at H $t = \dfrac{8U}{g}$

(b) $\dfrac{24U^2}{g}$ **(c)** $5U$

(d) $t = \dfrac{U}{g}$ and $t = \dfrac{7U}{g}$

4 (a) $3.45\,\mathrm{m}$ **(b)** $1.01\,\mathrm{s}$ **(c)** $4.04\,\mathrm{m}$

Index